Georeferencing

Digital Libraries and Electronic Publishing
William Y. Arms, series editor

Georeferencing

The Geographic Associations of Information

Linda L. Hill

The MIT Press
Cambridge, Massachusetts
London, England

MIT Press books may be purchased at special quantity discounts for business or sales promotional use. For information, please e-mail special_sales@mitpress.mit.edu or write to Special Sales Department, The MIT Press, 55 Hayward Street, Cambridge, MA 02142.

This book was set in Sabon by SNP Best-set Typesetter Ltd., Hong Kong, and printed and bound in the United States of America.

Library of Congress Cataloging-in-Publication Data

Hill, Linda L.
    Georeferencing : the geographic associations of information / Linda L. Hill.
        p.   cm.—(Digital libraries and electronic publishing)
    Includes bibliographical references and index.
    ISBN-10: 0-262-08354-X (alk. paper)
    ISBN-13: 978-0-262-08354-6
    1. Geographic information systems. 2. Information storage and retrieval systems—Geography. I. Title. II. Series.
G70.212H54   2006
910.285—dc22
                                                                                    2006043326

10 9 8 7 6 5 4 3 2 1

Contents

Preface

Georeferencing: The Geographic Associations of Information is an introductory-level book for individual study or to support formal education in fields such as library science, information science, museum informatics, and geographic information science. Given that a high portion of all types of information can be related to place and that users are best served by information systems that can access the total scope of these information resources, the book focuses on the common ground between placename-based referencing and geospatial referencing. It spans the fields of geographic information science, library science, and information storage and retrieval. For most people, this will be a new perspective and one that challenges the ways we have dealt with georeferencing up to this time. The focus is on the notion of *unified georeferencing*, where placenaming and geospatial coding are interchangeable to the degree that place-based information retrieval can be expected to work satisfactorily across the vast and dissimilar collections of data, images, library and museum holdings, news, online resources, and so on.

Using a *unified georeferencing* approach to draw information of all types together based on their relevance to a location on the Earth's surface is a powerful query capability and one that overcomes many query difficulties such as choosing the right words/terms/placenames to specify a location and accommodating expressions in multiple languages and through historical transitions. The ability to visualize the placement of information retrieved from collections as it is distributed across a landscape (a map) instantly conveys geographic distribution patterns that are hidden otherwise. Despite this potential, the uptake of geospatial referencing and retrieval techniques in digital libraries, museum informatics, online search services, and related information services has been slow. There are several reasons for this. One is the perception that geospatial systems are the domain of formal GIS software rather than an integral part of general information management and retrieval software. Another is that geospatial materials (e.g., maps, remote sensing images) are the province of map libraries and data centers and not integrated with general collections. Given this perception that geospatial referencing is "someone else's problem," library and information science professionals in general and the vendors that support them find themselves ill prepared to integrate geospatial technologies into their systems when they realize how useful it would be.

The approach of the book is to fill this gap in knowledge of georeferencing practices by covering the fundamental concepts, terminology, and standards for geospatial and placename georeferencing, as well as to introduce current approaches to the modeling of georeferencing concepts for documentation in gazetteers and metadata and for the purpose of geographic information retrieval.

This book evolved from a tutorial I developed to introduce the concepts of georeferencing to the digital library community. The tutorial was given twice in 2003— at the Joint Conference on Digital Libraries (JCDL) in Houston and at the European Conference on Digital Libraries (ECDL) in Trondheim, Norway. The tutorial resulted from the research and development activities of the Alexandria Digital Library Project at the University of California at Santa Barbara, where geographers, computer scientists, librarians, information scientists, and various user groups learned to work together and understand one another's vocabularies and ways of thinking and ended up creating the structure for and the reality of a georeferenced digital library.

Each chapter begins with an overview and ends with a summary. For most chapters, a list of sources for further information is provided, not an exhaustive list but some recommended sources to get started. A glossary of important terms and definitions appears at the end of the book. There is a special index to the named geographic places used as examples in the book. It includes a map showing the geospatial distribution of these examples to illustrate the potential of using the geographic associations of information in new ways.

Throughout the book, many of the examples are based on locations in California and elsewhere in the United States because that is where I live and the places are familiar to me. I do not want it to appear that the subject matter is in any way limited to California or to the United States. Georeferencing is universally applicable. To the extent that I have left out references to georeferencing projects in other parts of the world or used overly U.S.-oriented terminology that is foreign to you, I hope you will overlook this, fill in your own examples and terminology, and not let it get in the way of the main points.

Acknowledgments

Scattered throughout the book are personal statements from distinguished individuals who understand the value and the potential of georeferencing in our information systems. They are

Reed Beaman, Associate Director for Biodiversity Informatics, Peabody Museum, Yale University

Kate Beard, Professor, Spatial Information Science and Engineering, University of Maine

Larry Carver, Director, Library Technologies and Digital Initiatives, UC Santa Barbara

Leslie Champeny, Library Director, KIMEP (Kazakhstan Institute of Management, Economics and Strategic Research)

Kai Dragland, Department of Computer and Information Science, Norwegian University of Science and Technology, Trondheim, Norway

Michael Goodchild, Professor, Department of Geography, UC Santa Barbara and co-PI of the Alexandria Digital Library Project

Greg Janée, Lead Software Developer for the Alexandria Digital Library Project, UC Santa Barbara, and now continuing to work on georeference-related software development for project at UCSB

Tony Rees, Manager of the Divisional Data Centre, CSIRO Marine Research, Hobart, Tasmania, Australia

Susan Stone, Museum Informatics Project, UC Berkeley

John Wieczorek, Programmer, Museum of Vertebrate Zoology, University of California at Berkeley

I thank these individuals for their contributions, and I have added my own personal statement about the beginning of these georeferencing ideas for me.

I get the most satisfaction from work that involves the exchange of ideas and the unexpected consequences of working with a team and with colleagues. I say "unexpected consequences" because the results of teamwork always, in my experience, exceed what any one person could have done, at least what I could have done alone. I have learned a great deal from my colleagues through the years—particularly, in terms of georeferencing, from the Petroleum Abstracts Service at the University of Tulsa, the School of Information Sciences at the University of Pittsburgh, and from the stimulating environment of the Alexandria Digital Library Project at UC Santa Barbara. I have many to thank among that group of colleagues.

My dissertation advisor at the University of Pittsburgh, Edie Rasmussen, supported me in my desire to work in the area of georeferencing. She received her PhD at the University of Sheffield, UK, and therefore knew those who were doing early research in georeferencing for the British Library. She was my link to those projects and of considerable support in the research into the effectiveness of placenames versus coordinates in representing the geographic study areas of a test set of geoscience articles.

The Alexandria Digital Library Project—its researchers, developers, and the staff of the Map and Imagery Laboratory (MIL) in the Davidson Library of the UC Santa Barbara—has been the testing ground for much of the content of this book. I am thankful for the opportunity to work with them through the duration of the project. The project would not have existed without the efforts of Terence Smith and Michael Goodchild (the Principal Investigators) and Larry Carver, head of MIL, as well as other members of the executive committee who put the project together, the Digital Library Initiative at the National Science Foundation, and other funders who provided the resource support. Terry Smith invited me to join the ADL Project midway through the first round of funding and Lola Olsen of NASA's Global Change Master Directory program, with whom I was working at the time, encouraged me and supported me in making the transition. Mike Goodchild and I put the Digital Gazetteer Information Exchange (DGIE) workshop together several years ago, and he has involved me in many community-based activities to facilitate the use of georeferencing in new areas, particularly in the social sciences. Michael Freeston, James Frew, Greg Janée, and others have been very supportive of my work with gazetteer design and development. Jordan Hastings has taken up the core ideas of gazetteers as "mini-GIS systems" for his PhD research in the UC Santa Barbara Geography Department and has developed many interesting and forward-looking ideas for gazetteer data systems; he has been very helpful to me in continuing gazetteer development. Mary Larsgaard, Greg Hajic, David Valentine, and others of the MIL staff have also been companions through the ADL project's duration and have been sources of basic information about map libraries and their users as well as the information systems behind the operational Alexandria Digital Library.

I would also like to recognize Roger L. Payne, Executive Secretary of the U.S. Board on Geographic Names (BGN) and head of the gazetteer services of the U.S. Geological Survey, and Randall Flynn, Executive Secretary of Foreign Names for the BGN and head of the gazetteer services at the National Geospatial-Intelligence Agency (NGA). They have led the building of the U.S. government's gazetteer databases and services under the auspices of the BGN. These are valuable assets that have been made generously available and have been used for many georeferencing research projects and implementations, including the Alexandria Digital Library Project.

Many others have helped in putting the book together. Chief among them is Leslie Champeny, who has been my editorial assistant. She has edited and contributed to the book from cover to cover while living in Almaty, Kazakhstan—an example of the wonders of electronic communication and collaborative writing tools.

Susan Stone, Museum Informatics Project, UC Berkeley, and my son, Gregory B. Hill, read through a rough first draft and gave me useful feedback on ways to improve the content and the presentation. Thankfully, Patricia Frontiera's dissertation at UC Berkeley was finished in time to help me put my thoughts together on spatial information retrieval and evaluation. She reviewed the chapter on geographic information retrieval and also allowed me to use some of her graphics. Mary Larsgaard and Greg Hajic, MIL, UC Santa Barbara, reviewed the chapter on metadata (Larsgaard) and the chapter on the representation of geospatial locations (Hajic), making some things clearer to me and hopefully also to the reader. Rebecca Guenther, Library of Congress, reviewed the section on MARC and MODS metadata. Kathryn Ginger, Digital Library for Earth Systems Education (DLESE) Program Center, reviewed the information about the georeferencing elements of the DLESE metadata. Sharon Shin, Federal Geographic Data Committee (FGDC), reviewed the section on FGDC metadata. Patricia Harpring, Managing Editor of the Getty Vocabulary Program, contributed to the information about the *Getty Thesaurus of Geographic Names*. Jens Fitzke, Marcus Müller, and Hans Plum of "lat/lon GmbH" reviewed the sections discussing ISO and OGC standards. James Reid with the EDINA Data Centre in Edinburgh reviewed the information about their geospatial projects. Ian Johnson, Director of the Archaeological Computing Laboratory and the *Time*Map Project at the University of Sydney, reviewed information about *Time*Map and its application to Electronic Cultural Atlas Initiative (ECAI) data and the David Rumsey Map Collection.

Vivien Petras, School of Information Management at UC Berkeley, provided statistics showing the frequency of geographic subject headings and codes in a test dataset of records from Melvyl. Diane Vizine-Goetz, OCLC, provided statistics on the use of MARC georeferencing elements in OCLC's WorldCat database. Sharon Tahirkheli, American Geological Institute (GeoRef), provided information about GeoRef's current activities. Kim Etcheson and Doug Rippey of the Jefferson County Public Library in Wheat Ridge, Colorado, researched when spatial coordinates were added to the MARC bibliographic format. Karen Jungblut, Director of the Cataloging Department and Special Projects for the Survivors of the Shoah Visual History Foundation, confirmed the key importance of georeferencing in oral histories. Several staff members of Endeavor Information Systems and Tony Boston with the National Library of Australia helped me describe the geospatial capabilities of the Endeavor software. Simon Cox provided information about the spatial extensions he developed for the Dublin Core Metadata Initiative (DCMI). Tony Rees, Manager, Divisional Data Centre, CSIRO Marine Research, Australia, provided information about the c-squares coding system. Olha Buchel, who worked on the ADEPT Project at UC Santa Barbara (the second phase of the Alexandria Digital Library Project) provided insights into library cataloging practices in relation to georeferencing. Max J. Egenhofer, University of Maine, and Michael Wegener, Dortmund, Germany, verified some references for me.

I am grateful to Matt Rice, Cartomedia.com, who created original graphics for my book, and for those who allowed me to reprint their graphics. These included Murtha Baca, Getty Research Institute; Heather Ross, Geographical Names, Natural Resources Canada; Nan Hudes, Columbia University Press; and Steven Weinberger, Tibetan and Himalayan Digital Library, University of Virginia. Others are acknowledged in the figure captions.

The reviewers engaged by MIT Press were very encouraging from the beginning and have greatly improved the book by their careful thoughts and valuable suggestions. I do not, of course, know who they are and so will express my gratitude to them as a group.

I would like to thank Bill Arms for encouraging me to go ahead and write this book instead of just thinking about doing it as well as Douglas Sery, editor for computer science and new media at MIT Press, who also encouraged me and managed the process of getting it to press, ably assisted by acquisitions assistant Valerie Geary, senior editor Sandra Minkkinen, copyeditor Elizabeth Judd, and other editorial, design, production, and promotion staff at The MIT Press. This has all been done at long distance, so we have not met (so far)—it has been a productive team effort nevertheless.

Despite all of this help, I take full responsibility for any errors or omissions herein.

I am dedicating this book to my mother, Effie Irene Alexander Ladd, who died in 2001 at the age of 97. My sister and I grew up in a supportive and loving household in circumstances that now look idyllic from today's viewpoint. As I pursued my professional career, she was still there cheering me on even though she never understood what in the world I was doing.

1

Laying the Groundwork

Overview of Georeferencing in Information Systems

Georeferencing—relating information to geographic location—is a component of our lives and has been incorporated in our information systems in various ways. We are all familiar with information object types that represent geographic space and features of the Earth's surface—for example, maps and globes. We use online services that tell us where a named place or address is, how far it is from one place to another, and what route we should take or that has been taken (figure 1.1). In television news, it is no longer a novelty to be shown a "bird's-eye view" of the location of a story and to be taken on a virtual flight in for a closer view. Newspapers often supplement articles with maps showing the general location and details of the immediate area of the event. Increasingly, our scientific, engineering, governmental, business, and political practices are incorporating geographic information systems (GIS) to hold and analyze georeferenced data, leading to the discovery of geographic distribution patterns that support decision makers and planning (figure 1.2). In general, we are living in an age where technology and information techniques are enriching our understanding of geography and its effect on our lives and the lives of others.

In fact, "whatever occurs, occurs in space and time" (Wegener 2000) and can be visualized, explained, and understood in those terms. The route traveled by a scientific expedition, the path of a hurricane, the recounting of military battles, the individual paths we take through life, and the understanding of complex social and environmental dynamics all involve space and time dimensions. An elegant graphic by Charles Joseph Minard (1781–1870) of Napoléon's invasion of Russia in 1812–1813 (figure 1.3) illustrates the power of a space-time visualization to convey information. The graphic is described and praised by Edward R. Tufte in *The Visual Display of Quantitative Information* (1983, 40):

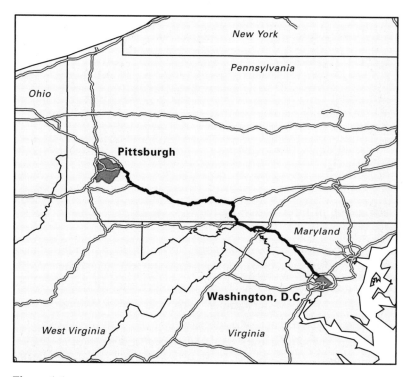

Figure 1.1
Route map from Pittsburgh to Washington, D.C. (Created by Matt Rice, Cartomedia.com. *Source data*: U.S. Census Bureau.)

Beginning at the left on the Polish-Russian border near the Niemen River, the thick band shows the size of the army (422,000 men) as it invaded Russia in June 1812. The width of the band indicates the size of the army at each place on the map. In September, the army reached Moscow, which was by then sacked and deserted, with 100,000 men. The path of Napoleon's retreat form Moscow is depicted by the darker, lower band, which is linked to a temperature scale and dates at the bottom of the chart. It was a bitterly cold winter, and many froze on the march out of Russia. As the graphic shows, the crossing of the Berezina River was a disaster, and the army finally struggled back into Poland with only 10,000 men remaining. Also shown are the movements of auxiliary troops, as they sought to protect the rear and the flank of the advancing army. . . . It may well be the best statistical graphic ever drawn.

The lowest temperature is roughly −24°C on December 6.

The scope of georeferencing includes the *informal* means of referring to locations, which we use in ordinary discourse using placenames, and the *formal* representations based on longitude and latitude coordinates and other spatial referencing systems, which we use in activities such as mapmaking and navigating. Formal rep-

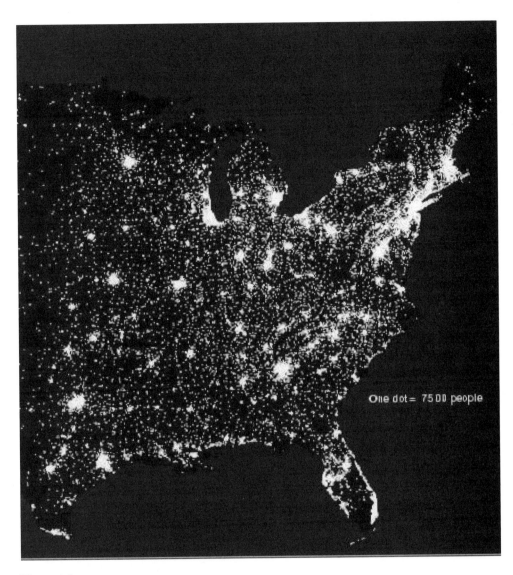

Figure 1.2
Eastern United States population distribution map for 2000 from the U.S. Census Bureau (*Source*: http://www.census.gov/geo/www/mapGallery/2kpopden.html.)

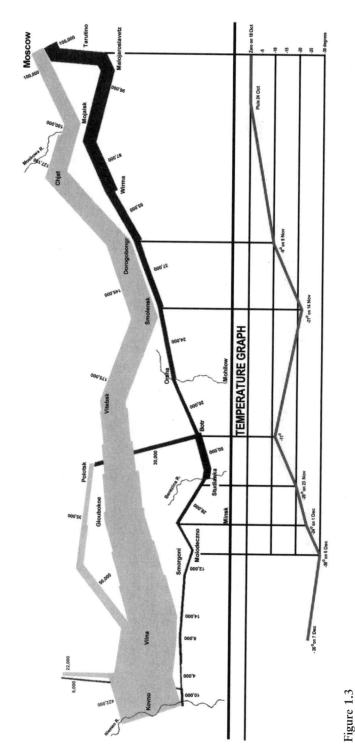

Figure 1.3
Graphic by Charles Joseph Minard in 1861, as recreated by John Schneider, showing the routes and the fate of Napoléon's invasion of Russia in 1812–1813 in geographic and temporal dimensions. (Reprinted with permission from John Schneider, *Napoleonic Literature: Losses Suffered by the Grande Armée during the Russian Campaign*, http://www.napoleonic-literature.com/1812/1812.htm.)

resentations are geospatial *footprints*—so called because they show on a map of the Earth's surface a particular spot or area where something is located. These footprints are the basis for mathematical calculations of distance and direction, and for definitions of spatial relationships (e.g., overlap and containment). That is, if we know that one place is located at one spot on Earth and another elsewhere, we can calculate the distance between them and the direction of travel to get from one to the other. We can calculate whether two areas overlap one another—that is, occupy some of the same area—and, if so, whether one is contained within the other. If we have the formal georeferencing of footprints, we can show where places are on a map and how they relate to administrative districts, coastlines, rivers, mountains, or any geographic point of interest. Placenames without geospatial referencing do not allow us to do this.

Most of the georeferencing we encounter daily is in the form of placenames. It has been estimated that at least 70 percent of our text documents contain place-name references (MetaCarta Inc. 2005a). Half (49.68 percent) of a set of five million library catalog records (1968–2000) of the University of California contain one or more place-related subject headings or codes (Petras 2004). The pervasiveness of place references in oral histories is very strong; a spokesperson for the Survivors of the Shoah Visual History Foundation reports that all of the testimonies in their archives, which are from survivors of the World War II Holocaust, contain one or more references to the places of importance in their lives, such as where they were born and the ghettos and camps to which they were forcibly transferred (K. Jungblut, personal communication, 2005).

Georeferenced information is everywhere (figure 1.4). Georeferencing is so ubiquitous that it seems that it should be an important component of all of our information systems, from library and museum catalogs to online searching services to data centers to scientific data services. And it is to some degree. Georeferencing is accomplished predominantly through text in today's information system, where searches to find information about a geographic area must be expressed as a text query—that is, query by placename. Sometimes this works just fine, as in cases where the information has been described with placenames for well-known administrative units. For example, many social statistics are collected by administrative areas (e.g., census tracts) and can be unambiguously retrieved using the names or codes for these administrative areas. But if the need is to find information about a location that could be identified by several placenames (or for an unnamed location such as a location at sea), then the retrieval of relevant information using text is more difficult. It could require some research to find all of the past and present

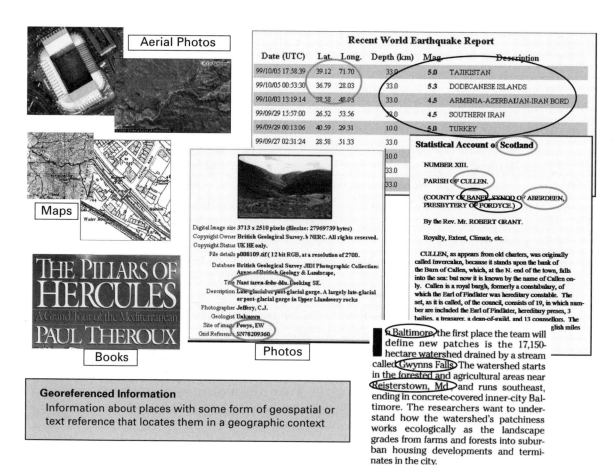

Figure 1.4
Examples of some of the sources of georeferenced information

placenames that exist for the area or its surroundings so that they can be included in the query; then the results have to be reviewed to find the useful results. An example of this situation is attempting to find maps that cover all or part of Los Angeles in an online catalog. The user may find "a map of Los Angeles" by a text search but will probably not find maps of suburbs of Los Angeles such as Long Beach, Hollywood, Beverly Hills, Torrance, Redondo Beach, or Inglewood, which may be equally useful.

An even larger problem is that text searching does not search the whole universe of information about a location. Maps, for example, are traditionally handled by special units of libraries or mapping agencies and they are accessed through special map indexes, filing systems, and agency contacts. Maps are also not indexed so that they can be found by all of the named features in a particular map; to use the previous example, the map of Los Angeles probably does include Hollywood, Beverly Hills, and so on, but the map cannot be found by using those names through a text search. Data such as remote sensing images and aerial photography is indexed by geospatial location instead of by placename; they cannot be found by the names of places covered by the image. Access to these resources must be directed through information services that are geospatially indexed—for example, GIS interfaces or georeferenced digital libraries such as the Alexandria Digital Library (ADL).

To take full advantage of placename referencing—to be able to map them and see the geographic patterns and associations of information—a translation between the formal and informal representations of geographic location is essential. This highlights the importance of *gazetteers*: dictionaries of placenames that include geospatial footprints for the named locations. Figure 1.5 illustrates the integration between placenames and associated geospatial information that has been implemented by the U.S. Geological Survey in its Geographic Names Information System (GNIS). The potential of georeferencing services is to extend this type of access to all types of information.

In ways that are ingrained in the information management practices of different communities, we have segmented the information associated with geographic locations by discipline. Much of the geographic data community interprets geographic information as geospatial data representing the Earth's surface (i.e., data that is formally represented with models of the Earth and coordinate and grid location notations). The advent of GIS technologies to manipulate and capitalize on such data has solidified this view. Within text-oriented communities, librarians have viewed the geographic associations of information as a type of subject heading (e.g., indicating that a document is about a place), an attribute of publication (i.e., place of publication), or a parameter of classification (e.g., the Library of Congress classification of DJK 1-77, which designates "Eastern Europe, History of"), and they have delegated cartographic materials to the care of map librarians in special map collections. Museum curators have represented the collection locations of specimens by descriptive narratives written in the field. Toponymic authorities—units of government with responsibility for establishing official placenames for government purposes—have bridged the gap between text (placenames) and geospatial locations (coordinates that identify the place) to produce freestanding gazetteers that have been seen to be useful but that are often not recognized as a key component

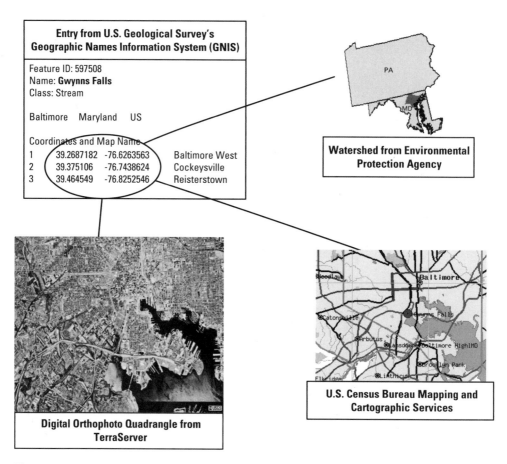

Figure 1.5
Example from the U.S. Geographic Names Information System (GNIS) of links between placenames and associated information about the location based on the coordinates

in information management systems for translation between the data and text domains (figure 1.5). Such integration is, in fact, an idea that has been slow to develop.

The premise of this book is that the users of information systems are best served through *unified georeferencing* where both placename and geospatial access works across all types of information resources and in all types of information storage and retrieval systems. Users should be able to start with what they know, whether a placename or a geospatial footprint, and create a query to find georeferenced information about a particular location from a variety of library catalogs, data centers,

Panel 1
Georeferencing for Natural History Museum Collections

Museums and herbaria worldwide curate over one billion biological specimens. Every one of these objects is associated with a biological identity and a place of collection. Although there has been much recent effort to digitally capture museum collection data, this task remains largely unfinished, and an even smaller percentage of the total has been digitally geospatially referenced. The natural history collection community would benefit greatly from a federated naming service for geographic names. This is especially true in light of our recent efforts to transform data captured by automated methods from original documents that are capable of directly accessing digital naming services.

Collections often house a vast array of primary archival material associated with biological specimens, including collectors' logs, original illustrations, bibliographical material, and maps. The collections community is therefore also in the position to contribute to gazetteer development. Access to primary collection information (e.g., collectors' maps) provides the ability to geospatially reference names that are often not found in existing [digital] naming projects; they may represent variant spellings or features known only in historical contexts.

Reed Beaman
Associate Director for Biodiversity Informatics
Peabody Museum, Yale University

museums, archives, directories, and web-based resources. Place-based research should not be hampered by the lack of unifying georeferencing practices to bridge across different domains of information resources.

Using geospatial footprints to gather information of all types together based on their relevance to a location on the Earth's surface is a powerful query capability and one that overcomes many query difficulties, such as choosing the right place-names to specify a region and working in a multilingual environment. In addition, the ability to visualize the placement of items retrieved from a collection as they are distributed across a geographic landscape instantly conveys information about their relevance to the region of interest that is hidden otherwise.

Within the field of information retrieval, the limitations of text searching are well known. In particular, Don Swanson's (1988, 96) research revealed that "literatures of different scientific specialties tend to develop independently of one another, but the connectedness inherent in the physical world suggests that there are many fertile, unintended logical connections between these distinct literatures." He found by searching the medical literature by hand, for example, an undiscovered relationship between fish oil and Raynaud's Syndrome—undiscovered because the nutritional effects of fish oil were discussed in one community and the causes of Raynaud's Syndrome in another and the literatures of the two communities were noninteractive; they seldom, if ever, cited one another (Swanson 1986). In similar situations that are associated with geographic locations, geospatial information retrieval has the potential of doing the same thing: bringing together information from multiple points of view and different communities of practice and research that otherwise operate in separate, noninteractive domains with different terminologies.

Despite this potential, the uptake of geospatial description and access in digital libraries and other information systems outside of GIS has been slow. There are several reasons for this that this book addresses. One reason is that geospatial referencing is perceived as the domain of GIS software rather than as an integral part of general information storage and retrieval software. Another is that geospatial materials (e.g., maps, remote sensing images) are perceived as the responsibility of map libraries and geospatial data centers. Given this perception that geospatial referencing and geospatial resources are "someone else's problem," many who could apply georeferencing practices in new ways find themselves ill prepared to integrate geospatial technologies and resources into their systems (e.g., in digital libraries, museum informatics, and online search services).

This book explains the potential of the integration of informal and formal means of georeferencing for information storage, retrieval, and visualization—for all cases where the geographic distribution of information and objects is of interest and where either placename or geospatial referencing is encountered. The application of georeferencing extends to almost all fields of academic and applied study, including the arts and humanities; social, physical, and life sciences; medicine; government administration; petroleum and mineral exploration; message understanding (text analysis); historical and genealogical research; and the documentation of personal histories. The approach of the book is to cover the fundamental concepts, terminology, and standards for georeferencing technologies, with the aim of educating those who would profit from integrating new georeferencing practices into their information systems and services. This includes library professionals, library software vendors, digital library designers, and managers of museum informatics, indexing and abstracting services, and online information services. From a GIS perspective, this book is about putting more emphasis on integrating formal and informal means of georeferencing and working toward a time when place-based resources of all kinds are shared easily among GIS services and services outside the specialized software environments of GIS applications.

A Little History

The term *distributed geolibrary* was advanced by a National Research Council workshop convened by its Mapping Science Committee in June 1998:

A distributed geolibrary is a vision for the future. It would permit users to quickly and easily obtain all existing information available about a place that is relevant to a . . . *geographically* defined need . . . relevant to a wide range of problems, including natural disasters, emergencies, community planning, and environmental quality. A geolibrary is a digital library filled with geoinformation—information associated with a distinct area or footprint on the Earth's surface—and for which the primary search mechanism is *place*. . . .

It is currently easier to find information about a named individual, an agency, or a field of scientific knowledge than about a place on the Earth's surface. (National Research Council Mapping Science Committee 1999, 1, 13)

The grand vision of the geolibrary was that it would not only enable place-based searching for and evaluation of useful information across distributed resources but that it would facilitate the retrieval, integration, manipulation, and analysis of that information. The analysis environment envisioned was a GIS environment, with mechanisms in the geolibrary architecture for capturing the knowledge resulting from such work (e.g., models, visualizations, reports, and statistics) and making it available to others. The broader construct of a *cyberinfrastructure* has expanded the scope of *digital libraries* in the last few years; the conclusions of this workshop apply equally well to the broader scope.

The Distributed Geolibraries workshop was held to generate ideas for the expansion of the vision and scope of the U.S. National Spatial Data Infrastructure (NSDI), which was established in 1994 by a presidential executive order as a means of "assembling" U.S. geospatial data from federal, state, local, and private-sector sources, as well as encouraging the reuse of data and a reduction in duplicative efforts to collect and archive geospatial data. A geospatial data clearinghouse was established to implement this directive and is administered by the Federal Geographic Data Committee (FGDC), which is part of the U.S. Geological Survey (USGS). As of January 2005, the Clearinghouse has 371 registered servers that are contributing geospatial data collected for local purposes to the NSDI for discovery and use by others (U.S. Federal Geographic Data Committee 2005b).

Also in 1994, the U.S. National Science Foundation (NSF) initiated its digital library program by funding six projects for four years. One of those projects was the Alexandria Digital Library (ADL) at the University of California at Santa Barbara (UCSB). The goal of the ADL project, as stated in the proposal to NSF, was "to develop a user-friendly digital library system that provides a comprehensive range of services to collections of maps, images, and spatially-referenced information." Researchers at UCSB and their partners proposed to "design, develop and test a distributed, high-performance digital library, in which collections of spatially-indexed information in digital form as well as users are dispersed geographically . . . [as] a major step towards the evolution of a distributed digital library supporting both textual and spatially-indexed sources of information and scalable to the national level." Acknowledging that technical issues relating to spatially indexed collections and services would require attention, the proposal states that the "long-term goal is to remove the distinction between mainstream libraries focusing on text and special libraries focusing on less conventional materials" (UC Santa Barbara 1994). The ADL project resulted in a series of prototype implementations and cycles of user evaluations to inform the next version, as well as a specification for the architecture of a distributed georeferenced digital library. At the end of the four-year funding period, ADL was, and continues to be, an ongoing operational service of UCSB's Davidson Library with collections of maps, remote sensing images, and aerial photography and an online user interface presenting geographic and other search parameters and visualization of the footprints of individual collection objects (figure 1.6). During the next round of digital library funding by NSF, UCSB applied its ADL experience to integrating digital library support into undergraduate education (known as the ADEPT project: the Alexandria Digital Earth ProtoType Project). Distributed digital library architectural and gazetteer design work continued through this funding period, resulting in digital library software available for downloading, content standards and specifications, and the integration of distributed collections of georeferenced collections to supplement the holdings at UCSB (Alexandria Digital Library 2005).

The precursors to the ADL project were (1) the exemplary collections and services of the Map and Imagery Laboratory (MIL) of UCSB's Davidson Library, and (2) a project of the Research Libraries Group (RLG) known as the GRIN project—the Geo-Referenced Information Network. Before the ADL project, MIL had already established itself as a forward-looking organization with a collection of historical aerial photography, a growing collection of remote sensing imagery, an extensive collection of maps, and income-generating services in addition to supporting on-campus education, interlibrary cooperative services, and professional map library associations. It participated in the GRIN project, which aimed to create a geoinformation control and retrieval system to provide access to descriptions of materials and data characterized by geographic location. The GRIN design included a name-coordinate thesaurus to associate placenames to geographic footprints and

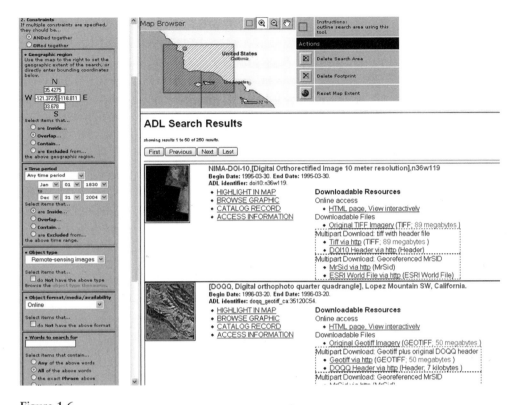

Figure 1.6
Screenshot of an in-process search using the Alexandria Digital Library search interface (Alexandria Digital Library 2005). At the top right, the map browser shows the search area as a striped box, which was drawn by the user. Within the box is a small square showing the geographic coverage of the top item listed below the map browser. The listings include thumbnail graphics of the images. On the left is a portion of the Catalog Search panel.

graphic displays of the footprints associated with the text description of collection items so that the user could see how the items related to the user's area of interest ("RLG Enters New Sphere with Geoinformation Project," 1989). Ideas from GRIN provided the model for the initial ADL demonstration prototype.

In the United Kingdom, the Joint Information Systems Committee (JISC), working on behalf of the higher education community's funding bodies, funds digital library development for the academic community. JISC has funded a range of geospatial services provided by EDINA, a National Data Centre in Edinburgh, and its partners (EDINA 2005; Reid et al. 2004). The goal of the services is to facilitate the discovery and use of the geospatial resources available for higher education for the widest possible audience. Among the services and projects are

• *Go-Geo!* (www.gogeo.ac.uk), an online resource discovery tool that allows for the identification and retrieval of georeferenced metadata records from distributed collections; the current geographic scope is the UK (figure 1.7).

• *geoXwalk* ("geo crosswalk"), a project that has developed a middleware proto-service for UK academia that incorporates gazetteer services into place-based information services to translate between placenames, postal codes, or other labels and the equivalent UK spatial reference system notations. This allows queries to be sent as geospatial queries to distributed collections of many types of georeferenced information (figure 1.8).

Leading up to and paralleling all of this activity was the CARTO-NET project at the University of Edinburgh and related research funded by the British Library, as well as the individual ideas and projects of professional map librarians. The CARTO-NET project was a shared cataloging system for maps that had a map interface for users. Users could zoom the map into an area of interest and match that area against the maps, gazetteer entries, aerial photographs, and satellite imagery held by the library (Morris 1988). Alan Griffiths and Michael Lynch (1987) at the University of Sheffield used British Library funding to investigate geographic information systems from a library perspective; they identified many of the key problems of placenames in information management systems, including the use of the same name for different places, named places with uncertain boundaries (e.g., "South of England"), name changes through time, and newly named places that are not clearly documented. Several years later, Daniel Holmes (1990), librarian for the Department of Geography at the University of California at Berkeley, published his thoughts about "Computer and Geographic Information Access" that drew from his experience as a member of a team that developed a prototype system called ImageQuery for geographic indexing and retrieval of photographic images using a graphic interface. He saw the need to expand this approach to "all types of media" to develop a powerful tool for "administering and cataloging the holdings of libraries, museums, agencies, organizations, and individuals," which would include "a comprehensive place name listing with appropriate footprint coordinates." Before all of this activity, visionaries such as Nancy Pruett (1986) foresaw graphical user interfaces for geoscience libraries and information services where a search for maps, journal articles, field-trip guidebooks, dissertations, data, and even the names of experts would be carried out by drawing on a computer screen the outline of the area of interest while interacting with an online bibliographic-type database.

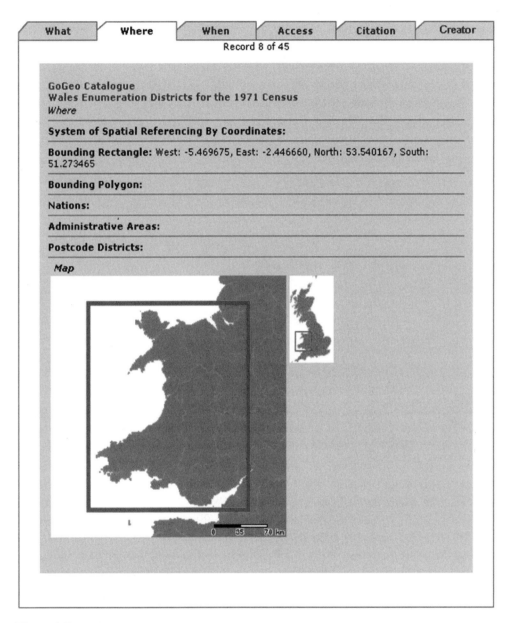

Figure 1.7
Screenshot of the search interface for the EDINA *Go-Geo* discovery service for georeferenced information in distributed collections in the UK. (Reprinted from Reid et al. 2004, with permission.)

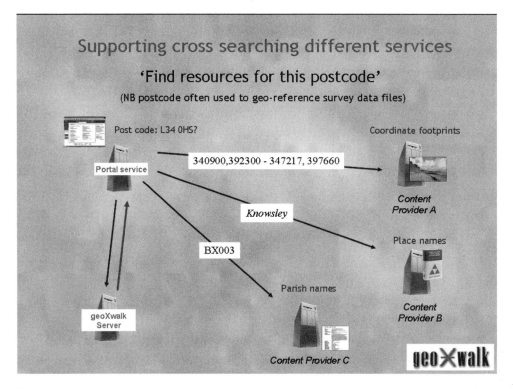

Figure 1.8
Illustration of the EDINA *geoXwalk* project, where the query starts with a postal code and is translated into coordinates, placenames, and parish names for distribution to distributed collections using different forms of georeferencing. (Reprinted from Reid et al. 2004, with permission.)

By the time of these early library-oriented georeferencing activities, developments in computer-aided mapping and theoretical work on geographic data structures and analysis software had advanced to the point that GIS was a well-known term for a mature technology. In the 1980s, a GIS infrastructure developed (e.g., books, journals, and conferences) and the NSF created the National Center for Geographic Information and Analysis (NCGIA), which developed a college curriculum and a research agenda for GIS. In the 1990s, many fields of study, professions, and work environments, including geology, archeology, epidemiology, and criminal justice, were transformed by the adoption of GIS as a desktop computer technology. The capabilities advanced rapidly: data capture directly from global positioning systems (GPS), the availability of high-resolution imagery as a reference base for data analysis, and the emergence of the Internet and e-commerce and web-based GIS (Clarke 2001).

Advancement in GIS has resulted in commercial products, standards, education and training, and infrastructures for professionals, services, and data management. Outside of the GIS environments, progress in the use of geospatial referencing has been less dramatic. This book is intended to provide some basics to introduce geospatial referencing into other types of information systems outside of the traditional GIS domains, and to facilitate the integration of placename and geospatial georeferencing in information systems of all types.

The Basics

Chapter 2 focuses on the users of georeferencing information services, providing a brief overview of some relevant insights from the field of cognitive psychology into how humans perceive and respond to geographic space. This is the basis of all of our attempts to represent geography in useful ways; in particular, it forms the basis for building information systems that incorporate georeferencing in ways that resonate with and are effective tools for users.

Chapter 3 contains basic information about types of geospatial information objects (e.g., maps, remote sensing images from spacecraft and aerial photography), and the scanning and digitizing processes that turn hardcopy maps and images into georeferenced datasets. To complete the picture of types of georeferenced information objects, examples of georeferenced text are included.

Fundamental concepts of geospatial referencing are covered in chapter 4 on a nontechnical level. This includes an explanation of why "longitude, latitude" is probably a better order of referencing than "latitude, longitude" and what difference the geodetic basis of coordinates makes. The meaning of "small scale" versus "large scale" for maps is explained as well as how "scale" compares to "resolution." Methods of projecting the Earth's three-dimensional surface onto a two-dimensional display are described, as well as some of the problems that result (e.g., distortions and discontinuities). Also included are issues of data uncertainty, ways of generalizing geographic footprints, and types of geospatial relationships between places.

Chapter 5 is devoted to gazetteers and to their role in georeferenced information systems. Ways of modeling gazetteer data—that is, descriptive and definitional information about a named geographic place—are covered, with diagrams to illustrate the arrangement and nesting of descriptive elements as structured by several gazetteer models. Sources of gazetteer data are discussed along with issues of gazetteer interoperability and gazetteer data conflation. Examples of applications of gazetteers in information services are given, including the process of computer analysis of texts to identify placename references so that the text can be related to spatial locations (known as geoparsing).

The ways in which georeferencing has been included in metadata structures is the topic for chapter 6. Because these formal descriptive structures for georeferencing have emerged through the last 35 years and have built on one another to some extent, the different structures are presented in roughly chronological order by when they first appeared, but described in their current versions. Diagrams are included in this chapter as well to provide a pictorial view of the structures of the descriptive elements used to document both the placename and geospatial associations of the information object represented by the metadata. The chapter ends with a discussion of general considerations for geospatial metadata elements for future metadata design.

This all leads us to the focus of chapter 7 on geographic information retrieval (GIR). Given that the geographic associations of information have been identified and documented and the information is held in accessible collections, how is GIR implemented? The basics of spatial matching operations are described, including methods of calculating spatial similarity between a query region and the geospatial footprints of the information objects in the collections. But how do we know how effective these methods are in returning relevant information to the user? Issues surrounding the evaluation of the effectiveness of GIR for both placename and footprint searching are presented.

Terminology and Meanings

In georeferencing, multiple fields of study and interest overlap and each brings its own terminology to the discussion, often with contextual, community-based meanings that are not apparent to others. Throughout the book, many terms with special meaning are used and an attempt is made to make their meanings, as used in this book, clear both in the chapters and in the glossary. Some terms with potentially confusing meaning are introduced here since they apply throughout.

For geographers, the terms *geography* and *geographic* are terms that are inherently *geospatial* and thus can be used to mean the geospatial representation of physical location by use of, for example, longitude and latitude coordinates. This is *geography* as the undivided, continuous surface of the Earth that contains discrete named locations and physical features but is not limited to such features. For others, the use of placenames alone and the use of hierarchical schemes for the administrative relationships of places is a sufficient representation of geography, with the addition of geospatial coordinates an added bit of information. For this discussion of a *unified georeferencing* framework and way of thinking, it is necessary to make a clear distinction between geospatial (continuous) and named-feature (discrete) georeferencing. Therefore, the terms *formal* and *informal* georeferencing are used. Others refer to this distinction as a difference between *quantitative* and *qualitative*, which indicates the difference between representations that can be treated mathematically and those that cannot. Geospatial representation is associated with formal quantitative georeferencing. This distinction is discussed more fully in the succeeding chapters.

The term *information systems* is meant to include a wide assortment of collections and information services, including but not limited to the collections and services associated with libraries and museums. Georeferencing applies to any information system where the associations of information and data to place are relevant and important. The focus in this book is on the design of georeferenced information systems—on users, collections, the representation of formal and informal georeferencing, metadata, and information retrieval—outside the realm of GIS environments.

In information systems, some confusion is caused because the *information object* of different systems and communities is not at the same level of *granularity*. Giving some illustrative examples is probably the best way to explain why this is important. Libraries have traditionally treated the book, journal, or map as their information object, which they describe in a catalog record with the author or producer, the title, the publisher and date, and so on. Digital libraries do this as well but also recognize collections (a higher level of granularity) and chapters of books (a lower level of granularity) as information objects. Archivists have traditionally considered collections of manuscripts or correspondence as the objects in their care, as well as the individual manuscripts and letters in those collections. Museums similarly treat collections as objects, as well as the individual artifacts, specimens, art works, and other holdings in those collections. Bibliographic indexes, such as *Engineering Index*, treat the individual journal article or conference paper as their information object, each of which is referenced to the journal or conference to which it belongs. Internet search services have evolved ways of handling nested web pages that variously represent collections of pages as a single object and individual pages as components of those objects. Granularity can be thought of as being a level of detail or a level in a hierarchy of object types. For example, an administrative hierarchy for named geographic places will have the nation/country level, a state or province level, a county or parish level, and so forth. An information system that uses such a hierarchy will choose the level of hierarchy (i.e., granularity) that best suits its purposes. Geographic information systems (GIS) typically consider individual features and data points as their information objects; this fine level of granularity supports analysis, visualization, conflation, and similar activities. The important point is that georeferencing can be and is applied at any level of *information object granularity*, and different communities will be dealing with different levels of detail. The principles and ways of thinking about georeferencing in this book are applicable across the board.

Some terms are introduced simply to make the reader aware of their existence in the context of georeferencing. These are terms that come up from time to time or add links to the way concepts are discussed in related literatures. Often they do not get full development because they are not central to the discussion. Useful terms are brought together in the glossary.

The one-word version of *placename* is used in this book. It represents an important concept in georeferencing—a concept that is strongly associated with *place* while also being a type of *name*. This is one of those terms that has been migrating from two words to a hyphenated term and now to one word by those who use it often. This happens to a lot of words in English. For example, such a migration happened to the word *today*. It started out as two words (*to day*) and then became a hyphenated term (*to-day*). Now, it is hard to imagine a time when it wasn't a single word. Similar concatenations are happening with many computer-related terms, such as from *on-line* to *online*. *Geo-referencing* is also seen as a hyphenated term. *Georeferencing*, however, is a concept and an activity that is mature enough to warrant its own one-word label; likewise *placename*.

Some of the concepts referred to in this book are commonly known by more than one term. Placename is one example; other terms that are used for this are *geographic name* and *feature name*. In these cases, one expression for a concept is used most of the time, though not all of the time because sometimes one of the other expressions seems to fit the context better. These equivalencies of terms are indicated every now and then with something like "placenames (aka feature names, geographic names)."

2

Spatial Cognition and Information Systems

This chapter focuses on how humans deal with geographic information, specifically on the aspects of spatial cognition that relate to georeferenced information system design. This includes some of the insights that are supported by research on how we acquire, store, and access geographic knowledge; how we categorize geographic knowledge; and how we communicate about geographic spaces, especially how we ask questions about geographic features and routes and what sorts of answers are useful to us. To some degree, this depends on individual, cultural, and disciplinary preferences that need to be taken into account when designing georeferenced information systems.

Some Basic Concepts of Spatial Cognition

Research supports the notion that our internal representation of geographic knowledge in long-term memory is fragmentary and incomplete. It is not a coherent maplike representation, as is implied by the *mental-map* metaphor, but more like a *cognitive collage* containing geographic knowledge stored in different formats, from multiple sources, and from different points of view (Hirtle 1998; Tversky 1993). From this collage, we mentally construct spatial models about particular places and environments for particular purposes, as needed for immediate use to navigate, give directions, ask questions, understand references to places in the news, and so on. Geographic knowledge in long-term memory has been characterized as being like architectural models that include the spatial relationships among the landmarks in the environment in a perspective-free manner that allows the taking of many perspectives on them (Tversky and Taylor 1998).

Because this knowledge is incomplete and most likely does not contain all the information we need for particular situations, we estimate and extrapolate, and in the process we routinely distort the information in predictable ways. Experiments have shown, for example, that the recall of distances and directions between geographic features is systematically distorted. One pattern is to estimate the distance *to* a well-known landmark from a less well known location as shorter than the distance *from* that landmark to that other location (e.g., Lloyd and Heivly 1987). For example, I might estimate that the distance from where I live to city hall is 4 miles, but if asked how far it is from city hall to my house I might estimate a greater distance—say, closer to 5 miles. A similar effect is seen in our treatment of the relationship between a well-known prototype and a variant of that prototype. It is immediately clear, for example, that the meaning of *robin* is closely related to the meaning of *bird*, but in tests that measure response time it takes us a bit longer to decide that *bird* is conceptually close in meaning to *robin* (Tversky 1977). Another effect is to remember shapes and geographic relationships as more schematic (e.g., straight lines and right angles) than they really are (Barkowsky 2002).

Our sense about the details of a place (e.g., how big, how high, exactly where it is) and about relationships between places (e.g., how far away and in what direction) can be based on *belief* or *knowledge*, with *belief* being something that we assert to be true and *knowledge* being justified by evidence or inference (Worboys and Duckman 2004, chap. 9). Geographic knowledge is acquired from observation and personal navigation in the environment, as well as from secondary sources such as verbal descriptions, maps, and texts. If the geographic facts and relationships we believe to be true are contradicted by actually being there, we can adjust what we *know*. Or as Gordon Livingston says, quoting a platoon sergeant in his book *Too Soon Old, Too Late Smart* (2004, 1–2), "If the map don't agree with the ground, then the map is wrong."

Researchers have classified human spatial cognition in several ways based on the research literature in the field (Golledge 1991; Mark 1993). One classification of three basic types of geographic knowledge is widely accepted:

• *Declarative geographic knowledge* consists of geographic facts that may or may not be associated with the map locations of the associated feature. For example, a person may know about the historical or current events that occurred in Somalia or Belgrade without a clear idea where to find these places on a map of the world.

• *Procedural geographic knowledge* allows us to find our way around our environment—that is, to find our way by using cues and learned responses or conscious decisions along a path. This navigation information contributes to a person's store of declarative geographic knowledge, and the accumulation of a set of routes in an area leads to the development of a survey-type mental model that can be used to derive shortcuts and paths to other destinations. Such conceptualizations are not necessarily grounded in the culturally defined and learned orientation of most maps, which have north at the top.

• **Configurational geographic knowledge** (aka *survey knowledge*) is maplike and ranges from a basic topological sense of the associations between features in the environment without any sense of direction or distance (i.e., *in the neighborhood of* or *far away*) to a general sense of directions and distances amongst landmarks and, at the most advanced stage, to nearly complete knowledge of the coordinates of features and the distribution of features in geographic space (Smith and Mark 2001). Configurational geographic knowledge incorporates and contributes to declarative geographic knowledge.

Golledge (1991) proposes that declarative and procedural knowledge develop quite easily in most people, but configurational knowledge develops less in some people and more in others (also see Nygeres 1993). Developing configurational geographic knowledge is related both to individual differences in spatial ability and exposure to map reading and spatial reasoning skills through formal education and through the use of maps in daily activities.

Psychological research has indicated that humans make use of different mental strategies for small-scale spaces in contrast to large-scale spaces. In this case, *small scale* is defined as a space in which the whole area and everything in it can be seen from one vantage point (*proximate space*) and *large scale* as a space where navigation or secondary sources (e.g., maps) are needed (*distal space*). Linguist David A. Zubin has also broken down the continuum between these extremes into a typology of geographic spaces that is based on the size of objects within the space compared to the human body, and whether or not spaces can be seen as a whole or must be mentally constructed from known components (Freundschuh 1998; Mark 1993). Based on such schemes, Daniel Montello developed four classes of "psychological spaces" depending on a person's point of view: *figural* space is the space of desktops, pictures, visualizations (including maps), and small three-dimensional objects—in other words, things we can view and perhaps handle without moving about; *vista* space is small-scale space such as a single room or a town square that can be seen from one vantage point; *environmental* space encompasses things such as neighborhoods and cities that surround us, so that the spatial layout can be understood given enough exploration and time; *geographical* space is much larger and must be learned through symbolic representations (i.e., maps and models) or from images taken from a great distance (e.g., from spacecraft). Maps and images themselves are small items that can be handled and are therefore part of *figural* space even though they represent *geographical* space (Montello 1993).

Panel 2
Geographic Points of View

> When I was a child, I was taught that there were seven continents in the world: North America, South America, Europe, Africa, Asia, Australia, and Antarctica. This could be seen on the map in any classroom: North and South America at the center of the world, Europe and Africa to the right (or the "east") and Asia and Australia to the left (or the "west"). Antarctica was the white blur spread across the bottom of some maps, missing from others altogether.
>
> Many years later, during a discussion of the continents among my first group of students of English as a Second Language, I was at first puzzled when my students insisted there were six continents. I thought that they had forgotten Antarctica, or even mistaken "six" for "seven." But of course, the geographic reality is that Eurasia is a single continent, an obvious, indeed, an undisguisable fact on any map that places Tokyo or Beijing at the center of the world.
>
> I now live and work at the imaginary continental divide of my childhood, in a place vaguely named "Central (Eur)Asia." The librarians at my university have been frustrated for many years in the search for good maps of this place, particularly for atlases in which the areas of greatest interest to our students do not disappear into the center binding of the book. We look forward to access to georeferenced materials that will demonstrate to the future policymakers studying here the larger consequences of local actions, in hopes of preventing future regional problems such as the shrinking of the Aral Sea.
>
> **Leslie Champeny**
> Library Director
> KIMEP (Kazakhstan Institute of Management, Economics and Strategic Research)

The geographic knowledge we store from procedural and secondary sources is more qualitative than quantitative. We are more likely to understand that a place is near or far than to know the exact mileage; more likely to know that the direction is generally north than the actual angle of the relationship; more likely to know generally where a city is within a state than its coordinates. But this general knowledge allows us to create more geographic detail than we actually know by estimating from our base of geographic knowledge and thus serves us reasonably well (Barkowsky 2002). Mark (1993, 57) also makes the observation that we are able to relate the spatial knowledge and reasoning skills acquired within familiar small-scale, procedural geographic knowledge spaces to geographic knowledge represented as maps, even though maps do not represent the world as it is experienced. Those who study map reading and spatial reasoning skills and teachers who teach these skills realize that learning to do it involves the juxtaposition of personal

Figure 2.1
Relative geographic orientations of Reno versus San Diego and North America versus South America. The map of California and Nevada was created by Matt Rice, Cartomedia.com. The GOES satellite image, provided by NOAA, was acquired on December 21, 2004, near the time of the winter solstice.

experiences in physical space to abstracted, symbolic map visualizations and learning to make the transition (e.g., Ishikawa and Kastens 2005).

Our mental processes for geographic information are the basis for some common errors in our geographic assumptions. If you ask a group of people what direction Reno, Nevada, is from San Diego, California, or to draw a sketch of the North American and South American continents, chances are that many of the answers will not agree with what is on the ground (figure 2.1). Since the state of California is west of the state of Nevada, many will factor this knowledge into their answers and assume that San Diego is further west than Reno (it is not). Since the North and South American continents constitute a *unit* separated by large oceans from other continents, many will draw South America more or less under North America rather than being offset to the east to the point where the west coast of South America is nearly in line with the east coast of Florida.

In an investigation using 108 students at the University of Alberta, Jean-Claude Muller (1985) found additional evidence that this type of distortion of spatial relationships at the global level is common. His research presented a list of fifteen cities distributed around the world and asked the students to put them in order from west to east. Another list of fifteen cities was presented for the task of ordering them

Table 2.1
Lists of city names used to test the geographic knowledge of students at the University of Alberta in 1985

To rank by longitude from west to east:	*To rank by latitude from north to south:*
Canton	Madras
Boston	Tananarive (Madagascar)
St. Louis	Bogota (Colombia)
Tunis	Dakar (Senegal)
Casablanca (Morocco) {rank #1}	Vancouver
Winnipeg	Cape Town
Sydney	Bombay
Washington	Los Angeles
Tehran	Anchorage (Alaska) {rank #1}
St. John's (Newfoundland)	Tashkent
Denver (Colorado)	Buenos Aires
Havana (Cuba)	Milan
Johannesburg	Saigon
Singapore	New Orleans
Caracas	Cologne

from north to south. The city lists are shown in table 2.1. The correct arrangement of these lists is printed in an appendix to this chapter for the curious.

Muller's lists made sense when this research was done twenty years ago—lists of places that were "fairly well known" for students in a Canadian university, with the addition of the country or state for "quicker identification" when needed. They are republished here just in case someone wants to try the experiment again. Muller reports that some of the distortions revealed by the north-south and east-west orderings were expected, such as "Europe being perceived much further south relative to North America"; some were surprising, such as "Buenos Aires being south of Cape Town."

These experiments are contrived in some sense because the participants did not have a personal need for the information they were asked for. They also depend on the ability to *recall* spatial knowledge. Our ability to recall what we have experienced or learned varies from person to person and to the degree that the information has been strongly or weakly integrated into our store of knowledge. *Recognition*, on the other hand, allows us to access knowledge that cannot be recalled since we are provided with cues that tap into our stored knowledge. Recognition often comes into play in geospatial contexts. We can recognize where we are by the surroundings, landmarks, and other contextual clues. Spatial displays (e.g., maps, globes, aerial photographs) can provide the spatial context we need to navigate and understand the relationships of features and objects in geographic space. On seeing the map and remote sensing image in figure 2.1, the orientations of Reno and San Diego and North America and South America are recognized even if we may not recall the orientations correctly.

There is research to suggest that choice of expression to describe geography to nonspecialists results in different interpretations and will therefore affect the results of tests of geographic knowledge, ease of navigation of user interfaces for information systems, and so on. Smith and Mark (2001) ran an experiment where they asked students in two large sections of an undergraduate "World Civilization" course to write down the first responses that came to mind during a thirty-second time period for each of these categories: "a kind of geographic feature," "a kind of geographic object," "a geographic concept," "something geographic," and "something that could be portrayed on a map." Some terms came up frequently for all of the categories—for example, *mountain*, *river*, and *lake*. But "geographic feature" elicited almost exclusively natural physical features; "geographic object" generated small, portable items such as maps and atlases; the only term for "something geographic" that did not show up elsewhere was *world*; the phrase "geographic concept" generated the lowest degree of agreement on what that meant; and only in response to "something that could be portrayed on a map" were "things produced by people, either through construction or by fiat," written down, like *city*, *road*, *park*, and *building*. The authors conclude that for the students participating in this exercise "being *geographical* and being *portrayable on a map* are definitely different concepts."

There is also research to suggest that when subjects are given tasks where they are introduced to objects in a spatial setting (e.g., an office layout with objects in file drawers, on desks, and so forth) and the objects are given names, the subjects can recall information about the objects by name more readily than by spatial location (Jones and Dumais 1986). This suggests that names carry a great deal of information concerning the object's content and its purpose and that an object's location appears to carry considerably less information (Jones and Dumais 1986, 61). This is an interesting result and can be related to our practice of georeferencing by place-name. Names can be used as cues for associated information and as a means of communicating about geographic locations. However, we may find that geospatially based georeferencing will become more familiar and an equally comfortable way to deal with geographic information in the future as we are more frequently exposed to map-based interfaces to computer-based information systems.

Vagueness of Georeferencing

A significant aspect of spatial cognition is the inherent *vagueness* of geographic places. The concept of *vagueness* applies to the use of placenames for locations with inexact boundaries (e.g., Southern California and the Great Lakes Region) and to spatial prepositions used in informal georeferencing (e.g., *near* and *in*) as well as to the use of placenames with specific boundaries but in a general way. An example of the latter is that you might say you are from Dallas when you are in fact from a small, less well known suburb and you are using "Dallas" in the sense of a general area in order to be understood ("Dallas area" would have been more correct). One physical condition that causes inexact borders and thus vagueness is when a feature's boundary is defined by another feature such as a river, a mountain range, or a coastline. Whether from the use of placenames and geographic references in a general sense or because of inexact boundaries, the vagueness of georeferencing implies the existence of *borderline* conditions where it is not clear whether an area near the border is part of the feature or not. The core of the area is considered to be 100 percent part of the feature and beyond that there is decreasing agreement about whether territory should or should not be included. For example, everyone agrees that Los Angeles is in Southern California, but is Santa Barbara also in Southern California? Reasonable people will disagree about this or will say that it all depends on how you divide the state up into districts. Essentially vagueness results in a range of interpretations for a place reference and a range of borderline values for the spatial footprint of such a reference.

A term often used in GIS for the opposite of spatial vagueness is *crisp*, where there is no debate about the boundary of a feature (Worboys and Duckman 2004, chap. 9). However, a *crisp*, spatial boundary is frequently used to represent a feature that is essentially vague so that mapping, formal reasoning, and mathematical processing can be performed. The problem with this is that such a boundary line is often accepted as being the "truth," when in fact the line represents a range of possibilities and uncertainties that are not represented with any indication of the fuzziness of the underlying data.

Vagueness and a consequent range of interpretations also apply to the category schemes we create to indicate types of geographic features. Most of the time, we are comfortable with an inherent looseness of definition and with multiple ways of classifying things. For example, think of types of *water bodies*. These could be subtyped into freshwater and saltwater bodies, or into standing- and moving-water bodies, or into natural and human-made features. In all such schemes, there are borderline cases and therefore judgment calls about what types to assign to particular features. In natural language, we talk about *lakes, ponds, rivers, streams, reservoirs, oceans,* and *seas* and, most of the time, avoid being precise in our classification of exactly what we mean by these terms. The water body one person calls a *pond* may be equivalent in size to what someone else calls a *lake.* We may not consciously consider the difference between a reservoir and a naturally formed lake when thinking in recreational terms where both function as "lakes" for boating, fishing, and so on, but the difference between human-made and natural will be recognized in other circumstances. Similarly, it may not occur to us that there is no clear boundary between a feature called a *hill* and one called a *mountain* until we try to classify such features according to some typing scheme; one or the other of these designations seems right for a particular feature, influenced by the local terrain and local placename usage. For example, an elevated mound in a flat terrain may be called a *mountain*, while an equivalent feature in a mountainous area may be called a *hill*.

Vagueness is a type of uncertainty; there are other types, including the uncertainty of measurement where the data itself is a definite value but where knowledge of it is uncertain. An example is a measurement of the depth of the sea in a particular location; the known value is compromised by our ability to measure it. Not all imprecision is vague in this sense, however. To say that I am in the United States is imprecise but not vague. Worboys and Duckman (2004, chap. 9) created a hierarchy of terminology for *imperfection* related to GIS that sorts this out: *imperfection* has two subtypes, *inaccuracy* and *imprecision*, and *vagueness* is a subtype of *imprecision*.

Vagueness is not handled well by GIS or by cartography in general where a boundary must be placed somewhere. Users place more confidence in such lines and points than they should. Specificity is forced on the representation even when the data may indicate that a range of values or probabilities for boundary data points is more appropriate. For georeferencing usage outside of GIS and cartography, though, we would like to be able to live with levels of uncertainty more naturally, without being forced to specify a line somewhere. This is an issue for both representation and spatial information retrieval.

Chapter 4 discusses the concept of *uncertainty* as it relates to the representation of geospatial locations.

Individual Styles of Spatial Cognition and Communication

Much research has been done to identify the contributing factors to individual differences in dealing with geographic knowledge. One of the most interesting differences is the choice of method for giving directions (i.e., procedures for navigating from one place to another) (e.g., Bosco, Longoni, and Vecchi 2004). One strategy (more associated with women than men) is to base directions on references to landmarks and topological directions (e.g., right, left, and straight ahead) in verbal directions: "To get to the auditorium, go straight down this street (pointing) until you get to the grocery store on your right; turn left and go down Main Street until you see the cathedral on your left at the intersection with Fifth Street. The auditorium is on your right; the entrance is down the street about half a block."

The other strategy (more associated with men) is to give the directions in more geometric terms: "Go north on this street for ten blocks, about half a mile, to the intersection with Main Street; turn west and go three blocks to Fifth Street and then turn north again. The entrance to the auditorium will be on your right about fifty yards down."

Or, both methods can be used when it is tough to come up with the answer to the question "How do I get to . . ." (see the panel for a great example from Maine's Down East storytellers, Marshall Dodge and Robert Bryan).

Another strategy is to draw a sketch map and avoid the verbal description altogether. Such a map can have some combination of landmarks, directions, and distances. It may be oriented with north at the top, as are most maps, or oriented to match the direction of travel (the so-called heading-up orientation).

In other situations, a time interval for travel may be the preferred method for indicating distance, particularly where time is of prime importance (e.g., catching a train or getting to the church on time) or where the time to get somewhere varies by time of day (e.g., car travel in the Los Angeles area during rush hours). In answer to a question about how far it is from Santa Barbara to Ventura, you might get the following answer: "It's about 30 minutes. After 4:00 in the afternoon, however, it could take an hour or more." This information can be more useful than the distance given in terms of geographic distance (about 30 miles), although again there may be personal preferences for one representation over the other.

Of course, asking for, giving, and receiving geographic advice is a form of communication that works best if both the giver and the receiver have the same preferences. The mismatch that often happens is well illustrated in one of my favorite *New Yorker* cartoons, by James Stevenson (figure 2.2).

There are also differences traceable to cultural, linguistic, and disciplinary contexts, particularly in the way features of the geographic space are categorized. The motivation to categorize things is universal and, in the case of continuous geographic space, classification is also required in order for us to communicate with one another

Panel 3
Giving Directions

I was standin' outside Southerlands IGA store one mornin' when I heard a flivver approaching down the street toward me.

[sound of an approaching old car that slows down and stops and a voice from the car says]

"Which way to Millinocket?"

Well, you can go west to the next intersection,
get onto the turnpike,
go north through the toll gate at Augusta,
'till you come to that intersection,
well, no . . .

You can keep right on this tar road,
it changes to dirt now and agin,
just keep the river on your left,
you'll come to a crossroads and, let me see . . .

Then again, you can take that scenic coastal route that the tourists use,
and after you get to Bucksport . . . ,
well, let me see now—Millinocket.

Come to think of it, you can't get there from here.

Transcription of "Which Way to Millinocket?" from *Bert and I*, starring Marshall Dodge and Robert Bryan. CD produced by Bert and I, Inc., PO Box 666, Ipswich, MA 01938.

---

about it. The category schemes reflect the cultures, climates, topologies, and features of local areas and points of view. For example, a forest to a forester is a stand of trees with a fixed boundary, while to an ecologist the same forest will be seen as a plant community and habitat without a sharp boundary (Mark 1993).

Summary

Georeferencing is a human activity based on processes of spatial cognition involving the knowledge of geographic facts and the ability to navigate around our environment, as well as the configurational geographic knowledge for the world at large that we acquire through exposure to and study of maps of the Earth. Much of our

Figure 2.2
New Yorker cartoon by James Stevenson, published February 16, 1976. © The New Yorker Collection 1976 James Stevenson from cartoonbank.com. All rights reserved.

spatial knowledge is not oriented to compass directions but rather to topological relationships (e.g., to the right or left, near or far) and to associations such as the administrative hierarchy of a place (e.g., Detroit is in Michigan). Research has documented that our store of geographic knowledge is fragmentary and that on recall we distort spatial relationships in predictable ways. Some research indicated that some of us make a distinction between geographic and mappable objects and other research, which measured response time for answering questions about objects for which we have both names and spatial locations, found that we perform faster when using names to recall what we have learned. Our geographic knowledge is more likely to be qualitative than quantitative and we operate comfortably with a sense of *vagueness* with the georeferences we use, not expecting them to have *crisp* boundaries and definitions. Individually we adopt different strategies for georeferencing and for navigating, showing a preference for using either landmarks or geometric descriptions when giving directions, for example. Further variations in geo-referencing practices are attributed to cultural, linguistic, and disciplinary influences. These aspects of spatial cognition are relevant to the design of georeferenced information systems.

Sources for Further Information

Egenhofer, M. J., and R. G. Golledge. 1998. *Spatial and Temporal Reasoning in Geographic Information Systems*. Spatial Information Systems Series. New York: Oxford University Press.

Medyckyj-Scott, D., and H. M. Hearnshaw. 1993. *Human Factors in Geographical Information Systems*. London: Belhaven Press.

Worboys, M., and M. Duckman. 2004. *GIS: A Computing Perspective*. 2nd ed. Boca Raton, FL: CRC Press.

Appendix: Answers to the Geographic-Order Test in Chapter 2

Correct rank by longitude from west to east	Correct rank by latitude from north to south
Casablanca (Morocco)	Anchorage (Alaska)
Tunis	Cologne
Johannesburg	Vancouver
Tehran	Milan
Singapore	Tashkent
Canton	Los Angeles
Sydney	New Orleans
Denver (Colorado)	Bombay
Winnipeg	Dakar (Senegal)
St. Louis	Madras
Havana (Cuba)	Saigon
Washington	Bogota (Colombia)
Boston	Tananarive (Madagascar)
Caracas	Cape Town
St. John's (Newfoundland)	Buenos Aires

Source: Muller 1985

3

Georeferenced Information Object Types and Their Characteristics

Georeferenced information objects are of two kinds when categorized on the basis of the predominant type of georeferencing used. They can be *geospatial information objects* that are explicitly grounded by geospatial referencing, such as maps and remote sensing images. They can also be information objects georeferenced by placenames, geocodes, and addresses but without explicit geospatial referencing, such as yellow page listings, text documents (e.g., environmental impact statements and journal articles), oral histories, and cataloging for collections of books, biological specimens, and so on. The placename type of georeferencing is sometimes called *indirect georeferencing*, implying that additional steps are required to identify the locations on a map. This chapter describes several familiar types of geospatial information objects and briefly describes examples of indirectly georeferenced objects. In fact, all types of information objects have the potential of being georeferenced through links to named geographic features (i.e., named geographic places), which in turn can be linked to geospatial locations.

Some familiarity with the characteristics, applications, and advantages of geospatial objects is necessary because they are major components of georeferenced information systems and key sources of information for user applications. Their availability has revolutionized our understanding of the Earth and our local and global cultural environments. They are dense in information value in terms of both data points and visualizations. They provide the framework and the thematic layers for map components of information systems as well as primary observational, interpretive, and administrative data.

Geospatial objects are most often under the management and care of the staff of map libraries, geospatial data centers, and government agencies. They are created by map production; remote sensing programs (i.e., data and images collected by spacecraft and seafloor mapping) and aerial photography; geospatially collected data (e.g., monitoring the environment with fixed or handheld devices); GIS analysis, modeling, and conflation; and digitizing maps. Other sources of geospatially referenced data include land- and sea-based monitoring instruments that capture seismic waves, oceanic conditions, stream flow, and so on. Land-based cameras and GPS units are beginning to be significant sources of geospatially referenced data also. While an in-depth understanding of the acquisition, management, and potential applications of geospatial information objects is beyond the intent and scope of this book, this chapter will introduce some types of these objects to the extent that their roles in georeferenced collections and systems can be appreciated.

The examples used in this chapter to illustrate familiar geospatial images and datasets are from U.S. federal government agencies, primarily the U.S. Geological Survey; similar types of images and datasets in other countries may have different names and formats. Several of the illustrations show the San Francisco area in different views for comparison.

Maps

Maps are probably the most familiar form of geospatial information objects, especially as printed maps but increasingly as digital maps displayed with map-viewing software. Maps are reports, representations, or visualizations of underlying data on a two-dimensional (planar) surface. They are cartographic products, containing a selection of features for a particular purpose, and created according to the design principles of *cartography* in terms of abstraction, symbology, colors, labeling, line styles, and legends. Maps are best considered to be a particular type of intellectual object that can be manifested in various physical formats, some fixed and some dynamic. We have known maps in the past primarily in their printed paper forms as map sheets and atlases and as illustrations in books and articles. Today, map displays are incorporated in online user interfaces and as integral components of handheld global positioning system (GPS) units and in other applications.

Maps are the ultimate outcome of the gathering (exploring, surveying, and remote sensing), processing, and analysis of georeferenced data points that document the "lay of the land" and the features of the landscape. Maps can be based on the conflation of data gathered from multiple sources, including domain-specific data. There are some classic examples of this merging of data from independent sources that resulted in significant new insights into previously unknown patterns of social phenomena. The website for the Center for Spatially Integrated Social Science (CSISS) describes some of these classic studies (Center for Spatially Integrated Social Science 2005). A well-known example is a study done by Dr. John Snow in 1854 in London. Through plotting on a street map the locations of buildings in which people died from cholera, Dr. Snow was able to identify the source of an epidemic of cholera in a neighborhood as a water pump at the corner of Cambridge and Broad Streets and thus to support his conclusion that cholera was spread through contaminated water and food supplies (figure 3.1). Mapping the data allowed him to document these facts more persuasively than tables of data could to community leaders who could do something about the problem. This innovation in medical geography and epidemiology required merging demographic and public health data with map data. With sufficient interoperability of georeferenced collections—enabled by the standards, services, and technologies discussed in this book—it will be possible to discover and combine data that pertain to a particular geographic area from distributed, independent collections and, using GIS technology, produce maps that reveal geographic distribution patterns impossible to document as clearly before.

The profession of map librarianship is well established, as are producers and distributors of major map series and special collections of maps and associated georeferenced materials. Historical maps found in these collections are of great value as they depict the geographic knowledge and cultural styles of their period and authorship. See the link to the David Rumsey Map Collection in *Sources for Further Information* at the end of the chapter for access to an extensive collection of digitized historical maps.

Key characteristics for maps are *projection* and *scale*, which are discussed in chapter 4.

Map Layers and Data Types

Maps are created by overlaying a set of *map layers* for types of features, such as a hydrographic layer for the depiction of lakes, rivers, and so on; a transportation layer for highways and railroad tracks; and layers containing other georeferenced datasets such as weather patterns and built-up areas (figure 3.2). Online map-viewing applications often give the user the choice of which map layers to turn on for the current display.

Map layers contain either cartographic information (e.g., boundary lines) or attribute data (e.g., population, elevation, symbols for features and their labels). The lines of boundaries, streams, transportation features, and so forth and single data points are represented as *vector* data; other data is represented as *raster* data. All of the layers in figure 3.2 are representations of underlying vector datasets. When a raster dataset layer is added (e.g., an image), it is the base layer on which the vector layers are superimposed.

Raster data is represented by a matrix or grid of cells. Each cell (aka pixel) has one or more discrete attribute values assigned to it. These attribute values can

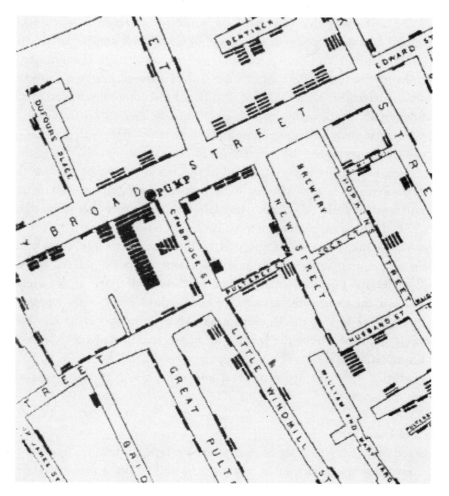

Figure 3.1
A portion of the original map by John Snow of the incidence of cholera during an outbreak in the Soho District of London in 1854 from *Snow on Cholera* (1836) by John Snow. By permission of Oxford University Press.

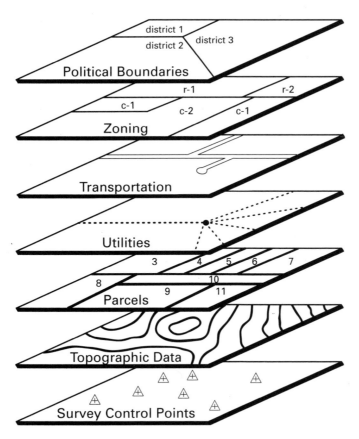

Figure 3.2
Example of a set of map layers. (Created by Matt Rice, Cartomedia.com.)

represent categories, such as that the location is an "urban area," "suburban area," or "rural," or they can be *density numbers* representing population, sea-surface temperature, and so on. Examples of raster datasets are remotely sensed images; digital elevation models; land-use land cover (LULC) data layers showing urban areas, forests, agricultural fields, and such; and socioeconomic data, which is often collected and reported by subdivisions of the coverage area (e.g., census tracks) and displayed as raster data. Cartographic representations of raster datasets often use colors, shades, and patterns to show variations in the data values. You can think of raster data as being like a hooked rug, where each square in the canvas is filled with a piece of yarn of varying colors to create patterns. A raster dataset similarly has data values filled in for each grid, which can then be visualized by applying

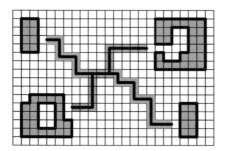

Figure 3.3
Illustration of vector data (shown as heavy black boundaries) over a raster data background.

colors or patterns to the data values. A scanned paper map is a raster dataset because it is a copy of the *image* of the map showing values for each pixel of the image; it does not show the underlying data or individual lines copied from the map.

Vector data is stored as unordered points or a series of ordered points, a point being a single pair of coordinates (i.e., longitude and latitude coordinates). A series of points that begins and ends with the same point encloses an area and is called a *polygon*. To interpret the polygon correctly, a sense of what area is enclosed ("in") and what is excluded ("out") is required, and this is supplied by the specification of a clockwise or counterclockwise ordering for the points. Arcs connect the points to one another to form the boundary of the polygon or the path of a line. For vector data, a comparison can be made to connect-the-dots type drawings where you start with dot 1 and draw a line from point to point to create a picture (although vector data is not as convoluted as connect-the-dots drawings). Examples of vector data are digital line graphs (DLGs) and TIGER/Line files; both are described in this chapter. Vector data can be displayed over or on top of a raster dataset, as in figure 3.3.

The set of layers for a map must be *georegistered* (aka geo*rectified*), which means that throughout the map's coverage area features on each layer are correctly aligned with features on other layers. If layers are properly georegistered, the lines, labels, and shaded and colored areas from the various layers appear in the correct relation to one another.

Typical map layers include

• Topography, representing surface differences in elevation from streambeds to mountain peaks
• Thematic data, showing locational patterns of types of data, such as social, biological, environmental, political, and historical data

Typical styles of maps are

• *Topographic*, showing horizontal and vertical positions of natural and cultural features, with the relief being shown in measurable form, commonly by means of *contour* lines. Surface features include administrative boundaries; transportation features (roads, railroads, pipelines, and transmission lines); hydrographic features (streams, lakes, wetlands); elevation contours; sand, gravel, lava, and glacial moraine features; survey control markers; cultural features, such as buildings; and vegetative surface cover.

• *Planimetric*, showing only the relative horizontal positions of natural or cultural features, by lines and symbols; distinguished from a topographic map by the omission of relief in measurable form (Jackson 1997).

• *Chloropleth*, showing thematic data for areas that are colored or shaded to represent the density of a particular phenomenon or to symbolize classes within it (Open Geospatial Consortium Inc. 2004).

Base Maps

Designers of online maps used for finding locations, getting directions, searching catalogs, visualizing data, or animating fly-through visualizations make a choice of a *base map* as the framework layer on which other layers of data are displayed. Simple online maps use planimetric base maps; more sophisticated and more computationally intensive applications use topographic maps where the representation of relief (elevation/depth differences) is shaded to give a three-dimensional view.

One dataset that is often used as a base map is the *Digital Chart of the World* (DCW) developed by ESRI from U.S. Defense Mapping Agency (now merged into the National Geospatial-Intelligence Agency or NGA). ESRI is a company specializing in GIS and mapping software located in Redlands, California. The DCW is a global dataset that includes major cities, rivers, lakes, coastlines, contours, vegetation, and transportation routes; "currency of the data varies from place to place, ranging from the mid 1960s to the early 1990s" (Princeton University Library 2005). DCW is distributed through online downloading from various sources and is available on CD-ROM.

Geospatially Referenced Images

Massive collections of digitized and geospatially registered aerial photography and image data captured by sensors carried by Earth-orbiting satellites have enhanced our knowledge of our planet—its surface features and atmosphere and changes through time. These collections supply the basic geographic visualizations so vital

Figure 3.4
View of the Earth as seen by the Apollo 17 crew traveling toward the moon in 1972. NASA officially credits the image to the entire Apollo 17 crew—Eugene Cernan, Ronald Evans, and Jack Schmitt.

to our understanding of environmental and social phenomena. Consider, for example, the famous image of the Earth, floating in the blackness of space, taken by Apollo 17 astronauts in 1972. It is known as the "blue marble" image and has had a profound impact on how we view ourselves and the world around us (figure 3.4). Aerial views were first obtained by enterprising photographers who sent their cameras aloft by balloon, pigeons, and kites, starting in 1858 (Aerial Arts 2004). We now have continuous views of our planet and its phenomena from miles out in space and have integrated this data and the images based on it into our lives.

One application of the new imagery is a realization of the imagination and skill of those who created the *bird's-eye views* popular in the 1800s. Compare the artistic rendition of San Francisco in 1878 featuring an imagined, oblique view from above (figure 3.5) to almost the same scene created from aerial photographs combined with a digitized topographic map (figure 3.6). Note that the recent aerial view is looking vertically down rather than from the side; vertical views are the only ones that can be used for measurement purposes and are most compatible with topographic maps.

In this section, three types of geospatially referenced images are introduced: remote sensing images collected by instruments carried by Earth-orbiting satellites;

Figure 3.5
The City of San Francisco. Bird's Eye View from the Bay Looking South-West. Sketched and drawn by Charles R. Parsons. Copyright 1878, by Currier & Ives, New York. (From the David Rumsey Map Collection, Cartography Associates, www.davidrumsey.com, Image #5683000.)

Figure 3.6
Digital orthophoto of San Francisco, January 29, 1998, North = 37.8125 South = 37.75
East = −122.375 West = −122.4375. U.S. Geological Survey (USGS). (From Alexandria Digital
Library, ID: C3712213.SES.829399.)

photography from handheld or mounted cameras from spacecraft and airplanes;
and digitized and georegistered maps.

Key characteristics of geospatially referenced images are *resolution*, *scale*, and
projection. These are discussed in chapter 4. Another key characteristic of images
is whether or not they are georegistered to a model of the Earth's surface. If an
image is georegistered, then it can be conflated with base maps and other georeferenced datasets.

Remote Sensing Images from Earth-Orbiting Spacecraft

Streams of *remote sensing images* are collected at an impressive rate. In FY 2004
NASA's Earth Observing System Data and Information System (EOSDIS), just one
of many international remote sensing programs, received a raw data stream of
approximately 424 gigabytes per day from 65 instruments on 18 satellites. These
raw data streams were automatically processed to create a range of products from
each image, increasing the data volume ten times to approximately 4.2 terabytes
per day of images and other products from this data (J. Frew, personal communication, 2005).

The captured data creates a snapshot of data points for portions of the Earth's surface that form the remote sensing images. Instruments are sensitive to particular wavelengths of electromagnetic radiation, and different sections of the electromagnetic spectrum reveal different phenomena. For example, visible and near-infrared wavelengths are used to measure surface chemical composition, vegetation cover, and biological properties of matter at the surface. Geologists can use such information to pinpoint geological formations typical of ore-bearing material or of petroleum deposits, while oceanographers can use the chlorophyll data to locate ocean regions of high biological productivity. Some instruments work by sensing radiation that is naturally emitted or reflected by the surface or from the atmosphere; others sense signals transmitted from the instrument and reflected back to it (Baker 1990).

The data received by the orbiting instruments is documented by time and by the area of the Earth's surface it covers, as well as by details about the project such as the instruments (sensors) used, the platform (e.g., plane or satellite), the path and location of the plane or satellite, and the orientation of the sensors (e.g., vertical or angled sideways). All of this documentation about the project is needed by end users to evaluate the "fitness for use" of the data for particular purposes. For individual images, the spatial footprint of the data and attributes such as "percent of cloud cover" can be factors in suitability. Remote sensing images come from sensors as raw data, which is processed to create image products with enhancements such as colorized ranges of data values that enhance pattern recognition (e.g., light-reflectance values are indicative of types of vegetation). This postcapture processing is also part of the documentation.

Typical examples of remote sensing image sets are AVHRR and Thematic Mapper images (both are raster datasets):

• *Advanced Very High Resolution Radiometer (AVHRR) images* (figure 3.7): AVHRR instruments collect four- to six-band multispectral data from the NOAA polar-orbiting satellite series. Fairly continuous global coverage is available since June 1979, including both morning and afternoon views. The resolution is 1.1 kilometer at nadir—that is, a vertical view directly under the satellite that can see features .68 miles (1,203 yards) across and bigger. This data is used to determine the weather conditions of a region (e.g., cloud cover and snow and ice coverage), to measure surface temperature (including sea-surface temperature), and for tracking forest fires and flooding and documenting land use.

• *Thematic Mapper (TM) images* (figure 3.8): The Thematic Mapper is a multispectral scanning radiometer that is carried onboard Landsat satellites. Nearly continuous global coverage from July 1982 to present, with a 16-day repeat cycle, is available. TM image data, with a spatial resolution of 20 to 30 meters (22 to 33 yards), is used to detect, measure, and analyze major characteristics and changes to

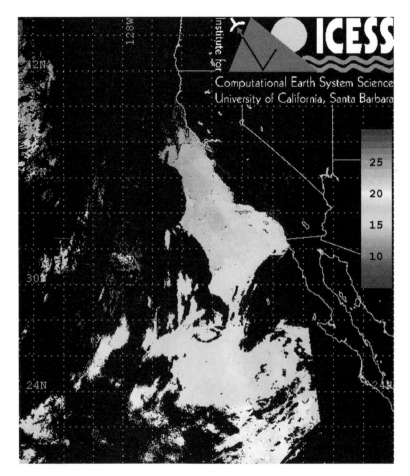

Figure 3.7
AVHRR image of coastal southwest U.S. (longitude 110 to 135 W, latitude 20 to 45 N) showing sea-surface temperature, taken January 20, 2005, at 0639 GMT. (Processed by the Institute of Computational Earth System Sciences, University of California, Santa Barbara, http://www.icess.ucsb.edu/avhrr/avhrr.html.)

Figure 3.8
Landsat Thematic Mapper image of San Francisco, June 20, 1990. (http://landcover.usgs.gov/urban/umap/htmls/sftm.asp.)

the surface of the planet. This includes the effects of desertification, deforestation, urbanization, agricultural development, pollution, development and degradation of water resources, cataclysmic volcanic activity, and other natural and anthropogenic events. TM images are being used to support a wide range of applications in such areas as global-change research, agriculture, forestry, geology, resource management, geography, mapping, water quality, and oceanography (Global Change Master Directory 2002a).

Photography from Spacecraft and Airplanes

Surveys of the landscape of the Earth have been conducted by aerial photography since the 1920s and continue today through national, regional, and project-oriented aerial photography-acquisition programs. The historical photographs are very valuable for documenting and understanding changes in the landscape, environmental conditions, and land use through time. Aerial photographs of battlefields and the surrounding countryside during the twentieth century are examples of the treasure trove of historical information contained in aerial photograph collections. Fast-forward to astronauts taking pictures with handheld cameras from orbiting spacecraft and the space station to see today's extension of this acquisition of photographic views from above.

The United States has an ongoing aerial photography survey program called the National Aerial Photography Program (NAPP), which collects "a standardized set of cloud-free aerial photographs covering the conterminous United States over five-to-seven year cycles" (U.S. Geological Survey Eros Data Center 2005). These are the photos that are used to create the digital orthophoto quadrangles described below.

When the camera is on a fixed mounting and the aerial survey is an orderly set of flight paths, then the geographic coverage of the photos is known, as well as the orientation of the camera to the ground. Such photos can be documented by the longitude and latitude points for the corners of the coverage area. Handheld photos, on the other hand, cannot be so easily georeferenced.

Digital Orthophoto Quadrangles (DOQs) are computer-generated copies of aerial photographs in which image displacement caused by terrain relief and camera angles has been removed—that is, the images have been georegistered to the Universal Transverse Mercator (UTM) projection on the North American Datum of 1983 (NAD83) (see chapter 4 for a discussion of the UTM projection and the NAD83 datum). A DOQ combines the image characteristics of a photograph with the geometric qualities of a map. The standard digital orthophoto quarter quadrangles (DOQQs) produced by the U.S. Geological Survey (USGS) are either grayscale or color-infrared images with a 1-meter (1.09 yards) ground resolution (figure 3.9). They cover an area measuring 3.75 minutes longitude by 3.75 minutes latitude, or

Over Christmas vacation in 1983, I typed out a paper describing a revolutionary idea—that the valuable collections of maps and aerial photographs in the Map and Imagery Lab (MIL) in the UC Santa Barbara campus library (and other libraries) could be made accessible through geospatial coordinate indexing and graphic interfaces, giving users simple processes to mark the geographic area of interest on the scene and view images of these resources. At that time, only the experts in special map collections understood the collections, the filing rules, and the printed indexes well enough to locate the pertinent materials. This new system would bypass the need to consult with the library staff to identify and retrieve cartographic and other geospatial materials.

This idea was inspired by systems newly developed for use by some government agencies that were providing such computer-aided access for agency personnel, albeit through systems that were complex both in the user interfaces and the computations that match the user request with the geospatial materials. That paper led to funding by the Keck Foundation to the Association of Research Libraries to develop a design for such a system. The system was called the Geo-Referenced Information Network (GRIN), and the funding resulted in a design document and conceptual drawings of initial search interfaces and how such a system would appear to the end user.

After this, the challenge was to convince potential funders to provide the means to develop this geospatial access for libraries. At a meeting of the few people working on this in 1993, Prue Adler of the Library of Congress mentioned the announcement by the National Science Foundation (NSF) of its Digital Library Initiative (DLI) and there was immediate recognition that this was an excellent opportunity to apply for funding. A research team was formed and a successful proposal for the Alexandria Digital Library (ADL) Project was submitted to the NSF. Through collaborative research with multiple partners through the four years of DLI-1 and the subsequent DLI-2 funding, ADL worked through multiple issues of designing such a distributed georeferenced digital library system. The MIL staff was involved in these research activities at every step along the way and then took the best of the results to build an operational ADL, which is widely used today.

Now finally, within the scope of library services, vast collections of geospatial information in the form of maps, aerial photos, and remote sensing images can be searched online for information that pertains to particular areas and particular projects and then, when permitted by intellectual property rights, selected digital images and datasets can be downloaded for local use. An indication of the value of this access is that onsite use of the ADL system by contractors provides a substantial income flow for the library (without interfering with ADL use in support of university-level education and by the general public). These contractors do research for lawyers, political bodies, developers, property managers, planners, and financial institutions for whom the historical and current geospatial information is critical to their work.

Getting ADL to this point has been a major accomplishment. We would now like to see use of the ADL technology integrated into general library catalogs and access systems to provide map-based access to all types of information including books, articles, and archives of all kinds.

Larry Carver
Director Library Technologies & Digital Initiatives
UCSB Libraries
University of California Santa Barbara
ADL Webclient: http://webclient.alexandria.ucsb.edu/mw/index.jsp

Figure 3.9
DOQQ of San Francisco North SW, North = 37.8125 South = 37.75 East = −122.4375 West = −122.5, 1998-02-18. Quadrangle Name: San Francisco North. (From Alexandria Digital Library, ID: C3712213.SWS.829400.)

approximately 5 miles on each side. They correspond to a quarter section of a 7.5-minute topographic quadrangle map produced by the USGS (that is, one-quarter of a topographic map measuring 7.5 minutes longitude and 7.5 minutes latitude on the sides). DOQs are designed to facilitate the creation of a mosaic of matched DOQQs and DOQs and to conflate with other geospatial objects (adapted from Digital Data Services 2004). DOQs serve a variety of purposes, from interim maps to field references for Earth science investigations and analysis. They are useful as a map layer for geographic information systems and as a tool for the revision of digital line graphs (DLGs) and topographic maps (Global Change Master Directory 2002b).

Digitized and Georegistered Maps

Georeferenced information that is represented only in analog form, such as a printed map or a photographic print, can be transformed into digital images or data through two processes: *scanning* or *digitizing*.

Scanning, on a desktop flatbed or a drum scanner, can produce a digital copy of the original map. Alternatively, a specialized scanner can be programmed to follow continuous lines on the map (e.g., contour lines). Scanned images can be further edited using graphic editing software, and they can be printed out using a *plotter* that draws with a moving pen. In scanned map images, the lines, features, text, and so on are scanned at their actual width in the original and must be preprocessed before further computer processing (Clarke 2001). Scanned maps and prints are raster datasets; they can, however, be converted to vector data with specialized software.

Digitization mimics the way maps were drafted by hand and involves tracing the features of the original document using a handheld electronic unit while the original document is held in place on a sensitized digitizing tablet—the digital equivalent of a drafting table. The handheld unit (the *cursor*) sends selected point coordinates to the host computer. Labeling from the original document is transferred manually to document the newly created digital version (Clarke 2001). Digitized maps and prints are vector datasets.

Georegistering of scanned and digitized maps and prints is done by accurately assigning the coordinate locations for at least three points from different parts of the digital images. For map sheets, these points are corners of the map coverage area; for photographs and other documents with less geospatial grounding, the points are recognizable features.

A *rubber sheeting* or *warping* process is applied to digitized maps to adjust the layout of the features in a systematic, statistically based way so that they match other georeferenced datasets, particularly for the purposes of matching a map to an image or photograph or for the edge matching of two adjacent areas so that continuous lines and features line up properly (Clarke 2001). This is just one of a suite of GIS editing tools available to eliminate errors in the georegistering of datasets.

Three of the well-known digital products from the USGS that use scanning, digitization, and georegistering processes are

• *Digital Raster Graphics (DRGs)* (figure 3.10): A DRG is a raster image of a USGS topographic map scanned at very high density. The scanned image contains the map, including the labeling for features and all of the marginal information outside of the map. The map is georegistered to the surface of the Earth. The USGS is producing DRGs of various topographic map series in scales ranging from 1:24,000 to 1:250,000, and others have made them available for online viewing and downloading. They are excellent resources for such activities as planning a hike or evaluating property for potential purchase or development and all the other uses of the printed topographic map series. When DRGs are combined with other digital products, such as digital orthophoto quadrangles (DOQs) or digital elevation models (DEMs), the resulting visualizations are useful for many purposes, including the extraction and revision of base cartographic information. Clarke (2001, 286) points out that "these maps make excellent starting points for GIS projects, and they often contain many features that can be extracted for use, such as contour lines and building footprints."

• *Digital Line Graphs (DLGs)* (figure 3.11): DLGs are digital vector representations of administrative boundaries; transportation features (roads, railroads, pipelines, and transmission lines); hydrographic features (streams, lakes, wetlands); elevation contours; sand, gravel, lava, and glacial moraine features; survey control markers; cultural features, such as buildings; and vegetative surface cover. They are derived from the vector layers of topographic maps. In contrast to DRGs, DLGs contain point, polyline, and polygonal data rather than raster images—for example, the symbol for a windmill in a DRG is replaced in the DLG with a longitude, latitude coordinate point and an associated attribute designates it as the site of a windmill (Longley et al. 2001). This geospatial data can be combined with other datasets and otherwise manipulated in ways not possible with raster data. DLGs are available in scales ranging from 1:20,000 (large scale) to 1:2,000,000 (small scale) and are used for base maps.

• *Digital Elevation Models (DEMs)* (figure 3.12): Another USGS product produced from topographic maps is the Digital Elevation Model series (DEMs). For DEMs, elevation values have been captured from the contour lines on topographic maps; more recently they are obtained from remote sensing techniques. They are available at various scales and range in resolution from about 10 to 80 meters (11 to 87 yards). DEMs are used to construct visualizations of the physical terrain that show landscapes of varying elevations and as a base level dataset for many mapping

Figure 3.10
Digital Raster Graphic of SAN FRANCISCO NORTH, CA. DRG o37122g4. North = 37.87
South = 37.75 East = −122.4 West = −122.5. 1973

Figure 3.11
Digital Line Graph (DLG) of California State Highways, January 2004. (From State of California, Caltrans Office of Geographic Information Systems, Data Library, http://www.dot.ca.gov/hq/tsip/TSIPGSC/library/libdatalist.htm.)

applications. When conflated with DOQ images, three-dimensional models can be constructed showing elevation; this is the basis for the software that provides the virtual experience of flying through a landscape. Strictly speaking, DEMs are not images; they are used in conjunction with geospatial images to construct three-dimensional visualizations. An interesting use of DEMs is in the analysis of "viewsheds," which are "areas that can be seen from a given viewpoint." Such visualizations are useful for protecting existing scenic views when, for example, adding a house to a neighborhood or an extra floor to a building (Longley et al. 2001, 342).

Geocoded Features

Closely related to the DLGs are the TIGER/Line files created by the U.S. Census Bureau. TIGER® is an acronym for Topologically Integrated Geographic Encoding

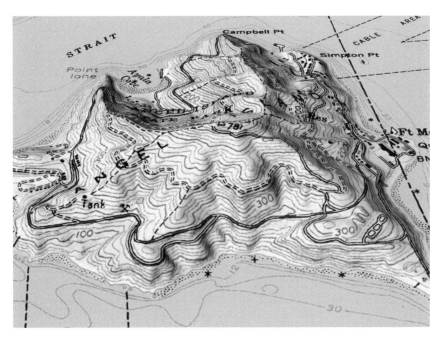

Figure 3.12
Angel Island, San Francisco Bay. USGS 7.5′ Digital Elevation Model (DEM) with Digital Raster Graphic (DRG) overlay. (Created by Richard Horne, using 3DEM software, http://www.visualizationsoftware.com/3dem.html.)

and Referencing, the name for the system and digital database developed at the U.S. Census Bureau to support its mapping needs for the decennial census and other Bureau programs. The Census Bureau has trademarked the term to distinguish clearly when products have been created by the Census Bureau; derivative products cannot use the acronym in product names. These files are not graphic images of maps, but rather digital data describing geographic features. TIGER/Line files contain geographic features, such as roads, railroads, rivers, lakes, administrative boundaries, census statistical boundaries, and so on covering the United States. The features are geospatially referenced; associated information includes the name, the type of feature, address ranges for most streets, and geographic relationships to other features. The data is often used to draw base maps such as the one in figure 3.13.

In the United States, TIGER files are key components of georeferenced studies and applications where the data is identified by street address and needs to be translated into coordinate-based georeferencing, a process called *geocoding*. A number of commercial services provide such geocoding services, and applications using such

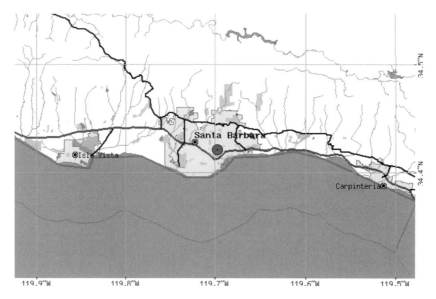

Figure 3.13
Map generated from TIGER files showing the location of the city of Santa Barbara, produced using a direct map request from the U.S. Census Bureau Mapping and Cartographic Resources at the U.S. Census Bureau, January 20, 2005 (through the query interface for the USGS Geographic Names Information Service (GNIS))

translations are the basis of services that provide driving directions and distance calculations (e.g., the MapQuest online service). The addresses in yellow page directories are used to link the names of businesses and public facilities (e.g., schools and museums) to coordinate locations. Driving directions can be provided to get to a given street address from another location by services using TIGER data, road-network data, and pathfinding software. Data associated with street addresses is used for many purposes and is often correlated with census statistics. Examples include (1) records of the occurrence of diseases (e.g., cancer), which are linked to the residence addresses of patients and are used in epidemiological studies and health planning, and (2) patterns of buying habits, which are used for marketing campaigns, choosing store locations, and product decisions.

Georeferenced Text

Text documents contain placenames, feature types (e.g., mountain, park), and spatial prepositional references (e.g., in, south of, near, 5 miles from) in both informal and controlled ways. Consider, for example, the ways geographic locations are referenced in

• Conversations: "While I was on a Nature Conservancy trip in the Front Range area of the Rocky Mountains in Montana in 2003, we saw some fresh Grizzly Bear prints on the banks of a pond but no Grizzlies 'in person,' so to speak—but we did see some black bears in Glacier National Park."

• Monographs: "There is a lovely road that runs from Ixopo into the hills" (the first line of *Cry, the Beloved Country* by Alan Paton).

• Correspondence: "I live at a village called Down near Farnborough in Kent, and employ myself in Zoology" (from correspondence between Charles Darwin and Francis Galton, http://www.mugu.com/galton/letters/darwin/correspondence. htm).

• Oral histories: "Never had no misfortune until I hit a town called Salina, in Kansas, where I had to change . . . to the next train to Lakeport. . . . But I forgot to tell you about Kansas City. I never see nothin' like that railroad station in my life." (from *American Life Histories: Manuscripts from the Federal Writers' Project, 1936–1940: Mr. Botsford on Travel—Kansas (1938)*, http://memory.loc.gov/ ammem/).

• Collections: *California Gold: Northern California Folk Music from the Thirties* (American Memory Project, http://memory.loc.gov/ammem/afcchtml/cowhome. html).

• Bibliographic indexing: The bibliographic record from *GeoRef* in figure 3.14 illustrates the use of georeferencing in titles, abstracts, and subject headings in scientific articles. Note that this entry is also an example of the coordinate indexing (*Latitude & Longitude* element of the record) that *GeoRef* has done on a portion of its bibliographic records.

• Book titles: *The Bridge of San Luis Rey.*

• Film titles: *If It's Tuesday, This Must Be Belgium.*

• Library cataloging:
Material type ⟨Book⟩
Author Loomis, Benjamin Franklin, 1857–1935
Title *Pictorial history of the Lassen Volcano*, by B. F. Loomis
Published [s.l.] California History Books [c1926]
Description 139p. illus., fold. map. 24 cm.
Subject Lassen Volcanic National Park
Subject Lassen Peak

• Environmental impact statements:
Hellgate Recreation Area: Proposed Recreation Area Management Plan and Final Environmental Impact Statement. [Medford, OR]: U.S. Dept. of the Interior,

---

Bibliographic entry from GeoRef

Title: Landslides, floods, and marine effects of the storm of January 3–5, 1982, in San Francisco Bay region, California

Author: Brown, William M, III (prefacer); Herd, Darrell G (prefacer)

Editor: Ellen, Stephen D; Wieczorek, Gerald F;

Affiliation: U. S. Geol. Surv., USA, (United States)

Sponsor: USGS, Publications of the U. S. Geological Survey

Source: U. S. Geological Survey Professional Paper, Report: P 1434, 310 pp., 14 sheets, 1988

ISSN: 1044-9612

CODEN: XGPPA9

Report Number: P 1434

Publisher: U. S. Geological Survey, Reston, VA, United States (USA)

Abstract: A catastrophic rainstorm in Central California on January 3–5, 1982, dropped as much as half the mean annual precipitation within a period of about 32 hours, triggering landslides and floods throughout 10 counties in the vicinity of the San Francisco Bay. Altogether, the storm damaged 6,300 homes, 1,500 businesses, and tens of kilometers of roads, bridges, and communication lines. Preliminary estimates of total storm damage exceeded $280 million. Landslides accounted for 25 of the 33 deaths attributed to the storm. The 16 chapters in this volume elucidate the processes of landsliding and flooding that operated during the storm and thereby provide basic information toward predicting hazards from future storms.

Latitude & Longitude: Latitude: N365300,N385600 Longitude:W1205500,W1233400

Descriptors: Alameda County California; California; Central California; Contra Costa County California; debris flows; engineering geology; engineering geology maps; geologic hazards; hydrology; landslides; maps; Marin County California; mass movements; Napa County California; rainfall; San Francisco Bay region; San Francisco County California; San Mateo County California; Santa Clara County California; Santa Cruz County California; shorelines; slope stability; Solano County California; Sonoma County California; storms; surveys; United States; USGS

Classification: 30 Engineering geology; 21 Hydrogeology

Copyright: GeoRef, Copyright 2004, American Geological Institute.

Accession Number: 1989-023395

Figure 3.14

Example of a bibliographic record (#1989-023395) from the *GeoRef* database showing the presence of both placename references and indexer-assigned coordinates

Bureau of Land Management, Medford District Office, Grants Pass Resource Area.

- Guidebooks:

  Geologic Guidebook to the Point Reyes Area, Northern California. Ventura, CA: Pacific Section, American Association of Petroleum Geologists, c1990.

The world is awash in such placename references in newspapers, journals, radio and television broadcasts, conversations, catalogs, and so on. These references are also ubiquitous in the way we ask for and give information for navigation (e.g., "Which way to Cucamonga?") and when asking for information or constructing a query to locate resources and answers in libraries and other information systems. It is not unusual for someone to feel that they are "in the middle of nowhere" when they cannot identify where they are by reference to a placename.

Natural History Museum Specimen Collections

Natural history museums often georeference the specimens in their collections using the narrative descriptions written by the collectors in the field. Descriptions from pre-GPS days (that is, before the use of satellites to determine position with global positioning systems) often refer to relative positions ("5 miles south of x on the bank of the y river") or stops along the way of an expedition ("on the second day near our camp site") (Moritz 1999).

Here are a few examples of collection-site descriptions where natural history specimens, now part of a museum's holdings, were obtained; some are more helpful than others (Mammal Networked Information System (MaNIS) 2005; Moritz 1999):

- "Congo River, three and one half miles down from Stanley Falls"
- "Fern Canyon, Mt. Tam., Marin County, CA"
- "E of Bakersfield, T29S R29E Sec. 34 NE 1/4"
- "left bank of the Mississippi River, 16 mi downstream from St. Louis"
- "10 mi E (by air) Bakersfield"

Some of these references, discovered when attempting to assign geospatial locations to the specimens they describe, have been identified by the MaNIS project as "classics" (Mammal Networked Information System (MaNIS) 2003a). Here are a few from that list:

- "between Los Angeles and San Francisco"
- "Bob Jones' yard" (This is actually a rather specific locality—if you know Bob Jones.)
- "Strawberry Canyon, 200 yards from nearest building, Berkeley"
- "Nevada border"

Obviously some of the georeferencing is generalized in such a way that deriving any geospatial location from the narrative can only be done with great uncertainty and only to the point of an enclosing region for the point of collection. Any geospatial footprint is useful, however; the aggregation of many locations associated with a particular species will reveal patterns and trends based on filtering out spurious data and weighting all data on the basis of confidence in the identification and location information. This revelation of spatial distribution patterns is crucial for environmental, ecological, and evolutionary biology research. In fact, without it much of the value of collections of biological specimens in today's museums is inaccessible, and this applies equally to other fields as well, such as archaeology and ethnology.

Music and Art

For museums and collections in general, georeferencing the locations associated with artifacts and other collection objects enriches our understanding of the Earth's and human history. This is especially true when the geographic locations associated with collection objects can be shown on base maps and researchers and others are given the option of finding just the set of objects associated with a particular geographic location. The georeferenced information linked with such objects can be of various kinds—for example,

• The geographic setting associated with a piece of music (e.g., Ferde Grofé's *Grand Canyon Suite* and *Meet Me in Saint Louis, Louis* by Sterling and Mills) or works of art (Georges Seurat's *A Sunday Afternoon on the Island of La Grande Jatte* and Picasso's *Guernica*)
• Where the piece was created or found
• The locations associated with the artist/composer
• Where the piece is housed or has been exhibited or performed

For these applications and others, the temporal dimension is often on equal footing with the geospatial. The Electronic Cultural Atlas Initiative (ECAI) (Electronic Cultural Atlas Initiative 2005b) is an excellent example of this approach. The system is based on a common metadata structure for distributed worldwide collections where both the geographic and the temporal details are documented. The ECAI Clearinghouse user interface is powered by the *Time*Map™ software developed by Ian Johnson and others at the University of Sydney. Users can search the distributed ECAI collections for historical and archaeological information or the David Rumsey Map Collection (Cartography Associates 2005), using both a map browser to identify the area of interest and a "time bar" to set the time frame of interest. Figure 3.15 shows the ECAI user interface for searching, as of summer 2005. The

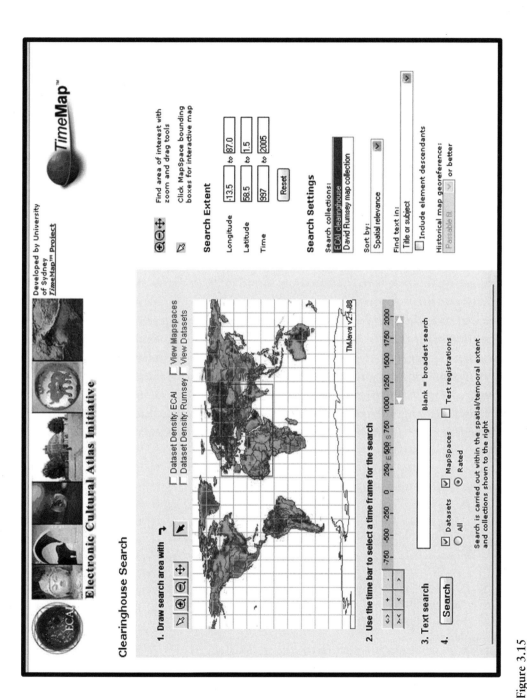

Figure 3.15

Screenshot of the search interface for the Electronic Cultural Atlas Initiation (ECAI) using the *TimeMap*™ software, as of August 2005. (http://www.geoplace.com/uploads/featurearticle/0508em.asp.)

box drawn over portions of Europe, Asia, and Africa is the search area and the time span has been set between the years 997 and 2005. The search can also be limited to items where specified words appear in the metadata. Datasets, images, and associated metadata can be downloaded for local use as permitted by ownership rights.

Summary

The major forms of geospatial information objects are maps, remote sensing images, aerial photography, and geospatial datasets. These resources range from historical hand-drawn maps representing the geographic knowledge of the author at the time to the streams of remote sensing data being captured from sensing apparatus carried by Earth-orbiting satellites. Increasingly, handheld digital camera photographs are accompanied by technical data, including the longitude and latitude position of the camera at the time the picture was taken. Scanning and digitization activities are converting a wealth of printed cartography into digital georegistered data.

In addition to these geospatial objects, all other types of information objects have the potential of being georeferenced through links to named geographic features or addresses that in turn can be linked to geospatial locations. The challenge for information system designers and implementers is to create systems that support the discovery of the information resources relevant to particular locations in a seamless way across all types of resources, using both geospatial referencing and placename referencing interchangeably. Once resources relevant to a user's need are identified, the challenge is to be able to visualize them on a common geospatial basis that will reveal patterns and relationships hard to discover and appreciate otherwise.

Sources for Further Information

Baker, D. J. 1990. *Planet Earth: The View from Space*. Frontiers of Space Series. Cambridge, MA: Harvard University Press.

Cartography Associates. 2005. *David Rumsey Map Collection*. http://www.davidrumsey.com/

Clarke, K. C. 2003. *Getting Started with Geographic Information Systems*. 4th ed. Upper Saddle River, NJ: Prentice Hall.

Larsgaard, M. L. 1998. *Map Librarianship: An Introduction*. 3rd ed. Englewood, CO: Libraries Unlimited.

Muehrcke, P., J. O. Muehrcke, and A. J. Kimerling. 2001. *Map Use: Reading, Analysis, and Interpretation*. 4th ed. Madison, WI: JP Publications.

4

Representation of Geospatial Location and Coverage

The planet Earth is a lumpy ellipsoid nearly spherical in shape. If it were a perfect sphere, developing methods of geocoding locations on its surface would be less complex. But as it is, there is not a single mathematical model of the Earth's shape and size but instead various models for different purposes and from different points of view. The science of determining the size and shape of the Earth is called *geodesy*, and all geospatial references are based on a particular Earth model (the *geodetic datum*). A coordinate system of longitude lines running north and south from pole to pole and latitude lines running east and west parallel to the equator is the most universally used scheme for referencing locations on the surface of the Earth; other spatial referencing systems similarly create ways to reference a location on the Earth, either for a portion or for the whole of the Earth's surface. These are means of *formal* georeferencing. To interpret these representations correctly, attention must be paid to issues of accuracy and precision as well as the associated issues of datum, scale, resolution, and projection. To calculate the relationships between geospatial locations, either *geometric* measurements of distance and direction based on mathematical models or *topological* relationships based on adjacency and connectedness can be used. This chapter explains these aspects of geospatial referencing at a general level to provide a foundation of understanding for applying formal georeferencing to information management practices.

There are other ways of formally geocoding a location. These include the cadastre schemes used to record property ownership, postal address systems, and the U.S. Public Land Survey System (PLSS) that results in the township and range geocodes in the western United States and western Canada. The geocoding of postal addresses is a particularly active process today because there is so much data associated with street addresses (e.g., crime statistics, customer buying patterns, real estate transactions, and hospital records that are indicators of the occurrence of diseases) for which geographic analysis provides valuable insights into cultural patterns. This translation of street addresses to coordinates is also the basis for the online services that provide the user with driving directions from a beginning point to a destination or that display a digital map or a remote sensing image for the area of a given street address. To be useful for georeferencing in information management systems, street addresses, cadastre codes, PLSS values, and other similar geocoding schemes are translated into longitude and latitude coordinates. This chapter describes the longitude and latitude georeferencing scheme but not any details about the other geocoding schemes, and it does not describe the process of converting street addresses and other geocodes into spatial locations. The reader is referred to chapter 4 in *Geographic Information Systems and Science*, by Longley et al. (2001), for a good explanation of these schemes.

Geospatial Coding Schemes

Coordinates and Coordinate Systems

There are many Earth-based georeferencing systems; in general, they are systems with all the necessary components of an origin, a type of unit distance, and two axes to locate a position in two- or three-dimensional space (Clarke 2001). The most familiar georeferencing system for the surface of the Earth uses longitude and latitude coordinates. The baseline (i.e., origin) for latitudes is the *equator* (0° latitude); the baseline for longitudes is the *prime meridian* (0° longitude) that runs from pole to pole through the original location of the Royal Greenwich Observatory in the United Kingdom, also known as the *Greenwich meridian*. The range of values for latitudes is 90° (from the equator to the poles in both north and south directions); the range of values for longitudes is 180° from the prime meridian around the globe to the east and to the west to the extension of the prime meridian on the other side, which is known as the *International Date Line* and also as the *anti–prime meridian*. Degrees of latitude, therefore, have up to two digits; degrees of longitude have up to three digits.

Although it is common practice to refer to "latitude, longitude" in that order, there are reasons why we should be retraining ourselves to say "longitude, latitude" instead and they have to do with the integration of traditional ways of talking about geospatial location and the way computer processing handles the same information. When a spherical coordinate system for the Earth as a globe is projected onto a flat surface, the result is a basic *x,y* graph representation that uses *Cartesian coordinates* based on the geometry developed by René Descartes; degrees of longitude run

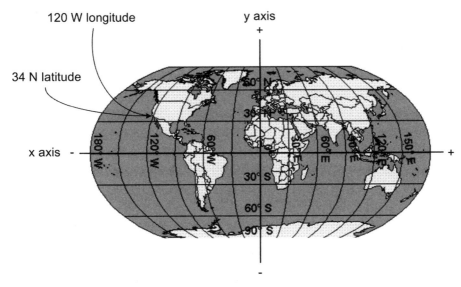

Figure 4.1
Illustration of the correspondence of *x,y* axes versus longitude, latitude coordinates

along the horizontal *x*-axis (i.e., distance between longitude lines) and degrees of latitude run along the vertical *y*-axis (i.e., distance between latitude lines). Notice that we almost always refer to points on such a graph (and in computer processing) as "*x,y*" values, while the same point on a globe or a map is often described with "latitude, longitude" coordinates. This unintentional switching of the order of the values potentially causes confusion. Figure 4.1 illustrates this difference. In the figure, the *x*- and *y*-axes cross at the intersection of the equator and the prime meridian—the dividing lines between north and south and between east and west. The point at the end of the curved pointed lines is at approximately 120° west longitude (i.e., 120° along the negative arm of the *x*-axis) and 34° north latitude (i.e., 34° along the positive arm of the *y*-axis). This point is written as −120,34 as a decimal coordinate representation (which is used for computer processing)—that is, in the order of *longitude, latitude*. This order of the coordinate values is the same order commonly used for *x,y* graphs.

The "latitude, longitude" order of reference may have become standard because latitude was formalized before longitude for navigation (as described in Dava Sobel's 1995 book: *Longitude: The True Story of a Lone Genius Who Solved the Greatest Scientific Problem of His Time*). Simply changing the order of the coordinates in speech and writing will be a small step toward removing some of the confusion during the current period, when we routinely digitize map data and move seamlessly between cartographic views and computer processing of the same data.

Longitude and latitude coordinates can be represented using degrees, minutes, seconds (denoted as ddmmss) or decimal degrees (denoted as dd.d). There are two terms that you may encounter for these two schemes. Decimal degrees are called *centesimal coordinates*, meaning coordinates based on divisions of hundredths; the degree, minute, second coordinates are called *sexagesimal coordinates*, meaning divisions based on the number 60.

This is a point representation for the location of Goleta, California, in both decimal degrees and degree, minute, seconds:

- Longitude: −119.8266 (119°49′36″W)
- Latitude: 34.4358 (34°26′8″N)

Note the way the positions west of the prime meridian and south of the equator are represented in the two forms of representation for these coordinates. For ddmmss representation, the position east or west of the prime meridian or north or south of the equator is noted with a letter either before or after the numerical string for direction (N, S, E, W). For decimal degrees, the convention is to consider a position east of the prime meridian or north of the equator as positive (+) and a position south of the equator or west of the prime meridian as negative (−) (with the + assumed in the absence of a sign). This follows the notation for *x,y* graphs.

Since ddmmss is the preferred coordinate representation for maps and other purposes and decimal degrees are needed in information systems for mathematical operations, conversion from one to the other is often necessary. When converting from ddmmss to decimal degrees, there is a possibility of introducing unintended precision if care is not taken to round the decimal to an appropriate length. For example, starting with 34°25′33″E, the conversion to decimal degrees should be limited to four decimal points—that is, to 34.4258 degrees. Any further extension will imply that the original value expressed a finer resolution than whole seconds—such as 33.5″. A four-decimal-point value will convert back to the original value because 0.0001 degrees is equivalent to only 0.36 seconds (J. Frew, personal communication, 2003). Although the mathematical operation of conversion from ddmmss to decimal degrees may result in an extended decimal value, it is misleading to use any more than is justified by the original value. There are services on the web to convert from one representation to the other; try a web search for "latitude longitude conversion" to find them.

Coordinate Footprint Types

The standard that is being adopted for the representation of geospatial footprints as well as for the "modeling, transport and storage of geographic information" is the Geography Markup Language (GML) (Open Geospatial Consortium Inc. 2003). The GML is a specification product of the Open Geospatial Consortium (formerly the Open GIS Consortium and known as OGC). Version 2 was released as a Recommendation Paper (Open Geospatial Consortium Inc. 2002). Version 3 is an Implementation Specification and it supersedes version 2, but the earlier version is still useful for basic constructs and is more accessible to nonspecialists. Section 4.3 of GML version 2 on *Encoding Geometry* provides some useful definitions for representing basic types of coordinate footprints. In this section, the possible types of footprints are listed with a technical specification for each. They are

- Point
- Box
- LineString
- LinearRing
- Polygon
- MultiPoint
- MultiLineString
- MultiPolygon
- MultiGeometry

The types of geometric shapes most frequently used in basic systems are described in the following paragraphs.

The simplest geospatial footprint is a *point* consisting of one pair of longitude, latitude values. In decimal degrees, a point is written as a comma-separated set of values—for example, "−120,34" represents a point 120° west of the prime meridian and 34° north of the equator. This point is illustrated in figure 4.1.

A *line* (i.e., a LineString in GML terminology) is a set of connected points in sequential order used to represent linear features such as streams and roads. In decimal degrees, a line is written as a set of points separated by spaces—for instance, "−120,34 −111,35 −110,36" represents a simple line. As a geospatial representation, a line has a beginning, an end, and a sequence of points, and it does not enclose a space as a polygon does.

A *polygon* is a closed set of points enclosing an area—that is, it is the boundary of an area such as an administrative district or a lake. In decimal degrees, a polygon is written as a set of points separated by spaces with the first and the last point being the same—for example, "−120,34 −111,35 −110,34 −111,33 −120,34" represents a simple polygon. The GML specifies a LinearRing type separately and says that such a ring is used in the construction of a polygon.

A *box* is a type of *polygon*, but boxes are used frequently and are separately defined by GML. A geometric box has four sides that are aligned with lines of longitude and latitude. That is, the latitudes of a box are parallel to the equator and the longitudes of a box are parallel to the prime meridian. GML specifies that boxes are represented by two points in diagonal corners of the box; specifically "the first of these is constructed from the minimum values measured along all axes, and the second is constructed from the maximum values measured along all axes," which translates into the SW corner followed by the NE corner (Open Geospatial Consortium Inc. 2002, sec. 4.3.3). For example, this set of points "−116,36 −115,37" is sufficient to represent a geometric box.

GML specifies that the coordinates for any geometric shape can be encoded in XML either as a sequence of ⟨coord⟩ elements representing points, as in this example of a box specification:

```
<gml:box>
    <gml:coord>
        <gml:X>-116</gml:X>
        <gml:Y>36</gml:Y>
    </gml:coord>
    <gml:coord>
        <gml:X>-115</gml:X>
        <gml:Y>37</gml:Y>
    </gml:coord>
</gml:box>
```

or as in this representation of the same box as a single string contained within a ⟨coordinates⟩ element:

```
<gml:box>
    <gml:coordinates>-116,36  -115,37</gml:coordinates>
</gml:box>
```

When the coordinate footprints are represented by a single string containing a sequence of points, GML specifies the default syntax as separating the coordinates in a tuple by commas, and separating successive tuples by a space character (Open Geospatial Consortium Inc. 2002). That is, in a list of coordinate points, the longitude and latitude values for a single point are separated by a comma and spaces are used to separate one point from the next point in the string.

Another way to specify a box that is not included in the GML specification is to declare all four sides explicitly, with the easternmost and westernmost longitudes and the northernmost and southernmost latitudes as four distinct values, as in this example using the FGDC geospatial metadata format (see explanation of the FGDC metadata standard in chapter 6):

```
Spatial_Domain:
        Bounding_Coordinates:
        West_Bounding_Coordinate:  -116.0000
        East_Bounding_Coordinate:  -115.0000
        North_Bounding_Coordinate:  37.0000
        South_Bounding_Coordinate:  36.0000
```

This is referred to as a *geodetic box* and has the advantage of avoiding the difficulties that arise when boxes extend across the discontinuity of the International Date Line (the anti–prime meridian) (Janée and Frew 2004). This is illustrated in figure 4.2, where the use of minimum and maximum values for a box as specified by GML to represent Russia leads to a false interpretation. Russia's western boundary is at approximately 025° longitude and its eastern boundary is at approximately –175° longitude, which is across the anti–prime meridian. The correct two-point representation of the box is 025,42 for the SW corner and –175,77 for the NE corner. But since "–175" is literally less than "025," the GML specification flips the SW corner to –175,42 (minimum values) and the NE corner to 025,77 (maximum values). If the four sides of the box are represented completely, there is no problem understanding that the area crosses the 180° line. But if only the two points specified by the GML standard are used, the points reorient the intended diagonal line of the box and the box is interpreted to bound the area outside of Russia's boundaries instead (Janée 2004). This is a good illustration of how a general treatment works most of the time but where caution is needed in boundary areas or at discontinuities.

A *bounding box* (aka minimum bounding box (MBB) or minimum bounding rectangle (MBR)) is the smallest box that completely encloses a spatial footprint. Bounding boxes are frequently used generalizations of irregular polygons in georeferenced information systems. They are discussed in more detail in the section of this chapter titled "Generalization of Geospatial Representation" and their use in geographic information retrieval is discussed further in chapter 7.

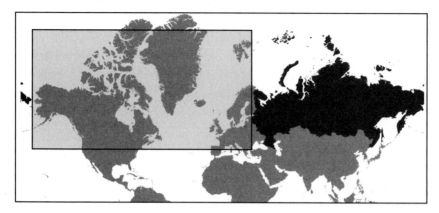

Figure 4.2
Computer misinterpretation of the bounding box for Russia when represented by two diagonal points according to the GML specification for the area that crosses the anti–prime meridian. (From Greg Janée, *Simple Geometry Language*, http://www.alexandria.ucsb.edu/~gjanee/archive/2004/geometry/writeup.html. Graphic was recreated by Matt Rice, Cartomedia.com.)

Other Spatial Referencing Systems

Other spatial referencing systems exist that are used to represent geographic locations for the whole Earth or local regions such as countries. A well-known system is the Universal Transverse Mercator (UTM) coordinate system (figure 4.3). The name comes from the modification of the Mercator projection into its transverse form in 1772 by Johann Heinrich Lambert. In the modified form, the equivalent of the "equator" runs north-south from pole to pole; the effect is to minimize distortion in a narrow strip from pole to pole. Others worked out additional formulas for the projection: Carl Friedrich Gauss in 1822 and Louis Kruger in 1912 and 1919. The projection is alternatively known as the Gauss conformal or the Gauss-Kruger projection. The UTM projection has been used for mapping most of the United States and many other countries (Clarke 2001).

For the UTM system, the Earth is divided into 6° zones running from pole to pole and numbered from west to east, from 1 to 60, starting at the International Date Line (figure 4.3). In UTM notation, Goleta, California, is located in Zone 11S at easting = 240265.77, northing = 3814106.2. *Eastings* are measured in meters from a *false origin* about half a degree beyond the western limit of each zone; this position is set so that the central meridian of each zone has an easting of 500,000 meters. *Northings* are measured from the equator in the northern hemisphere and from the South Pole in the southern hemisphere. The zone letter for east-west running zones

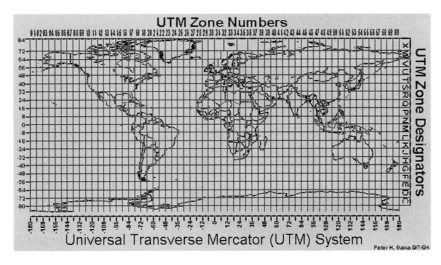

Figure 4.3
UTM System. (From Peter H. Dana, *Coordinate Systems Overview: UTM Zone Numbers.*
Geographer's Craft Project, University of Colorado at Boulder, http://www.colorado.edu/
geography/gcraft/notes/coordsys/gif/utmzones.gif.)

("**S**" in the Goleta example) adds additional identification for the location. Since
distortions increase in the polar regions, it is customary not to use UTM referencing beyond 84° north and 80° south (Clarke 2001). UTM geocoding is sufficiently
complex to limit its use to "spatially aware professionals" (SAPs) or to hide in the
background of systems that use it; it does, however, show up on many topographic
maps (Longley et al. 2001).

Local spatial referencing systems have been developed for U.S. states, known as
state plane coordinate systems (SPCSs), and for countries. An example of a country-
level system is the one for the United Kingdom, known as the British National Grid
(figure 4.4). An example of a geocode in this system is SK624852: SK identifies a
100 km square; 624 is an easting location and 852 is a northing location within the
box. The code represents a point to the nearest 100 meters (Longley et al. 2001).

Tony Rees of CSIRO Marine Research in Australia has developed a grid-based
system called *c-squares* for *Concise Spatial Query and Representation System* (figure
4.5). In this system, a series of grid squares is used to represent geographic coverage areas; point locations can be represented using the code for the square in which
they reside, and a text string of grid notations is the representation of an area. The
c-squares grid system is based on "a successive subdivision of World Meteorologi-
cal Organization (WMO) 10 × 10 degree squares for the Earth's surface" (described

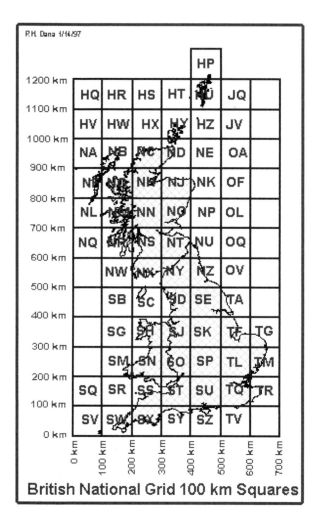

Figure 4.4
British National Grid System. (From Peter H. Dana, *Coordinate Systems Overview: British National Grid 100 km Squares.* Geographer's Craft Project, University of Colorado at Boulder, http://www.colorado.edu/geography/gcraft/notes/coordsys/gif/bng100km.gif.)

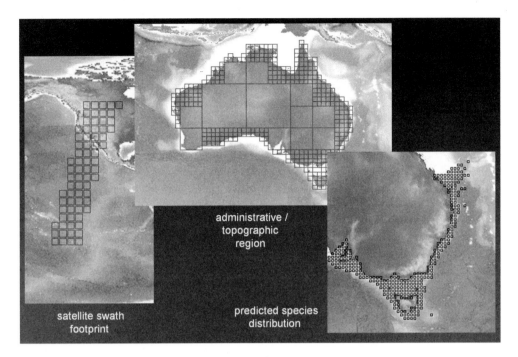

Figure 4.5
C-squares examples. (From Rees 2003a.)

in Rees 2002). The notation scheme for the squares is thus globally applicable and the size of the squares is adjustable for individual locations, from 10 × 10 degree squares to 0.1 × 0.1 squares and smaller. There are several advantages to this approach. This grid representation can represent an irregular or diagonal shape, such as a ship's track or coastal zone, with a set of squares that is faithful to the shape of the feature. Another is that place-based queries can be implemented as a text-string comparison on the c-squares grid notation (see chapter 7 for more on geographic information retrieval) (Rees 2002, 2003a, 2003b).

In c-squares, Goleta, California, is located by the grid string notation of 7311: 249:248:132:456:486:226:498 at a resolution of a 0.000001-degree square; this notation represents a successive refinement from the 10-degree square 7311 that includes Goleta to the 0.000001 square of 498 that includes it. If the resolution is set to 0.1, the notation for Goleta is truncated to 7311:249:248.

For an area represented by a set of c-squares notation strings, the strings are separated with a bar (|) symbol. For example, the string 7311:248|7311:249 represents an area that extends across two adjacent 1-degree squares.

Panel 5
Developing C-Squares Georeferencing

During the late 1990s and early 2000s I was involved with designing metadata specifications for indexing and retrieval of scientific data resources for a large, multidisci-
plinary research agency (CSIRO in Australia), and the perennial question arose of
which would be a suitable method for text-based retrieval—by geographic identifier
or location keyword. What quickly became apparent was that a system based on
administrative areas was unsuitable to the biologists (who preferred bioregions), bioregions were no use to the geologists, and so on. In my own specialist area (marine
data), location keywords—at least, away from the coast—were frequently so vague as
to be only marginally useful (e.g., "southwest Pacific Ocean" or "Tasman Sea").

Instead, I was attracted to a "discipline-neutral" approach such as the geometrically
regular series of mapsheets produced by our local national mapping agency, which at
the 1:100,000 scale corresponded to squares measuring 0.5 × 0.5 degrees of latitude
and longitude. It occurred to me that specifying the location of data by a list of the
mapsheets on which it occurred would form a possible "ideal" spatial index, which
then could be equally useful to researchers from any discipline. From this idea grew
my "c-squares" spatial representation method, which takes the grid-based approach
and extends it to a global coverage, and also embeds the "example" resolution of 0.5
× 0.5 degree squares within a more flexible hierarchy, ranging from 10 × 10 degree
squares (largest) to any decimal fraction of either 10 or 5 degrees, as fine as may be
required. While this spatial indexing method is still fairly new and applied in a limited
number of systems at present, I will be interested to discover whether a system I have
developed in the first instance for use within my own agency's applications, may have
a value in solving similar problems for other users as well.

Tony Rees
Manager, Divisional Data Centre
CSIRO Marine Research
Hobart, Tasmania
Australia

One useful feature of the c-squares notation is that it incorporates literal digits
of longitude and latitude into the code to represent a corner of each grid square.
The truncated example for Goleta corresponds to latitude 34.4 N, longitude 119.8
W (7311:249:248 and 7311:249:248), while the full resolution example can be
inspected to reveal the extended coordinates of 34.435829 N and 119.826668 W.
The first digit (7) indicates the quadrant of the globe in which the square is located:
7 indicates the NW quadrant. This coding method functions as a spatial index that
reduces the two-dimensional coordinate representation to a single indexable term
that can be expressed and used for spatial queries at variable levels of spatial resolution. The relatively large number of codes required to represent spatial objects

at continental scales and above can be an issue, although this is moderated to a degree by the use of larger grid squares for the interior areas and smaller squares for the boundary areas.

The c-squares system is deployed in a limited number of applications as of this writing, but as software is developed to process the data, it has potential for general use. There is a "lat/long to c-square converter" accessible from the c-squares website.

These spatial referencing systems are based on *projections*—that is, mathematical transformations of an ellipsoidal Earth onto a two-dimensional surface (discussed in a later section of this chapter). Systems have also been developed for the unprojected Earth—in other words, the Earth as a globe. These schemes are known as *discrete global grids* (DGGs) and provide spatial frameworks for purposes such as environmental data sampling, spatial simulations, geospatial data indexing, and geographic location coding. One popular one, which is used for spatial indexing by the *Encarta Atlas* and for other purposes, is based on an octahedron treatment of the Earth and consists of triangular cells that can be progressively subdivided to finer detail with a hierarchical cell referencing code (figure 4.6) (Dutton 1999; Goodchild, Yang, and Dutton 1991).

Geodesy

Geodesy is the science of determining the size and shape of the Earth. Since the Earth has an elliptical shape and a lumpy surface, no one geodetic model of the Earth works for all purposes. Different geodetic referencing systems have been developed and exist as global or regional geospatial referencing standards; they are called *geodetic datums*. These datums pertain to the horizontal space on the Earth's surface. The vertical datum for the measurement of elevations and heights is most often referenced to *mean sea level* (MSL) as the zero elevation for a local or regional area.

Specifying the geodetic basis of a geospatial representation is often ignored outside of the GIS and mapping communities, the assumption being that it does not really matter when the locations tend to be represented imprecisely anyway. In fact, "referencing geodetic coordinates to the wrong datum can result in position errors of hundreds of meters" (Dana 1999b). Since this degree of error may be significant in some cases, it is important to begin paying attention to the geodetic datum when documenting geospatial references for non-GIS and noncartographic objects and data.

Figure 4.7 shows the displacement of a coordinate point in Texas (the Texas State Capitol Dome) that can be caused by interpreting a coordinate location based on one datum by reference to another datum. The World Geodetic System (WGS) of

11.25
grid

QTM
facets

Figure 4.6
Octahedron grid system for the Earth globe, known as the Quaternary Triangular Mesh (QTM). (Courtesy of Geoff Dutton, Spatial Effects, http://www.spatial-effects.com/SE-research1.html.)

1984 is used as the basis for the illustration. The location of the point for the Capital Dome is also shown as if the same coordinates were interpreted on the basis of other datums. The datums showing the greatest displacement were designed for regions far from Texas, such as Europe and Tokyo.

A common datum used for general purposes is the World Geodetic System of 1984, known as WGS-84. It is equivalent, for all practical purposes, to the North American Datum of 1983, known as NAD-83. This is the datum used for global positioning system (GPS) referencing.

Projection

For geospatial data, *projection* is the transfer of the Earth's surface features onto a flat (planar) surface, such as a sheet of paper or an electronic display. Only a globe can represent accurately the shape, orientation, and relative area of the Earth's surface features; any display of those features on a flat surface produces some dis-

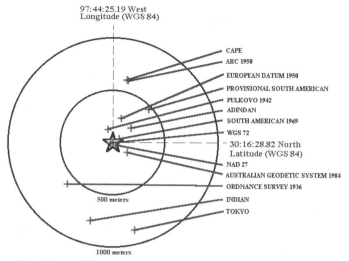

Position Shifts from Datum Differences
Texas Capitol Dome Horizontal Benchmark

Peter H. Dana 9/1/94

Figure 4.7
Illustration of the effect of geodetic datums in the placement of a coordinate point. This was created by Peter H. Dana using the location of the Texas State Capitol to show the displacement of a point based on the WGS-84 when it is interpreted according to various other datums. (From Peter H. Dana, *Geodetic Datum Overview: Position Shifts from Datum Differences.* Geographer's Craft Project, University of Colorado at Boulder, http://www. colorado.edu/geography/gcraft/notes/datum/datum/gif/shift.gif.)

tortion, and the larger the area, the more the distortion. Even when viewing the Earth from space we do not get the full picture: the center of the view shows the most detail, detail becomes progressively less on the edges, and the back of the Earth is invisible (Longley et al. 2001). Many different map projections have been created with the goal of preserving selected aspects of the globe's surface characteristics for particular purposes (e.g., navigation, data presentation, comparative density analysis). Some projections preserve correct relative distances but only along one or a few lines between places on the map (*equidistant projections*); some preserve the relative sizes of areas (*equal-area* or *equivalent projections*); and some preserve the property of local shape, such as an administrative boundary or a coastline as well as the directions (i.e., directional relationships with other features) around any given point (*conformal projections*). Other projections are some combination of two or more projections to achieve some end result (adapted from Clarke 2001 and *Columbia Electronic Encyclopedia* 2003).

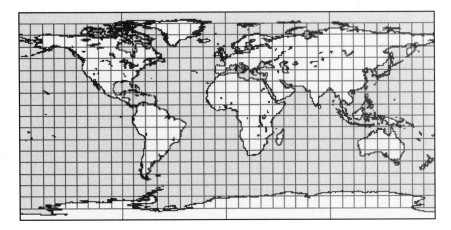

Figure 4.8
World map in the plate carrée projection. (From C. A. Furuti, *Map Projections: Cylindrical Projections*. Progonos Consulting, http://www.progonos.com/furuti/MapProj/Normal/ProjCyl/projCyl.html.)

The simplest projection is known by the French term *plate carrée* (often seen as "plate carree" without the accent and often seen capitalized), which means "flat square" (figure 4.8). For this projection, the longitude and latitude lines are directly plotted on a regular *x,y* graph, forming an implicit grid of squares (*graticules*). A *plate carrée* map of the world is a 2:1 rectangle; the equator is twice as long as the meridians (longitudes). This projection is not conformal and not an equal area projection. It is called an *unprojected* projection (yes, the terminology is confusing) because this regular *x,y* graph representation cannot be achieved through a process of projecting an image of the surface of the Earth onto a flat surface, cylinder, or cone by a light source in the center of the globe, which is the theoretical basis of most of the map projections. It is frequently used for computer-drawn world maps when the extreme distortion in the polar regions can be tolerated.

Another familiar projection is the Mercator Conformal Projection (figure 4.9), which is designed for ocean navigation and produces a map on which a straight line between two points (the *rhumb* line, aka *loxodrome*) matches the route that a ship or airplane would take along a *great-circle* path around the globe, keeping to a constant directional bearing—the shortest distance between the two points on the surface of the globe. The following exercise may help you envision how the Mercator projection is achieved: "Make a globe out of a spherical balloon. Place it in a larger glass cylinder. Blow it up slowly so that it first touches at the equator. Con-

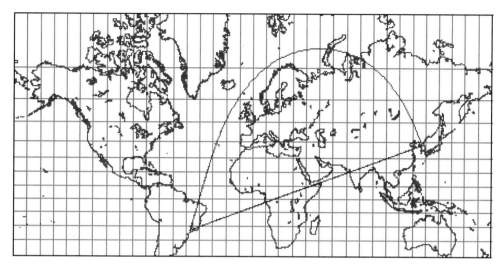

Figure 4.9
Mercator map of the world between 70°N and 40°S, showing a rhumb line (straight) between Campinas, Brazil, and Seoul, Korea, and the corresponding great-circle line (arched) as it would be on the globe. (From C. A. Furuti, *Map Projections: Projections for Navigators and Radio Operators*. Progonos Consulting, http://www.progonos.com/furuti/MapProj/Normal/ProjNav/projNav.html.)

tinue blowing it up slowly. Each point on the balloon globe is blown up until it is pressed against the wall of the glass cylinder. Higher latitudes are blown up more. The final result is a Mercator projection" (Weimer 1998).

One of the most frequently used projections for large-scale mapping is the Lambert Conformal Conic projection (see the discussion of large versus small scale for maps below). For this projection, meridians (longitudes) radiate out from a single polar point and the parallels (latitudes) are curved, parallel to the equator and at right angles to the meridians. Figure 4.10 shows a map of North America using this projection.

Figure 4.11 illustrates the difference that choice of map projection makes in the orientation of the United States around the same central point using the three projections just described.

All projections create *discontinuities* at the edges for world maps, such as splitting the Pacific Ocean or the Asian continent so that portions of these features appear on the far right and left of the map, and only projections specifically designed to represent the polar regions do so adequately. Creators of world maps usually position the edges of their maps away from highly populated areas to minimize the

North America
Lambert Conformal Conic
Origin: 23N, 96W
Standard Parallels: 20N, 60N

Figure 4.10
Lambert Conformal Conic map of North America. (From Peter H. Dana, *Map Projection Overview: North America Lambert Conformal Conic.* Geographer's Craft Project, University of Colorado at Boulder, http://www.colorado.edu/geography/gcraft/notes/mapproj/gif/nalccna.gif.)

difficulties such discontinuities cause. For the visualization of other georeferenced data, the map edges are chosen to frame the areas of greatest interest.

Consideration of projection in georeferenced information systems is primarily in regard to digitization, visual displays, and the interpretation and analysis of data. As long as the underlying data is expressed in longitude and latitude coordinates that are associated with a geodetic datum, it can be interpreted within the framework of any projection. The choice of projection and location of the discontinuities can be crucial for the proper interpretation and understanding of the underlying data.

Levels of Detail

Scale
The scale of a map is reported as a ratio between the linear distance on the map and the corresponding linear distance on the Earth's surface. For example, a scale of 1:24,000 indicates that 1 inch on the map equals 24,000 inches on the ground.

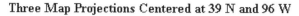

Peter H. Dana 6/23/97

Figure 4.11
Three map projections centered at 39°N and 96°W, created by Peter H. Dana to illustrate the difference that map projections make in the placement of features. (From Peter H. Dana, *Map Projection Overview: Three Map Projections Centered at 39°N and 96°W.* Geographer's Craft Project, University of Colorado at Boulder, http://www.colorado.edu/geography/gcraft/notes/mapproj/gif/threepro.gif.)

This is the scale of the USGS 7.5-minute topographic maps, with sides equal to 7.5 minutes of longitude and 7.5 minutes of latitude. A map of the world in an atlas, on the other hand, will have a scale of something like 1:58,000,000—that is, 1 inch on the map equals 58,000,000 inches (915.4 miles).

Large scale and *small scale* as applied to map displays are relative terms that are often misunderstood. The best way to think of the meaning of these terms in this context is that *large-scale maps* show a large amount of detail in a small area, while *small-scale maps* show a small amount of detail in a large area. See figures 4.12 and 4.13 for examples.

If you find this interpretation of *large scale* and *small scale* confusing, it may be because the opposite meaning is used in other circumstances. For example, a *large-scale study* usually means a study with a large scope or coverage area. This is the meaning used in chapter 2 in reference to human mental strategies for small-scale places in contrast to large-scale spaces. Perhaps geographers and cartographers developed their opposite use of the terms by thinking from the perspective of the view you see from far above the scene compared to what you can see when you are closer. When you are far above the scene, you can see a wide swath of territory but

Figure 4.12
Example of a large-scale map. (Created by Matt Rice, Cartomedia.com; source data: USGS 1:24,000 topographic map for the Santa Barbara area.)

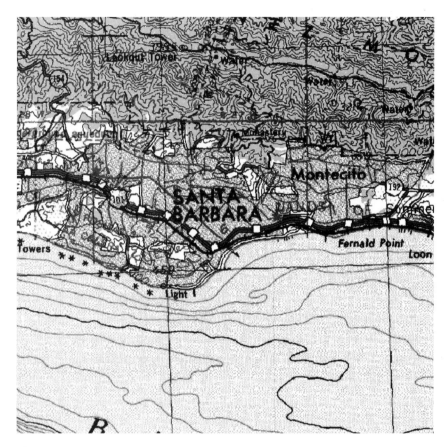

Figure 4.13
Example of a small-scale map. (Created by Matt Rice, Cartomedia.com; source data: 1:250,000 USGS topographic map for the Los Angeles area.)

all of the features are small (hence, small scale); while when you are closer you see less territory but the features are large (hence, large scale). That is, the designation of *small scale* and *large scale* for maps applies to the *features* rather than to the extent of the territory covered. In fact, a large-scale map refers to one that shows greater detail because the representative fraction (i.e., 1/24,000 or 1 inch on the ground to 24,000 inches on the map) is a larger fraction than in a small-scale map with a representation fraction of 1/250,000 to 1/7,500,000. Large-scale maps have a scale of 1:50,000 or greater (i.e., 1:10,000). Maps with scales between 1:50,000 and 1:250,000 are of intermediate scale. Maps of the world that fit on two 8 1/2 by 11 inch pages are very small scale, about 1 to 100 million (Rosenberg 2004).

Resolution

Resolution is a term closely associated with *scale*. Resolution, however, represents the fineness of detail in the image, which translates to the pixel size. It is like the number of stitches per square inch in needlepoint or the number of dots per square inch in a color illustration. There is a limit to how far you can zoom into any digital image because you eventually reach the limit of the pixel size; beyond this point, the image gets progressively blurrier. The resolution of images is expressed as a matrix of dots. For example, a 640 × 480 resolution monitor has a matrix 640 dots wide and 480 dots high, and a 300 dpi (dots per inch) print or scanning resolution means that each linear inch contains 300 dots.

When applied to geospatial data, resolution may be limited by the method of gathering the information, the processing steps, or the choice of representation detail. Consider, for example, a dataset that was gathered as a 1-meter sample (i.e., the data points were spaced 1 meter apart, thus 1-meter resolution). This data can be applied to smaller-grid, say half-meter resolution, only by an interpolation process to estimate the data values between the 1-meter data points. The resulting 0.5-meter resolution product is a mix of original and estimated data points. On the other hand, a dataset can be used to create a product in which the original data points are averaged together to produce a product or visualization with reduced resolution.

Scale is more appropriately associated with products, such as printed maps, with fixed ratios of representation distance to the actual distance on the ground. The degree of detail in the underlying sets of data is more appropriately expressed as resolution. However, *scale* is also sometimes used as a surrogate expression for the resolution of the data and *resolution* is used to express the smallest resolvable object in a fixed product. For example, in the ISO TC 211 metadata standard for Geographic Information (described in chapter 6), s*patial resolution* can be documented by an *equivalent scale* element, which is the "scale of a comparable hardcopy map or chart." If the digital data has been derived from a printed (fixed) representation, then both the scale of the original product and the resolution of the scanning process are defining characteristics of the digital dataset. If, for example, the map in figure 4.13 is digitized, it will not contain the degree of detail present in the map in figure 4.12 even if it is digitized at high resolution.

Uncertainty

In chapter 2 on spatial cognition, there is a discussion of vagueness in the way we conceive of and refer to geographic locations. We think about places such as the

Rocky Mountains without concern for the exact placement of the boundaries of the area, and we talk about regions such as southern France where some of the edges are open to interpretation. Vagueness introduces a degree of uncertainty in specifying the location and boundaries of a place. Other contributors to uncertainty are imprecise measurements, the side effects of processing, and judgments based on the reliability of the providers of the information (i.e., the *provenance* and *lineage* of the data). In this section, we consider some aspects of these *uncertainties* in georeferenced information.

Accuracy and Precision

Accuracy and *precision* are closely related attributes of geospatial information. An accuracy value documents the degree to which the geospatial data adheres to the real world. Accuracy is often estimated and expressed as a value with a plus/minus extension to indicate a range of possible values. For example, a location may be represented as being "5 ± 1 miles" from a reference point, which means that the distance is estimated to be 4 to 6 miles. Accuracy values are sometimes based on the characteristics of the measuring instruments and the data-capture processes, and sometimes on the confidence of knowing the exact location and distances.

Precision refers to the specificity or exactness of the representation. In GIS, the term *crisp* is used to mean precisely represented data boundaries such that a location can be clearly designated as being either in or out of an area. A location represented to the extent of degrees, minutes, and seconds (e.g., 119°49′36″ W and 34°26′09″N) is more precise than one represented by degrees only (119°W and 34°N). There is a danger in representing a higher precision than is warranted by the degree of confidence in the knowledge (e.g., the false precision that can result from converting ddmmss coordinates to decimal degrees explained earlier). Such *false precision* implies more knowledge than is justified and can lead to false conclusions. The level of precision that is "right" is judged not only by the level of confidence in the data but also by the detail needed for a particular purpose and for foreseen future uses.

Keep in mind that precision does not imply accuracy in any way. Representations of geospatial location can be accurate but imprecise; to say, for example, that a certain species of plant can be found in a particular county is accurate, but the information is not precise enough to provide directions to a specimen of the plant or to do anything more than the most general interpretation of the significance of the information. Just as a set of coordinates for a location can be accurate but imprecise, the opposite is also true: a set of coordinate values can be precise but inaccurate (that is, wrong).

Panel 6
Georeferencing Guidelines for Natural History Museums

December 2000. Here I am in a tent in Argentina, on location to do fieldwork in animal behavior. The NSF proposal for the Mammal Networked Information System (MaNIS) has been resubmitted. It dawns on me that there are no precedents for the georeferencing task ahead—300,000 different locality descriptions from 18 natural history museums. We need guidelines. It so happened that there were a few days in a row of nasty weather that December, during which I sat in my office (the cab of our '77 Datsun pickup) and worked out what became the *MaNIS Georeferencing Guidelines* and the accompanying Java *Georeferencing Calculator* to take care of the sometimes nasty combinations of uncertainties in the descriptive localities. This approach has now been used by other projects, such as BioGeomancer, MaNIS, HerpNet, and ORNIS, to georeference over a million localities related to over 20,000 species.

John Wieczorek
Programmer
Museum of Vertebrate Zoology
University of California, Berkeley

When working with written documentation of location, many of the geographic references contribute to an inherent uncertainty of place definition. The *Georeferencing Guidelines* for the Mammal Networked Information System (MaNIS) contain instructions for calculating the maximum error in estimating geospatial location from specimen descriptions in natural history museum collections (Mammal Networked Information System (MaNIS) 2005). The document categorizes types of uncertain location information encountered in such descriptions, including the following:

• Uncertain collection site ("Bakersfield?")
• Vague offset from a named place ("near Bakersfield")
• No direction for offset ("5 mi from Bakersfield")
• An indication of uncertainty ("about 3 mi E of Bakersfield")
• Questionable precision of offset distance (e.g., "10.5 mi N of Bakersfield" probably means 10.5 mi ± 0.5 mi)
• Questionable precision of direction of offset (e.g., "10 mi NE of Bakersfield" probably implies a directional uncertainty of ± 22.5 degrees)
• Having to work from point locations for named places with extents (e.g., a point location for Bakersfield instead of a boundary for the region)
• Characteristics of the gazetteer used to look up the coordinate locations of named places (e.g., level of precision and interpretation of points given for areas)

- Uncertainty due to GPS reading accuracy
- Uncertainty due to unknown datum
- Uncertainty due to coordinate precision (calculation of possible range of location values based on a particular datum and given coordinates)
- Uncertainty due to the map used to reference the location (related to map scale and map source)

A *Georeferencing Calculator* (a Java applet) is available that uses the methods described in the MaNIS *Georeferencing Guidelines* (Mammal Networked Information System (MaNIS) 2003b).

There are situations that call for deliberately imprecise footprints. One example of this is the representation of a sensitive location in a public database, such as an archaeological site or a bird's nesting site. In such cases, a common practice is to show the general location of the site without giving enough information to contribute to damage to the site from human mischief or use of the site as a reference point in sensitive situations.

Representation of Uncertainty

When it comes to recording uncertain regions or locations in information systems, uncertain boundaries and locations are usually represented by some boundary or point that is judged to be good enough for the purpose. However, several theoretical and practical approaches to representing and working with uncertain boundaries are worth knowing about.

One is the notion of assigning a probability that an area or point is or is not in a particular region, with a value of 1 for a location that is definitely *in*, 0 for a location that is definitely *out*, and values between 0 and 1 for boundary areas where in and out is not definite; this is known as a *fuzzy-set* approach to representing an imprecise boundary. If such in/out judgments were represented in a grayscale illustration of the footprint of a feature, you would see a dark center and progressively lighter shades of gray toward the outer edge (Worboys and Duckman 2004, chap. 9).

Another way of expressing a range of values for a geographic location is with a *point and radius* footprint, where the point represents the estimated location, the length of the radius represents the degree of certainty about where the actual location is, and the circular area is intended to enclose the real location. This method works for locations represented by points and is used by the MaNIS Project (Mammal Networked Information System (MaNIS) 2005; Wieczorek, Guo, and Hijmans 2004).

It should be noted that one of the obvious responses to the uncertainty of much of the georeferenced information we have available to us is to get information from multiple sources and to document the source of each piece of information.

Generalization of Geospatial Representation

Another issue with representing geographic boundaries for georeferenced information systems (in metadata, gazetteers, and queries) is the advisability of using generalized footprints, such as minimum bounding boxes (MBBs), rather than or in addition to more detailed polygonal boundaries. Points are also a form of generalization when they are used to represent the footprint of a feature that has an extent (e.g., an area of coverage) in the assumed scale of representation. That is, a point for a well (e.g., for water, oil, or natural gas) may be the most appropriate footprint for all but the most detailed (large) map scale; a point for a county, on the other hand, is a generalization of such a feature at the same scale. There is more discussion of the use of point locations in gazetteers in chapter 5.

Minimum bounding boxes (MBBs) are the smallest longitude/latitude aligned boxes with sides that enclose the maximum and minimum coordinates for the area of coverage. They are also known simply as bounding boxes or as minimum bounding rectangles (MBRs) (figure 4.14).

The arguments for using bounding boxes for footprints are

- They are relatively easy to obtain and they are better (more expressive) than points.
- They are efficient to store and process for information retrieval.
- Systems that are not capable of spatial matching operations based on polygons can process bounding-box data using ordinary mathematical operations.
- They are good enough for many purposes, including most information retrieval.

The arguments against depending on bounding boxes are

- They are not faithful to the shape of the area, especially when the area is diagonal in orientation, irregular in shape (e.g., has a panhandle), or consists of disjoint regions (e.g., the United States).
- They contribute to lack of precision in spatial information retrieval because they retrieve items relevant to adjacent areas.
- They apply to projected coordinates (i.e., boxes on a flat projection) and thus may not behave as expected on the Earth's surface in some cases (e.g., in the polar regions).

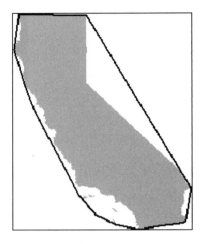 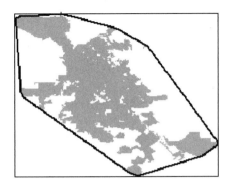

Figure 4.14
Minimum bounding boxes are shown as the gray (thin) lined boxes; convex hulls are shown by the black (thick) lines and more closely follow the shape of the state of California on the left and the city of San Jose on the right. (From Larson and Frontiera 2004.)

Another form of footprint generalization is the convex hull. A convex hull consists of the smallest set of points that encloses a boundary (or set of points) without dipping inward, as illustrated in figure 4.14; it is sometimes described as being like a rubber band around the boundary of a polygon. In contrast to MBBs that can be represented by only two corner points or four sides, convex hulls have a variable number of points depending on the shape of the boundary. They create a generalized boundary with a *manageable* number of points and are thus candidates for footprint representation in information systems.

Chapter 7 provides further discussion of the use of MBBs and convex hulls in spatial information retrieval.

Summary

Geospatial referencing rests on a mathematical foundation of models of the Earth and on formal methods of representation, processing, and analysis. Georeferenced information systems include a spectrum of objects and processing that ranges from those that are less sensitive to variations in geospatial values to those that are highly sensitive. That is, the variations caused by differing geodetic datums, projections, scales, resolutions, and levels of accuracy and precision may not be significant in some cases, and generalized data points and footprints can be "good enough" for some purposes (e.g., general information retrieval). Uses involving conflation, visualization, and analysis, however, can be affected significantly by such variations. In any case, some general knowledge of the mathematical aspects of geospatial referencing as well as an acquaintance with the terminology used in the field is needed to understand georeferenced information systems. This chapter has given a nontechnical introduction to concepts to provide a starting point for deeper study as needed.

Sources for Further Information

Clarke, K. C. 2003. *Getting Started with Geographic Information Systems*. 4th ed. Upper Saddle River, NJ: Prentice Hall.

Dana, P. H. 1999a. *Coordinate Systems Overview*. Geographer's Craft Project, University of Colorado at Boulder. http://www.colorado.edu/geography/gcraft/notes/coordsys/coordsys.html.

Dana, P. H. 1999b. *Geodetic Datum Overview*. Geographer's Craft Project, University of Colorado at Boulder. http://www.colorado.edu/geography/gcraft/notes/datum/datum.html.

Dana, P. H. 1999c. *Map Projection Overview*. Geographer's Craft Project, University of Colorado at Boulder. http://www.colorado.edu/geography/gcraft/notes/mapproj/mapproj_f.html.

Furuti, C. A. 2005. *Map Projections*. Prógonos Consulting. http://www.progonos.com/furuti/MapProj/CartIndex/cartIndex.html.

Longley, P., M. F. Goodchild, D. Maguire, and D. Rhind. 2001. *Geographic Information Systems and Science*. Chichester: Wiley. (See especially the chapter on "Principles.")

Pidwirny, M. J. 2002. *Fundamentals of Physical Geography*: *Chapter 2: Maps, Remote Sensing, and GIS*. Department of Geography, Okanagan University College, British Columbia, Canada. http://www.physicalgeography.net/fundamentals/2a.html.

Sobel, D. 1995. *Longitude: The True Story of a Lone Genius Who Solved the Greatest Scientific Problem of His Time*. New York: Walker.

Wikimedia Foundation Inc. 2005. *World Geodetic System*. http://en.wikipedia.org/wiki/World_Geodetic_System.

Wolfram Research. 2004. *Mathworld: Geometry: Projective Geometry: Map Projections*. http://mathworld.wolfram.com/topics/MapProjections.html.

5

Gazetteers and Gazetteer Services

Georeferencing by placename (aka feature name) is the most common form of referencing a geographic location and is an *informal* means of georeferencing. We use placenames in conversation, correspondence, reporting, and documentation. We have used them through time to refer to places, and the names for those places have been adjusted to changing times. We reuse names, as is evident in the number of U.S. placenames that are the same as, or based on, names familiar to residents that immigrated from elsewhere (Crane 2004; Smith and Crane 2001). We name all sorts of features (e.g., continents, countries, towns, mountains, rivers, wetlands, buildings, parks, railroads, radio towers, and airports). A study of the etymology of names—the origins of the names—reveals much about our history and culture.

Dictionaries of placenames are called *gazetteers*. They contain descriptive information about named places, which can include their geographic locations, types (categories), and other information. The *Columbia Electronic Encyclopedia* (sixth edition, 2003) provides some interesting information about the origins of gazetteers:

The term *gazetteer* originally was applied to one who wrote a gazette. It was first used in its modern sense early in the 18th cent., after the publication (1703) by Lawrence Echard of the *Gazetteer's or Newsman's Interpreter,* a geographical index. But lists of place names, with descriptions, had been made as early as the 6th cent.; part of the gazetteer of Stephen of Byzantium, of this time, is extant. The 19th cent., when geographical knowledge and the need for having geographical facts readily available had both increased greatly, was the great period of development of gazetteer making. Attempts were made to produce complete gazetteers, necessitating several volumes. Famous gazetteers include Johnston's (Scotland, 1850), Blackie's (Scotland, 1850), Bouillet's (France, 1857), Ritter's (Germany, 1874), Longman's (England, 1895), Garollo's (Italy, 1898), and Lippincott's (United States, 1865; now *The Columbia Gazetteer of the World*, 1998); later editions of many of these have appeared.

The gazetteer model has changed significantly from its early manifestations as printed alphabetical or hierarchical lists of placenames with associated information

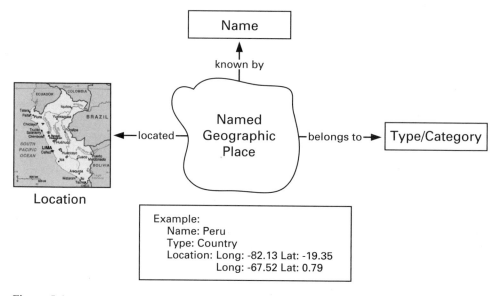

Figure 5.1
Basic components of an entry in a digital gazetteer for a named geographic place: name, location (footprint), and type/category

(often not including the geospatial coordinates). Now gazetteers are considered to be a type of *knowledge organization system* (KOS) that organizes information about named geographic places. This type of KOS relates textual labels for places (i.e., placenames) to geospatial locations (e.g., longitude/latitude coordinates) and to a scheme of categorization (e.g., administrative areas, mountains, buildings). They form the primary tool for translating between textual and mathematical forms of georeferencing—between informal and formal ways of georeferencing. These basic elements of a digital gazetteer are illustrated in figure 5.1.

Gazetteers play several roles in information management. For information retrieval, gazetteers provide translation between informal and formal means of georeferencing; to do this, they link placenames to geospatial footprints (e.g., longitude/latitude coordinates). One application that uses this translation capability is known as *geoparsing*—where placename references in text are looked up in a gazetteer so that geospatial coordinates can be associated with the text. Also useful for information retrieval, gazetteers categorize places according to a scheme of classification; this enables answers to questions like "what schools are in or near Baltimore, Maryland?" As basic reference sources, gazetteers answer the "where is" questions and also describe places in terms of their histories, their placename origins, and other descriptive information. For scholarly research, gazetteers record the basic facts known about historical places or link to research sites and the corpus of research and maps pertaining to those places. For administrative management of placenames for a jurisdiction, locale, or country, gazetteers are the primary dataset.

Information about named places is essentially local in nature. That is, the best, the most detailed, and the most up-to-date information about named places is known locally. Gazetteer data is typically created either for local purposes (e.g., naming parks, neighborhoods, administrative districts, buildings, facilities) or is related to some activity such as travel, genealogical research, historical research, scientific research, business activities, or documenting collections of information and objects. Official toponymic authorities of countries and their subdivisions, which have responsibility for establishing official names for their jurisdictions, depend on and choose among locally created placenames. This local nature of gazetteer data leads to scattered, independent gazetteers holding rich data about places. Add to this the constantly changing nature of gazetteer data (e.g., placenames change through time) and it is clear that there is a need for agreed-on standards of access and data sharing specifically designed for distributed, independent gazetteers. The *ADL Gazetteer Protocol* and the protocol being developed by the Open Geospatial Consortium (OGC), which are described at the end of this chapter, are steps in this direction.

These protocols are useful for applications that need to consult more than one gazetteer to find the information they need—often a combination of online gazetteer services plus a local gazetteer. A case in point is the following scenario from the British Geological Survey:

A user has heard that there are remains of oil fields in the Widmerpool Gulf, but has no idea where this is or what type of feature it is. A place name gazetteer returns "Widmerpool" as a populated place in the UK, but our gazetteer (a separate *specialized* gazetteer server as part of the network of servers) would also return "Widmerpool Gulf" as the name of a sedimentary basin, and the identifiers of related features such as the named faults that bound it. The locations (as lines, polygons as appropriate) could be displayed on our website map, and the user could then select to display locations of boreholes, site exploration data, models, reports etc. (R. E. Heaven, personal communication, 2004)

A principle for gazetteers is that there should be one entry for one place in a particular gazetteer. For example, if the information in a gazetteer about the Black Sea, located in southeastern Europe and Asia Minor, comes from multiple sources, all of that information needs to be gathered into one entry. If instead it is scattered into several entries, confusion is created because it is not clear if all entries are about the same place or about distinctly different places. If the pieces of information about a place all use the same name (e.g., all say they are about the "Black Sea"), that may still not be enough to determine if they are about the same Black Sea because the same name can be used for multiple places. Only if both the geographic locations (i.e., footprints) and the *feature types* (e.g., "lakes") are similar can information about similarly named places be combined in a gazetteer with confidence.

Chapter 4 describes geospatial referencing at a general level and gives only a brief overview of the constructs and technologies of formal georeferencing because there are many other sources for this information. The present chapter goes into more depth about gazetteers as knowledge organization systems in information systems because this is a new area of development and, except for a few published papers and conference presentations, very little has been published. The beginning sections provide a history of gazetteer development and describe the sources of and applications for gazetteer data. Next, core elements for basic gazetteer data entries are described. The section titled "Models of Gazetteer Data" may contain more detail than some readers want to know. This section can be skipped if that is the case. Four structures are described that model the linguistic (informal) and geospatial (formal) aspects of gazetteers in different ways and that will give gazetteer and information system designers an understanding of variations in structuring this data to meet specific user and application environments. Diagrams of the gazetteer models provide a quick way to grasp the commonalities and differences in the choice of descriptive elements. This is followed by a discussion of *Gazetteer-level Metadata*—what needs to be said about a gazetteer to identify it and describe its contents—and protocols for the searching of distributed, independent gazetteers through the Internet. Aspects of information retrieval that involve gazetteers are discussed further in chapter 7.

Background of Gazetteer Development

There is remarkable diversity in approaches to the description of geographic places and, until recently, no standardization beyond authoritative sources for the geographic names themselves. There are many types of printed gazetteers. Some gazetteers, such as the *Columbia Gazetteer of the World*, provide descriptive information about places, including a history of the locale, population data, elevation, or the pronunciation of the name. Figure 5.2 shows an entry from the *Columbia Gazetteer of the World's* online service (http://www.columbiagazetteer.org/). Atlases, such as the *New York Times Atlas,* have gazetteer sections that serve as indexes to the map page(s) and grid reference(s) where the corresponding features are shown.

Name of place: **Timbuktu**
Type of place: **city**
Location: **Mali**

Timbuktu (tim-buhk-too), city (1987 pop. 31,925; 1998 pop. 31,973; estimated 2005 pop. 32,460), (cap.) Sixth Region, central Mali, near the <u>Niger River</u>; 16°46'N 03°01'W. Connected with the Niger by a series of canals, Timbuktu is served by the small river port of <u>Kabara</u>. Its salt trade and handicraft industries make it an important meeting place for the nomadic people of the <u>Sahara</u>. Timbuktu was founded (11th century) by the Tuareg people as a seasonal camp. By the 14th century, when it was part of the Mali empire, it had become one of the major commercial centers of the W Sudan region, famous for its gold trade. Under the Songhai empire (15th–16th century) the city was a great Muslim educational center, with more than 100 Koranic schools and a university centered at the Sankoré mosque. Timbuktu was sacked in 1593 by invaders from Morocco and never again recovered its leading position. It was repeatedly conquered by neighboring peoples until it was captured (1894) by the French. This "pearl of the desert" is now a crumbling mud-house town. Was designated a UNESCO World Heritage site in 1988. Also spelled Tombouctou.

CITATION "Timbuktu." *The Columbia Gazetteer of the World Online.* New York: Columbia University Press, 2005. http://www.columbiagazetteer.org/. Accessed: August 16, 2005.

Figure 5.2
Example entry from the Columbia Gazetteer of the World Online. (Courtesy of Columbia University Press.)

Some sets of placenames are available as hierarchical thesauri designed for information retrieval; these are used to describe documents, museum objects, or other information resources. The *Getty Thesaurus of Geographic Names* is used widely as a controlled vocabulary of current and historical names to describe (i.e., catalog) art and architecture literature and museum holdings. The U.S. federal government's mapping agencies maintain gazetteers that document the official names of places for government purposes as well as alternative names. These gazetteers are the U.S. Geological Survey's *Geographic Names Information System* (GNIS) and the National Geospatial-Intelligence Agency's *GEOnet Names Server* (GNS). Both of these are maintained under the aegis of the U.S. Board on Geographic Names (BGN). Many other examples could be cited for local areas, for other countries, and for special purposes.

The Alexandria Digital Library (ADL) has been engaged in major gazetteer development since the beginning of the National Science Foundation's (NSF) digital library funding in 1994. Early in the research, the ADL Implementation Team combined the two major U.S. federal government gazetteers into one gazetteer containing over four million entries. As a result of this experience, ADL developed the *ADL Gazetteer Content Standard* and a *Feature Type Thesaurus* and then rebuilt the *ADL Gazetteer* to this new model. This gazetteer is integrated into ADL's search interface to provide translation from placename to coordinates for queries of the ADL collections. It is also searchable through the ADL Gazetteer client and through the *ADL Gazetteer Protocol*.

During the period of time that ADL was researching and developing its gazetteer model and services, the International Standards Organization's (ISO) Technical Committee 211 (TC 211) with responsibility for "standardization in the field of digital geographic information" developed a standard for gazetteers, and the Open Geospatial Consortium (OGC) developed a proposed gazetteer protocol based on the ISO standard.

Details of the Getty, ADL, and ISO gazetteer models are presented in the section below titled "Models of Gazetteer Data," and links to related online sites are given in the *Sources for Further Information* section at the end of the chapter.

Starting in 1998, several workshops have been held focusing on gazetteers or highlighting their importance. The reports and presentations from each of these workshops are available online. The *Distributed Geolibraries* workshop was held in 1998; included in its findings is the following statement: "A comprehensive gazetteer, linking named places and geographic locations, would be an essential component of a distributed geolibrary" (National Research Council Mapping Science Committee 1999, 78). The following year, a two-day workshop on *Digital Gazetteer Information Exchange* (DGIE) was held at the Smithsonian Institution in Washington, D.C. The workshop was funded by the NSF and the sixty-six participants were from federal and state government, academic institutions, and for-profit as well as nonprofit organizations, with international participation. The goals of the workshop were to develop an understanding of the potential of indirect spatial referencing of information resources through geographic names and to identify the research and policy issues associated with the development of digital gazetteer information exchange. (See Hill 1999 in the Sources for Further Information section.)

In 2002, a workshop on *Digital Gazetteers: Integration into Distributed Digital Library Services* was held as part of the Joint Conference on Digital Libraries (JCDL) in Portland, Oregon, sponsored by the Networked Knowledge Organization Systems/Services (NKOS) group. The focus of this workshop was on digital gazetteers as components of digital libraries, protocols and tools for gazetteer and thesaurus services, and geoparsing applications that recognize and geospatially reference placenames and placename types in text. (See Networked Knowledge Organization Systems/Services Group 2002 in the Sources for Further Information section.) The following year, a workshop on the *Analysis of Geographic References* was held as part of the North American Association for Computational Linguistics (NAACL) in Edmonton, Alberta. The focus of this workshop was on adapting existing and creating new natural language processing techniques to advance geographic reference analysis of text. (See Kornai and Sundheim in the Sources for Further Information section.)

Uses of Gazetteers in Information Services

Gazetteers are stand-alone resources on their own, used to find out where a place is and to get some basic information about it. Frequently, this is a very useful function—for example, when you are not sure where a place is that is the focus of the news or a book reference. The author of a book talks about "Mesoamerica"—what is the extent of that region, you wonder. The news says that new research is being done on King Tut's tomb in the Valley of the Kings near Luxor—where is that? You find out that your grandfather lived in a small town in Norway named Svolvær—where is it? Curiosity drives you to want to know the location of Bugtussle, Kentucky. Knowing where a named place is in terms of its county, state, and country is useful, but it is more useful to *see* where a place is on a map in order to get the context of the place—its nearest neighbors and, possibly, how big it is and the terrain of the area. Brief descriptive information, if available, provides a sense of the history and character of the place.

As a component of georeferenced information systems, gazetteers provide translation capability between formal and informal means of georeferencing. Here is a specific example of the type of information search where this is an important matter (from Janée, Frew, and Hill 2004). Say you want to find maps, aerial photos, remote sensing images, or ground-based photos of the Flatirons—a popular rock-climbing and bouldering spot outside of Boulder, Colorado. You will start your search using "Flatirons" as the query, but you will not find all of the information you need if you cannot do a spatial search. Aerial photographs and remote sensing images that cover the area will not be tagged with "Flatirons" so that you can find them with a placename search. The USGS topographic quadrangle map for this area is titled "Eldorado Springs," a fact you may only discover after some research. With a gazetteer as a component of the information system though—one that contains an entry for the Flatirons—your query can start with the placename and be converted into a spatial area. The query can then be done on the basis of both the placename and the spatial footprint. The footprint query will find information about the area no matter what placenames have been used.

Gazetteers can also be the source of labels for identifying features in georegistered images. For example, if you did find an aerial photo that covers the Flatirons, it will be practically useless without labeling unless you know the region well, as illustrated in figure 5.3 (Janée, Frew, and Hill 2004).

Gazetteers are useful as aids to cataloging and indexing when coordinates are to be added to metadata. For this purpose, there is a gazetteer lookup stage, selection of the appropriate gazetteer entry, and then the transfer of the coordinates from the gazetteer to the metadata. This process can be accomplished by embedding a protocol to search a gazetteer in the cataloging software and then processing the information that is returned from the gazetteer query. Gazetteer protocols are discussed toward the end of this chapter.

For existing collections, the metadata or bibliographic records often contain either structured placenames from controlled vocabularies, as in library cataloging records, or free-text statements describing a location, as in the narrative statements that accompany natural history museum specimens and observation data. In both cases, a gazetteer lookup process can locate appropriate coordinate values to add to the metadata, thus geospatially referencing what can be vast collections of library resources and scientific evidence. Two articles in the May 2004 issue of *D-Lib Magazine* describe such applications, one working with library cataloging records (Buckland and Lancaster 2004) and one using customized software to estimate coordinate locations based on the narrative descriptions of natural history museum collection metadata (Beaman, Wieczorek, and Blum 2004).

A related use is the geospatial referencing of photographs. For example, you have several collections of digital photographs and the individual photographs are geo- and time-referenced by placenames and dates: Grand Canyon, May 5, 2002; Dillon, Colorado, May 10, 2002; Tokyo, September 2003; and so on. These can be geospatially tagged through a gazetteer lookup process followed by adding the coordinates to the metadata for the photographs. The result is the capability to show the locations of the photographs on a map and retrieving photographs taken in specified locations. When the photographs were taken is also a key piece of data for such collections (Naaman et al. 2004). Processing existing photograph collections in this way would allow them to be integrated with photographs taken with GPS-enabled cameras; this is a technology that will become more widely available in the coming years.

Figure 5.3
Example of an aerial photo without and with feature labeling to illustrate how feature identification gives context and thus promotes understanding of the image. (From Janée, Frew, and Hill 2004. Satellite and aerial imagery provided courtesy of GlobeXplorer.com and Partners. Copyright 2003. All rights reserved.)

Panel 7
Georeferencing and Bibliographic Indexing

In the late 1980s I was working with the Petroleum Abstracts Service (PA) at the University of Tulsa as head of the staff of geologists, geophysicists, and petroleum engineers who reviewed the published literature in the field of petroleum exploration and production and created abstracts and indexing so that subscribers could browse the *PA Bulletin* or search the database to find items of interest. One day, an indexer, Arthur (Chico) Seay, brought to my attention a situation where the indexing could have been improved if geospatial footprints had been available to him for named locations in the article. It was a petroleum-exploration-type article about a lake region in Africa. The author did not include any discussion of the geologic provinces relative to the area—information that would have been useful for the indexing. Chico realized that if he could enter the name of the lake into a reference system and get in return information about the named regions that spatially included the lake, he might have been able to discover the name of the relevant geologic provinces to add to the indexing. This was an insightful comment and intriguing enough to generate the ideas that led to my dissertation topic and subsequent research and development—the linking of placenames to geospatial coordinates for information description and retrieval purposes.

Linda L. Hill
UCSB Alexandria Digital Library Project (Retired)

Geoparsing Applications

The process of recognizing place references in text and associating geospatial coordinates with them is called *geoparsing*. The steps of this process are illustrated in figure 5.4.

1. Digital text is input into a process that applies natural-language techniques to recognized placenames, feature types, and related text. For example,

   a. Detection of geographic reference strings, such as "LaGuardia," "a mile from downtown Manhattan," and "Mesoamerica."

   b. Detection of references to type of location, such as "LaGuardia *Airport*," "the *town of* Manhattan," and "the *region of* Mesoamerica."

2. The output of the first step is a set of "georeferenced facts." The placenames in the "facts" are passed to a gazetteer in the "gazetteer lookup" step, using feature types as added clues for the query.

3. If the gazetteer query is successful, the results consist of a set of one or more gazetteer entries.

4. If more than one gazetteer entry is a possible match, steps have to be taken to disambiguate the entries and choose the most appropriate one.

5. Coordinates from the selected entry are added to the georeferencing in the text with a measure of confidence in the coordinates; this can include assigning coordi-

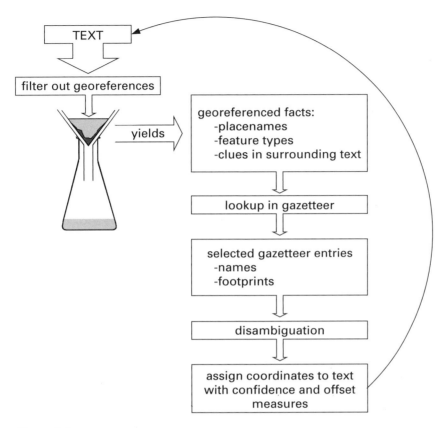

Figure 5.4
Geoparsing process: natural language "filter" finds georeferences in text, and coordinates are found for these references through gazetteer lookup and assignment steps

nates to a location that is offset from a named place, such as a point for "5 miles west of Bakersfield."

6. Optionally, an overall set of coordinates for the whole document can be assigned based on the individual georeferencing occurrences in the text.

An interesting example of geoparsing is the work done by Woodruff and Plaunt (1994) with Ray Larson at the University of California at Berkeley, on *GIPSY: Automated Geographic Indexing of Text Documents*. They applied enhanced automated geoparsing techniques to a set of publications of the California Department of Water Resources to derive polygons representing the spatial coverage of the text. These polygons were represented on a base map and were, in effect, stacked on top of one another when their areas overlapped. The results were visualized as a

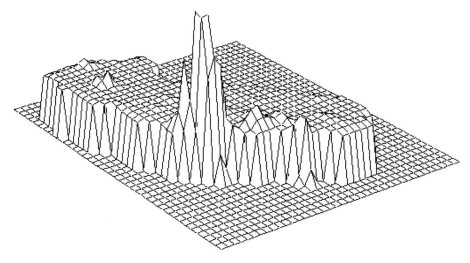

Figure 5.5
Surface plot produced by the GIPSY software representing a paper that talks about Santa Barbara County, San Luis Obispo, and the Santa Ynez Valley area in California at some length. (From Woodruff and Plaunt 1994. Copyright © 1994 Woodruff and Plaunt; reprinted with permission of John Wiley and Sons, Inc.)

three-dimensional "skyline" whose peaks approximated the "importance" of the georeferences in the text, and from this the most significant georeferences in the text could be identified for indexing and retrieval purposes (figure 5.5).

Geoparsing is a growing field of research and application. Research projects include the Perseus Digital Library at Tufts (Smith 2002; Smith and Crane 2001), the *Going Places in the Catalog* project at Berkeley (Buckland, Gey, and Larson 2002), and numerous projects within the natural language processing community (Kornai and Sundheim 2003). The Mammal Networked Information System (MaNIS) project has developed a set of guidelines and algorithms for deriving and documenting geospatial location from the narrative descriptions of location that accompany objects in biological collections (Beaman, Wieczorek, and Blum 2004; Mammal Networked Information System (MaNIS) 2005). A follow-on project, the BioGeoMancer Project, is building a suite of web-based services to support the process of adding geospatial coordinates to specimen records through geoparsing (Ball 2005; Peabody Museum of Natural History 2005). A group working specifically on cross-language information retrieval—Cross Language Evaluation Forum (CLEF)—has announced the first effort to develop and test multilingual geographic information retrieval (GIR) using geoparsing techniques (Gey and Clough 2005).

Panel 8
Georeferencing and Multilingual Applications

> One of the things I find most useful about georeferencing is that it provides a language-independent way of searching for or displaying data related to locations. In multilingual projects it is helpful to think of place—along with time—as something that can be represented without having to worry about language or script or spelling. And furthermore, georeferenced location can be used to relate different linguistic representations of placenames through multilingual gazetteers, which can be constructed to provide further detail such as historical information on their period of use.
>
> **Susan Stone**
> Museum Informatics Project
> University of California, Berkeley

MetaCarta is a company in the business of "geographic text search systems" using geoparsing services that evolved from research projects at MIT (MetaCarta Inc. 2005b). The OGC has published a draft specification for a geoparser service (Open Geospatial Consortium Inc. 2001).

Sources of Gazetteer Data

Giving names to places and using them for reference is a pervasive characteristic of human society. Thus, placenames come from innumerable sources around the world and are forever being created for new purposes or rediscovered from historical documents and artifacts. There are numerous sources of data about named places available for building new gazetteers and adding to existing gazetteers.

Toponymic authorities, such as the U.S. Board on Geographic Names (BGN) and the Geographical Names Board of Canada, are primary sources of gazetteer data. They are tasked with standardizing placenames for governmental purposes, from the country/nation level to local government councils. They use sets of rules to standardize the form of official names and to exclude some names that would be offensive or otherwise unacceptable (e.g., Orth and Payne 2003). Formal toponymic authorities focus on placenames and generally use point locations for footprints, which are sufficient to disambiguate one feature from another. They also use typing schemes that make sense for their operations.

The two publicly available gazetteers maintained by the U.S. government under the aegis of the BGN are rich sources of gazetteer data. They are particularly valuable sources of placenames and the point locations giving the general locations of the features. Both of the U.S. federal gazetteers are searchable through online user interfaces and both make it easy to download sets of their data for local use. The USGS Geographic Names Information System (GNIS) gazetteer is the official repository for domestic placename information. It obtains its data primarily from USGS topographic map sheets and from the network of state-level toponymic agencies; in 2004 it added an online form to facilitate the submission of new gazetteer data or corrections to the GNIS staff (U.S. Geological Survey, Geographic Names Information System (GNIS) 2005). The NGA GEOnet Names Server (GNS) is the official repository of foreign placename decisions approved by the BGN. Approximately 20,000 of the database's entries are updated monthly; the online database is updated on a biweekly schedule (National Geospatial-Intelligence Agency 2005). These gazetteers contain names for administrative units and physical and cultural features; they do not contain entries for regions such as "Southern California," which are used often in normal discourse but are not formal administrative units.

Other governmental agencies also collect and create gazetteer-type data as a result of community planning, zoning, the legal recording of property ownership, and community infrastructure building. These are the agencies that were early adopters of GIS technology. GIS data is rich in complex polygons and official location boundaries, with limited attention to the placenames—one label for a place is often sufficient and the label may be nonspecific (e.g., "pond") or abbreviated.

Creators and publishers of maps, both governmental and private, hold vast quantities of gazetteer data in the form of labels for features in map layers. These maps in turn are the sources traditionally used as a basis for gazetteers. From these map series, coordinate points or grid references for features can be obtained as well as supporting evidence for officially authorized names, alternative names, and variant spellings. Charts that identify the locations of landmarks for air, sea, and coastal navigation are ready sources of gazetteer data, as are the gazetteers included as indexes for atlases. There are also thousands of printed gazetteers in the library collections of the world and digital versions available on the web, some with coordinates and some without. Books such as guidebooks for travel and field studies (e.g., guidebooks to the geology of an area) contain many references to named geographic locations, too.

Gazetteer data is also the result of scientific research projects where locations along the path of an expedition, the boundaries of research areas, or specimen collection sites are recorded. Scholarly historical research rediscovers and locates places referenced in the past and genealogical archives, oral histories, and memoirs contain many placename references. Field research to discover and record placenaming conventions among indigenous native peoples results in collections of names and cultural meanings of places heretofore not included in official gazetteers. A form used for this purpose by the Canadian Permanent Committee on Geographical Names is shown in figure 5.6.

Many of the controlled vocabularies that support library cataloging and bibliographic indexing contain placenames. Most of the time, these sets of placenames do not include coordinates. An exception is the *GeoRef Thesaurus*, which does include points or bounding-box locations with its entries for geographic features; 75 percent of the entries in the *GeoRef Thesaurus* are for geographic features as of November 2004 (S. Tahirkheli, personal communication, 2005). A sample *GeoRef* entry for a named geographic place is

Skomer Island
    In Saint Georges Channel off Dyfed.
    CO N514500N514500 W51800W0051800
    BT Pembrokeshire Wales
    BT Dyfed Wales
    BT Wales
    BT England
    BT United Kingdom
    BT Western Europe
    BT Europe

With a GPS in hand—that is, a global positioning system unit that calculates your position by receiving signals from orbiting satellites—gazetteer data can be collected by almost anyone. These locations could be the routes of hiking trails or bicycle paths, the boundaries of a school's athletic field, or the locations of grave sites of interest for family histories. The possibilities of building special-purpose gazetteers in this way are just beginning to be realized. For example, collecting information about named features in a local area would make a good school project that combines social studies, map reading, and mathematics.

Criteria of Gazetteer Quality

In an extended abstract and presentation titled *Towards a Reference Corpus for Automatic Toponym Resolution Evaluation* for a workshop on geographic information retrieval, Jochen Leidner identified key criteria of gazetteer quality that he used as selection criteria for his research project. He included the following

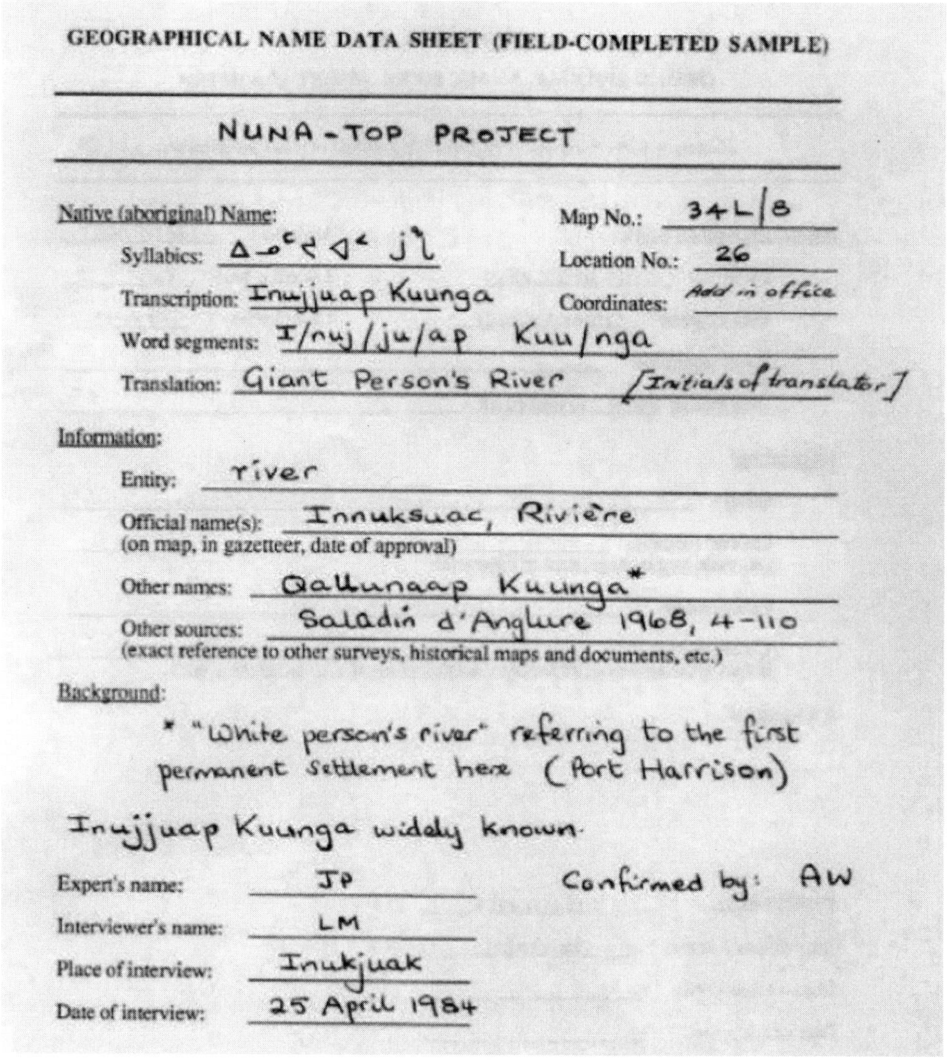

GEOGRAPHICAL NAME DATA SHEET (FIELD-COMPLETED SAMPLE)

NUNA-TOP PROJECT

Native (aboriginal) Name:

Syllabics: ᐃᓅᑊᔾᔪᐊᑉ ᔪᖢ

Map No.: 34L/8

Location No.: 26

Transcription: Inujjuap Kuunga

Coordinates: Add in office

Word segments: I/nuj/ju/ap Kuu/nga

Translation: Giant Person's River   [Initials of translator]

Information:

Entity: river

Official name(s): Innuksuac, Rivière
(on map, in gazetteer, date of approval)

Other names: Qallunaap Kuunga*

Other sources: Saladin d'Anglure 1968, 4-110
(exact reference to other surveys, historical maps and documents, etc.)

Background:

* "White person's river" referring to the first
permanent settlement here (Port Harrison)

Inujjuap Kuunga widely known.

Expert's name: JP   Confirmed by: AW

Interviewer's name: LM

Place of interview: Inukjuak

Date of interview: 25 April 1984

Figure 5.6
Example of a filled-out form for the collection of native geographic name information used by the Canadian Permanent Committee on Geographical Names. (From *Guide to the Collection of Native Geographical Names* (provisional edition). Canadian Permanent Committee on Geographical Names, 1992. http://geonames.nrcan.gc.ca/pdf/native_field_guide_e.pdf. © 2005. Her Majesty the Queen in Right of Canada with permission of the Minister of Public Works and Government Services, 2005.)

considerations, some of which can be documented by the gazetteer owner/curator and others that are based on user evaluation:

1. Availability: degree to which the gazetteer is freely available and not limited by restrictive conditions of use

2. Scope: small communal database, regional/national coverage, or worldwide coverage

3. Completeness: degree to which the scope of the gazetteer is covered completely

4. Currency: degree to which the gazetteer has incorporated changes

5. Accuracy: number of detectable errors in names, footprints, and types

6. Granularity: includes large, well-known features only or features of all sizes and those that are less well known

7. Balance: uniform degree of detail, currency, accuracy, and granularity across scope of coverage

8. Richness of annotation: amount and detail of descriptive information beyond the basics of name, footprint, and type (adapted from Leidner 2004)

Core Elements of Gazetteers

As the ADL *Gazetteer Content Standard* shows (discussed in the "Models of Gazetteer Data" section below), the description of named geographic places can become quite complex if you design for documenting all aspects of placenames, place typing, geospatial referencing, relationships between places, changes through time, and other descriptive information. On the other hand, it is well established that a subset of this information is all that is needed to support basic documentation of named places for information management and retrieval. There are three core elements of a gazetteer entry:

• A name (could have variant names also)
• A class/type (selected from a typing scheme of categories for places/features)
• A location (a footprint; coordinates representing a point, line, or areal extent)

These three elements can be represented as a tuple of **N,t,g,** meaning that the gazetteer entry has at least one name, one type, and one geospatial footprint. Table 5.1 shows three examples of gazetteer entries containing these basic elements.

These core elements permit translation from one place element to another, and this capability supports powerful functions in information services, such as allowing searchers to

• Search a catalog by starting with a placename and expanding the search to the geospatial location, thus retrieving items such as remote sensing images or maps

Table 5.1
Three examples of gazetteer entries containing only the basic elements of description

Name	Type	Footprint
Goleta	populated place	−119.93,34.44
Goleta Beach	park	−119.83,34.42
Hearst Castle	building	−121.17,35.69

that are about the place but that do not actually mention the place by name. For example, "What images does the library have showing the terrain in the La Plata Mountain area in southwestern Colorado?"

• Search a gazetteer by starting with a geospatial footprint (drawn on a map) and ask, for example, "What places named Goleta are in this area?" or "What national parks or forests are near Goleta?"

• Search a gazetteer by asking questions based on placenames such as

• "Where is Hearst Castle?"

• "What museums are in the Houston area?" and get names and locations based on a search using the geospatial footprint of the area around Houston and a feature-type term

Note that users may not be aware that their questions are going to a catalog in some cases (e.g., for remote sensing images) and to a gazetteer in other cases; the interface to the information system may hide this detail.

Next we will look at the details of these three basic gazetteer elements.

Names

Placenames (aka toponyms or geographic names) have rich histories; they often reveal significant cultural and environmental aspects of a community's identity (Canadian Permanent Committee on Geographical Names 1992). Placenames exist in all of the world's languages and character sets. They are tied both to local ways of naming and to official registers of names authorized by toponymic authorities. Even for particular names, the way they are spelled and punctuated may vary from one document to another.

For some information management purposes, one placename may be sufficient for each feature. For query translation and other purposes, however, all of the names associated with a place are useful; an information system should be able to recognize a place no matter what form of name is given by the user. Beyond the names themselves, gazetteers may hold information about placenames, such as the language and etymology (derivation) of the name, the historical period(s) in which it was used, transliterated forms of the name, or certainty about the assignment of a name to an ancient place. The fact that a particular name has been designated as the official name by some naming authority is also useful information. Some examples of these descriptive aspects of placenames are

• Ho Chi Minh City: formerly Saigon (to 1976); aka Thanh Pho Ho Chi Minh (in Vietnamese)

• Some of the variant names for the Mississippi River: Balbancha, Chucagua, Father of Waters, Fleuve del Missisipi, Mee-chee-see-bee River, Missicipy River, Rio de la Espiritu Sancto (U.S. Geological Survey, Geographic Names Information System (GNIS) 2005)

• Beijing (pinyin transliteration); Peking (Wade-Giles transliteration)

• Dominica [island]: called Waitukubuli, meaning "tall is her body," by the native populations; call Dominica by Columbus, who arrived there on a Sunday ("domingo" in Spanish); called Dominique by the French (Fontaine 2002)

• Variant names for South Hamilton (in Massachusetts): Hamilton Village, Hamilton and Wenham, Wenham Depot, Wenham Station, Wenham and Hamilton Station

• Variant spellings for one location from inscriptions on cups from the Roman imperial era carrying the names of western forts along Hadrian's Wall: Camboglans, Camboglanna, Cambogs, Cammoblanna (Ancient World Mapping Center 2004)

A placename is a proper name for a geographic feature or location such as "Santa Barbara County," "Mount Washington," and "St. Francis Hospital." These formal names are typically found in gazetteers, but names such as "Abbeville 30 × 60 Minute Topographic Quadrangle," "Great Fort Tejon Earthquake Epicenter," and "Habitat of the Red-Legged Frog" are also placenames; they are named geographic locations. The first is the name of a U.S. topographic map but can also be considered the name of the area covered by that map, the second is the point on the Earth's surface identified as the epicenter of an earthquake, and the third is a collection of areas identified as the habitat of an endangered species.

Names that may be considered to be more like geographic identifiers are also suitable for gazetteers, such as census tract numbers and postal code zones; footprints can be associated with these named regions. Locations identified by street addresses are usually not included in gazetteers as placenames, because these locations are often calculated based on data about streets, blocks, and intersections and therefore accessed through systems designed to do that. However, such systems could be considered a special case of gazetteers. More frequently, in gazetteers the street address is included as a piece of information about a named place such as a library.

A placename is composed of parts—the toponym itself, often an administrative *modifier*, and sometimes an indication of the type of place. To illustrate how we typically use the components of placenames and how the components are treated in gazetteers, the following examples will be used: "Ford Hospital"; "Detroit, Michigan"; and "Paris, France."

When these names are in the same sentence, you probably guess, assume, or know that Ford Hospital is in Detroit, Michigan, but typically we do not *modify* the name of the hospital with its administrative placement. That is, the placename is not "Ford Hospital, Detroit, Michigan" but only "Ford Hospital." For uniform treatment of placenames in gazetteers, the toponyms of these three places are "Ford Hospital," "Detroit," and "Paris," and the administrative hierarchy can be expressed as a relationship (e.g., Detroit *is part of* Michigan). You can think of placenames as composed of the name itself, known as the toponym, and the modifying administrative units when the place itself is an administrative unit.

You will notice a difference in the way the modified names "Detroit, Michigan" and "Paris, France" are composed—one with a state modifier and one with a country modifier. These patterns are based on localized conventions of forming placenames and, in the case of library cataloging, on sets of rules by which catalogers decide what modifier to use. Actually, in both cases there are additional administrative areas involved and, if you were to construct a modified placename strictly from the information in a gazetteer containing comprehensive administrative relationships for features, you would get "Detroit, Wayne County, Michigan, United States" and "Paris, Arrondissement de Paris, Département de Ville-de-Paris, France." This same approach would result in "Ford Hospital, Detroit, Wayne County, Michigan." This uniform treatment of placenames and administrative modifiers is the basis of placename treatment in gazetteers. Note that the use of explicit statements of administrative relationships is not the only way that *part of* relationships are represented in a gazetteer. The other way is the implicit spatial relationships based on the footprints. The fact that Ford Hospital and Detroit are in Michigan and this particular Paris is in France can be determined from their geospatial coordinates, at least in principle. The actual ability to do this at all or reliably is dependent on the quality and specificity of the footprints. You will find more about this in the section on footprints.

Toponyms often contain a proper name part and a generic part that indicates the type of place it is. "Ford Hospital" is an example of this. "Ford" is the proper name and "Hospital" is the *type* of place it is. For populated places, the generic terms are often assumed but not included (e.g., "Detroit," not "City of Detroit," and "Michigan," not "State of Michigan"). This mix of proper and generic parts to placenames presents some issues for the translation of placenames from one language to another. For example, the place "Hill Auditorium" might be properly translated to "Hill Auditorio" in Spanish but not to "Cerro Auditorio." The generic terms in placenames can be used to help categorize places by type, but with caution. Names like "The Library Bookstore" and the "Jefferson Market Courthouse Library" give multiple clues that must be sorted out. In some cases, the clues are completely misleading, especially when marketing is involved (e.g., "The Study Hall" for a beer parlor in a college town and "Happy Hollow" for a housing subdivision).

Placenames alone, especially unmodified placenames, do not always uniquely identify a location. Gregory Crane (2004) describes the situation in his article in *D-Lib Magazine*: "Americans used the same placenames over and over again: the *Getty Thesaurus of Geographic Names* lists 48 Lebanons in the United States and 58 Springfields. Thus even knowing the state does not always resolve ambiguities: the designation Lebanon, AL describes three distinct inhabited places."

On the other hand, one place can have a variety of names. Some are official—that is, authorized by a toponymic authority that is usually a governmental agency. Others are colloquial, either local names or a nickname generally used for the place. Placenames come in all languages, have transliterated forms, have different spellings, and the original name can be written in non-Roman scripts. See, for example, the entry from the *Gazetteer of Tibet and the Himalayas* in figure 5.7. This is a project of The Tibetan and Himalayan Digital Library as part of its Environmental and Cultural Geography Collection, which is supported and managed by the University of Virginia Library.

Some are names formerly used for a place. For example, here is the beginning of the *Wikipedia* entry for Russia's Saint Petersburg:

Saint Petersburg (Russian: Санкт-Петербу́рг, English transliteration: **Sankt-Peterburg**), colloquially known as Питер (transliterated **Piter**), formerly known as **Leningrad** (Ленингра́д, 1924–1991) and **Petrograd** (Петрогра́д, 1914–1924), is a city located in Northwestern Russia on the delta of the river Neva at the east end of the Gulf of Finland on the Baltic Sea (Wikimedia Foundation Inc. 2005).

Abbreviations are a special class of names. That is, "NYC" is an abbreviation for New York City; it is not a variant name like "The Big Apple."

Toponymic authorities exist all over the world. They coordinate their activities through the United Nations Group of Experts on Geographical Names (UNGEGN) (2005). In the United States at the federal level, the Board on Geographic Names (BGN) has legislative authority "to establish and maintain uniform geographic name

Names
'gag kha (tib-wylie, currently used)
Gagka (chi-roman, phonetic, currently used)
岗卡 (chi-simplified, phonetic, currently used)
剛卡 (chi-simplified, phonetic, currently used)
崗卡 (chi-traditional, phonetic, currently used)
Gangka (chi-pinyin, phonetic, currently used)

Classifications/Codes
f235 [THDL id]
鄉 [90Census] (chi-simplified)
xiang (chi-pinyin)
Township (without urban registered population)
(eng)
ADM5 [NIMA]
5421266200 [GB91ext-Ryavec]

Spatial References
1. Latitude: 30.733°, Longitude: 97.767°
Authority: Ryavec Township GIS "vtarpt.e00"
Accuracy: Township seat

2. Latitude: 30.258°, Longitude: 97.270°
Authority: TAR93

Related Features
partof f222

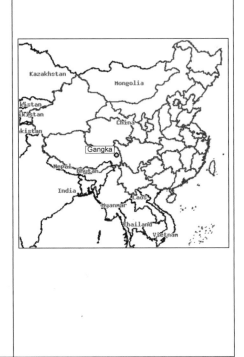

Figure 5.7
An entry (#235) from the *Gazetteer of Tibet and the Himalayas*, release 2.0, which contains detailed data for the Tibet Autonomous Region. (See http://orion.lib.virginia.edu/thdl/xml/gazinfo.php?page=f235.)

usage throughout the Federal Government. Sharing its responsibilities with the Secretary of the Interior, the Board has developed principles, policies, and procedures governing the use of both domestic and foreign geographic names as well as undersea and Antarctic feature names. Although established to serve the Federal Government as a central authority to which all name problems, name inquiries, and new name proposals can be directed, the Board also plays a similar role for the general public." (U.S. Geological Survey, Geographic Names Information System (GNIS), 2004). In the United States, toponymic authorities also exist at the state level; the Council of Geographic Names Authorities in the United States (COGNA) is their organization (Council of Geographic Names Authorities in the United States (COGNA) 2005). Figure 5.8 shows an entry from the Canadian Geographical Names gazetteer. Among the details it includes is the status of "Official" and the "Decision Date" documenting the action taken by the Canadian Permanent Committee on Geographical Names to make this name official. This is important administrative data for toponymic authorities.

Name authorization is also established in the form of *authority files*, which set the names, spelling, and punctuation to be used for cataloging and indexing purposes. These authorities designate which placenames are used when documenting the places associated with information objects. Typically, they do not include other information about the places.

An article appeared in the *Santa Barbara News Press* on November 20, 2004, about a lake in Massachusetts and its interesting name. The article was written by Pam Belluck of the *New York Times*; she said that the name of the lake is "Lake Chargoggagoggmanchauggagoggchaubunagungamaugg." The name is reported to mean "English knifemen and Nipmuck Indians at the boundary or neutral fishing place." It is often misspelled and some have taken to calling it "Lake Webster" for the nearest town. If you look up "Lake Webster" in the GNIS gazetteer, you can find an entry for this lake and some of the numerous ways its American Indian name has been written. The *official* toponym according to the U.S. government is "Chaubunagungamaug, Lake."

Unicode capability is a basic software requirement for gazetteer systems so that they can store and process placenames in all languages and scripts. Unicode may not handle all cases, but it will handle the majority. Currently many gazetteers use transliteration methods to convert non-Roman alphabet names into English for processing but may also be able to display names in other languages and scripts with Unicode characters. Treatment of multilingual text in information systems is an area of research and development that will be more evident in gazetteers of the future.

When a place is known by more than one placename, gazetteers usually designate one name as the *primary* name and the others as *variant* names. In the section "Models of Gazetteer Data" in this chapter, structures to manage the diversity and richness of name information are discussed.

Types

Categorizing (aka typing or classing) places in a gazetteer involves having a scheme of classes from which to choose—that is, a knowledge organization system (KOS)

Figure 5.8
Screenshot showing part of the results on a search for the placename "White Rock." (From Canadian Geographical Names website, http://geonames.nrcan.gc.ca/index_e.php. GNBC Secretariat, Natural Resources Canada. © 2005. Her Majesty the Queen in Right of Canada with permission of the Minister of Public Works and Government Services, 2005.)

that classifies types of geographic features in a logical scheme. This means establishing a hierarchical structure of classes (a thesaurus), an authority list, or a classification system that is comprehensive in the sense that it contains a category for all features within the scope of the gazetteer.

Creating good, serviceable typing schemes is difficult to do and many system designers would rather not have to do it. They might argue that a gazetteer only needs two core elements, names and footprints, because these two elements support the translation function between formal and informal georeferencing. However, knowing what types of places a gazetteer contains is useful information. More importantly, being able to select types of places from a gazetteer is a frequent user requirement. Some examples of this have been given already; here are some more:

· Where are the hospitals in the Kansas City area?
· Show me the distribution pattern of {religious facilities, cemeteries, parks, wetlands} included in the gazetteer.
· How many named lakes does the gazetteer include in Minnesota? in Oklahoma?

The situation in 2005 is that the typing schemes for most gazetteers are local and limited to use by just one gazetteer, and the structure and content of these schemes vary widely. This, of course, is understandable since these systems were developed when local management of data was a higher priority than interoperability with other systems. The creation of the *ADL Feature Type Thesaurus* (FTT) in 2001 was an effort to create a scheme that could be used more generally (Hill 2002). An inventory of representative classification schemes for gazetteers with wide coverage as of October 2004 is shown in table 5.2; reference links to these schemes is included in the Sources for Further Information section.

Note that the list in table 5.2 does not include schemes that cover only specific types of places, which are typically not used in gazetteers. There are many of these— for example, the *U.S. Standard Industrial Classification* (SIC) system and the *North American Industrial Classification System* (NAICS) for type of businesses that could be used to type commercial facilities in gazetteers, and the *Classification of Wetlands and Deepwater Habitats of the United States*, by L. M. Cowardin et al., U.S. Fish and Wildlife Service, Office of Biological Services, U.S. Department the Interior.

The categories required for typing schemes to cover the broad range of features for gazetteers fall roughly into two major categories: natural and cultural (aka human-made) features. Natural feature types include physiographic features (e.g., continents, mountains), hydrographic features (e.g., lakes, seas, channels), and

Table 5.2
Representative type schemes in current online gazetteers

Organization	Description
U.S. Geological Survey	*GNIS Feature Class Definitions*: alphabetical list, with definitions, of 65 categories.
U.S. National Geospatial-Intelligence Agency (formerly NIMA)	*Geonames Feature Designation Codes*: 643 categories in 9 classes, with code names and definitions.
National Resources of Canada	*Canadian Geographical Names Feature Types*: 38 categories with codes and terms in both English and French, organized into two classes (populated places and physical features) and with "generic" terms associated with each category.
Geoscience Australia	*Feature Codes Used by the Gazetteer of Australia*: alphabetical list of 117 categories with codes and "included terms."
Getty Thesaurus of Geographic Names	"Place types are indexing terms based on the structured vocabulary of the AAT where possible." An alphabetical list of 595 category terms is linked to the TGN search page.
Alexandria Digital Library (ADL)	*ADL Feature Type Thesaurus*: a hierarchical thesaurus with 210 preferred terms, 1,046 nonpreferred terms, and 6 top terms.

biogeographic regions (e.g., forests, grasslands). Cultural feature types include administrative areas (e.g., countries and their divisions), buildings, transportation features, hydrographic structures (e.g., piers, dams, reservoirs, canals), and an array of other constructions. Some classifications, however, cut across the natural-cultural division. For example, GIS feature classifications tend to use the category *water bodies* as a top-level category that includes both natural and human-made features: lakes and reservoirs, channels and canals. Such schemes often include subcategories that distinguish between *still water* and *moving water* and/or between *freshwater* and *saltwater*. A scheme for categorizing gazetteer entries needs to adopt a method of classification that makes sense for the particular gazetteer, while keeping in mind that it is often better to adopt an existing scheme than to develop a new one and that there is an interoperability advantage to using a scheme that others use if possible.

See the illustrations of gazetteer entries in this chapter for examples of feature typing and the references in the Sources for Further Information section for links to feature-typing schemes.

The best practices for feature-typing schemes are to

• Base them on the guidelines given for the construction of thesauri by U.S., British, and ISO standards.

• Publish them as independent schemes with metadata documenting the responsible party, scope and purpose, update frequency and versioning, statistics of number of terms, details of structure, and terms of use.

• Avoid the use of categories such as "Other"; an alternative for features that cannot be classified is to give them a very broad category until more is known.

• Adopt, adapt, or translate existing schemes if possible in lieu of creating a new one from scratch.

• Adopt the metadata structures emerging from the W3C (as of 2005), namely, the Extensible Markup Language (XML), Resource Description Format (RDF), and Web Ontology Language (OWL) as well as the *SKOS Core Vocabulary Specification*, which will provide the basis for greater collaborative building of such schemes, integrating them into operational applications, and improving their interoperability (Worldwide Web Consortium (W3C) 2005).

The first point in this list covers a multitude of best practices for constructing thesauri and other types of knowledge organization systems (KOSs). Suffice it to say that knowing these principles is the basis for building a KOS that will be applied consistently and logically, which is the key to providing reliable, predictable information retrieval results.

A gazetteer usually uses a single feature-typing scheme to classify all of its entries. More than one feature type per entry is possible, in which case one of them is usually designated as the primary feature type for the convenience of short displays. It is also possible to assign feature types from more than a single category scheme. For example, a forest might be classified according to the general scheme used for the whole gazetteer as a *forest* and by a forest classification scheme as a *temperate deciduous forest*.

Geospatial Footprints

Gazetteer footprints document the location of named places on the surface of the Earth using longitude, latitude coordinates, or other spatial references. They can be detailed polygons representing the boundaries of the location or generalized as points, bounding boxes, and so on, as discussed in chapter 4. They may also be a group of disjoint (unconnected) polygons representing, for example, the individual islands in an island group such as Hawaii. Gazetteer footprints are used for various purposes, including spatial information retrieval and spatial similarity analysis (see chapter 7) and the display of named locations on a background map.

Footprints are also used to establish the spatial relationships between features. This is similar to using footprints for information retrieval, but it has a slightly different application. For instance, using footprints, it can be deduced that the Farmington located at –108.19,36.74 (a longitude,latitude point) is the Farmington in New Mexico because the point falls within the bounding box for the state (north: 37.3; south: 31.04; east: –102.7; west: –109.35). Since there are many cities named Farmington, this is a useful disambiguation. This *implicit* spatial relationship can substitute for or support an *explicit* relationship statement, such as that this Farmington *is part of* New Mexico (more discussion of relationships is provided below). Note that spatial relationships are sensitive to the quality of footprints, especially in border regions. For a place like Detroit, Michigan, which is at the boundary of both Michigan and the United States, determining that Detroit is *within* Michigan and the United States by comparing footprints might not work. If the three footprint boundaries do not match up exactly, the Detroit boundary may extend beyond the Michigan boundary or the Michigan boundary beyond the U.S. boundary at some point, in which case the best that can be determined is that the areas *overlap* substantially.

Another use of footprints is to show the spatial coverage of a gazetteer. Figures 7.8 and 7.9 illustrate this use with a graphic showing the extent and depth of spatial coverage for a gazetteer. And one more use of footprints worth mentioning is to show spatial distribution patterns of specific types of places or places with common names or parts of names—for example, distribution patterns for the world's volcanoes, distribution patterns for Presbyterian or Baptist churches in the United States, or distribution patterns for wetlands named "bayou," "fen," "marsh, "slough," and so on to illustrate the regional use of words in placenames.

Single points for footprints are often found in gazetteers. Such points serve to disambiguate one place from all others with the same name and type. For instance, it is common practice in gazetteers to use a point at the mouth of a river to represent the location of that particular river. This works because the point is sufficient to distinguish that river from all other rivers. Official gazetteers have also relied on point locations for another reason: the focus of toponymic authorities is on the naming of places and not on establishing official footprints for those places. In a similar way, indexes in the back of atlases (a form of gazetteer) point to a particular page or map number and a grid reference for a place because that is sufficient georeferencing for an index to an atlas.

Point locations for features are the easiest type of footprint to obtain. They are the most widely used footprints even outside of formal gazetteers for specifying where a feature is located. Points are generalizations of footprints for all but the most pointlike locations (e.g., drilling sites). They are of limited usefulness when they are representing countries or mountain ranges; they are more useful for features such as city parks or farms. They are almost totally useless for information management systems when they are representing a river that extends miles across the surface of the Earth or for features as large as oceans.

Despite these limitations, point features are still useful for gazetteers. For information retrieval, they can be used in user interfaces to center a map window whose edges form the query area. They can show the general location of a feature on a map. They can be used as the center of a zone around the point that estimates the extent of the feature.

A footprint that represents the extent of the feature (e.g., how much territory it covers) or the detailed boundary of it gives more information and is needed for many purposes, but such footprints have not typically been included in or linked to gazetteer entries. The reasons for this are historical and technical. It is a recent development that gazetteers have been recognized as playing a major role in geo-referenced information systems for information description, retrieval, and visualization. Only with that realization has the need for more expressive footprints in gazetteers been recognized. There are issues, both technical and cost-related, to be weighed when choosing between using bounding boxes or polygons as footprints in gazetteers; these are discussed in chapter 7.

The best practices for footprint representation for gazetteer entries are to

• Document the source and time frame for the footprint.
• Document the geodetic datum for the coordinates (or other representation) (see the example of this in figure 5.8).
• Plan for multiple footprints per gazetteer entry—for instance, detailed footprints and their generalized versions, footprints from different sources, and footprints for different times.
• Use standard representations of footprints that can be shared with other applications.
• Document known uncertainties about the footprints.
• Choose the type of footprints used on the basis of the current and anticipated uses and users of the gazetteer.

Other Key Elements of Gazetteers

There are three other important elements of gazetteer data: the relationships between named places (e.g., administrative hierarchies), the temporal aspects of gazetteer data, and documentation of the sources of information about a place.

Relationships

The spatial relationships between gazetteer entries are implicitly documented by their footprints. By comparing footprints, it can be determined, for example, whether one feature is spatially contained within another feature, whether they are some distance from one another and their areas do not overlap, or whether they do overlap—and if so, the degree of overlap. Other types of relationships, such as that one feature is the administrative parent of another, can be explicitly represented. Spatial relationships are automatically available when footprints are present. Deriving accurate relationships between named geographic features from footprints, however, depends on the quality of the representation of the borders of the footprints. Therefore, gazetteers usually include explicitly stated relationships for administrative units and sometimes for other *part of* relationships that are not administrative (e.g., that a mountain peak is *part of* a particular mountain range). Explicitly stated relationships must be *predocumented* by inclusion in the gazetteer data.

The range of possible explicit relationships extends beyond administrative hierarchies and includes

• *part* of: this is a general relationship that could be applied to physical as well as administrative relationships (e.g., Pikes Peak is *part of* the Rocky Mountains)
• *administrative seat* of (e.g., one feature could be documented to be the capital of another)
• *partition of*: administrative or physical units can be partitioned into subunits (e.g., states are *partitions of* the United States and drainage basins are *partitions of* the North American continent)
• *flows into*: a stream could be documented as *flowing into* a river

Note that a hierarchical thesaurus model for gazetteer data (discussed further in the "Models of Gazetteer Data" section below) is usually based on a partitive relationship—that is, the organizational structure of the thesaurus conveys that one feature is *part of* its parent term—a reciprocal broader-narrower term relationship. In the catalog model of a gazetteer, where each gazetteer entry is represented by its own record, each entry can include a statement of the relationships it has with other named features. For example, the entry for "Detroit" can have a *part of* relationship with "Wayne County," which in turn has a *part of* relationship with "Michigan," and so forth. These explicitly stated relationships can be traversed to build a *display name* for a gazetteer entry, such as "Detroit, Wayne County, Michigan, United States." Note that these relationships are stated only in one direction with the reciprocal relationship assumed—that is, the *part of* relationship implies the corresponding *has part* relationship.

Documenting explicit relationships in the catalog model (i.e., not a thesaurus model) for gazetteer data requires the use of a scheme of relationship types. Even if only the partitive relationship is used, that *part of* relationship should be declared as an authorized relationship term so that it is used uniformly throughout the gazetteer. Ideally, the scheme of relationship types would be established as a formal KOS with hierarchical relationships between terms so that, for example, the scheme could include subtypes of the partitive relationship.

To document explicit relationships between gazetteer entries, the best practices are to

- Select relationship terms from a formal scheme of relationship types.
- At a minimum, use the *part of* relationship to document the administrative hierarchy for an administrative feature, showing its relationship to its nearest parent in the administrative chain of relationships.
- Plan for allowing multiple explicit relationships to be documented (e.g., "Michigan" is also *part of* the "Great Lakes Region").
- If the related feature is an entry in the gazetteer, the relationship can be documented using the unique ID of the related feature as well as its primary name; if the related feature is not in the gazetteer, the primary name alone can be used.

Temporal Ranges

Time is an important attribute in gazetteers. A gazetteer that does not have a temporal component cannot represent the changes that happen through time to place-names, spatial footprints, relationships, and other characteristics of named geographic places. Even the features themselves appear and disappear through time. Examples from recent times include the emergence of Slovakia and the Czech Republic in Europe as well as the building of the Three Gorges Dam in China and the impact the new reservoir will have on the named places in the surrounding countryside.

Time ranges are like *temporal footprints*. Beginning and ending dates are the *boundaries* of the linear span of time. There are issues of temporal specificity and generalization and uncertainty to deal with, just as with spatial footprints. With spatial footprints, we assume that the *center* of the box or polygon is certainly *in* the right area for the feature, even though we are uncertain whether specific points in the boundary areas are in or outside of the feature's spatial extent. We also often represent the location of a feature by a point that represents the center of the footprint (i.e., a centroid). With temporal footprints, it is less clear that this can be done. For example, does the expression "in the 1920s" mean that the real time is more likely to be in the midrange of the decade (e.g., 1923–1927) than to be at the beginning or end (e.g., 1928–1929), or that 1925 can be used to represent the decade? The expression "circa 1920," on the other hand, is more like a point location and implies that the year 1920 is the center point of the time range before and after it.

The time periods that are associated with features and their names, footprints, and so on can also be categorized or associated with named time periods. For example, the *ADL Gazetteer* and the *ADL Gazetteer Protocol* have adopted three categories of time to characterize named geographic features—*former*, *current*, and *proposed*—for purposes such as retrieving only historical named geographic features or eliminating historical features from a search result. Also, information about named cultural features is often associated with named time periods, such as the political entities or towns existing during the "Middle Ages." This raises the issue of translating such named time periods into date ranges for information management and retrieval (Feinburg 2003).

The best practices for the documentation of the time associations of gazetteer data are to

• Include temporal periods (i.e., date ranges, time categories, or named periods) for the features themselves and for their names, footprints, type categories, and relationships.

• Add whatever dates are known to be associated with the feature or one of its descriptive aspects, even if the dates are not precise (e.g., only expressed to the decade or the century) to support some degree of searching and display by date range.

• Use international standards for date representation (e.g., ISO 8601—Representation of Dates and Times).

• Qualify the degree of uncertainty of dates by using, for example, a probable range of values (e.g., 1925 ± 5 years).

• Support the use of temporal categories (from a scheme of categories such as *former*, *current*, *proposed*) and the association of gazetteer data with named time periods.

Attribution

A single entry in a gazetteer can contain information from different sources. For example, a placename may come from one source (e.g., a map or a toponymic authority), the footprint may come from another source (e.g., a GIS database or from direct measurement with a GPS unit), and the type category may be assigned by the gazetteer managers or obtained from an external source. Some users of gazetteers will just "take the information and run." For others, however, and for the managers of gazetteers, the source of the information provides the context needed to evaluate its cultural context, reliability, and currency. Only gazetteer information with documented lineages can be trusted, understood, and interpreted correctly. Although the importance of documentation of sources is true for all information systems, it is worth making a point of it for gazetteers because in too many cases gazetteer data is presented as if it is the *truth* without acknowledgment of sources. The *Getty Thesaurus of Geographic Names* documents and displays its contributors and sources particularly well; see figure 5.15 for an example.

The best practices for documenting the sources of data in gazetteers are to document the contributor and the contributor's sources for individual pieces of gazetteer data as well as the date of the entry into the gazetteer.

Models of Gazetteer Data

In this section, four models of gazetteer structure are presented:

- The abstract model of the gazetteer on which the *ADL Gazetteer Protocol* is based
- The comprehensive *ADL Gazetteer Content Standard* (GCS)
- The ISO TC 211 model for gazetteers called *Spatial Referencing by Geographic Identifiers* (ISO 19112:2003)
- The thesaurus model used by the *Getty Thesaurus of Geographic Names*

The objective is to give a framework for considering the design of information systems to hold gazetteer data and to provide some standards against which to evaluate other structures, such as the set of tables holding placenames likely to be found in a GIS application. The graphics of the models included here are for illustration of the main structures only; they do not completely represent the actual schemas or structures. Readers are encouraged to follow up through the Sources for Further Information for the actual details of each model. See Understanding the Schema Diagrams as an appendix to this chapter (p. 154).

Abstract ADL Gazetteer Model

The *ADL Gazetteer Protocol*, developed by the Alexandria Digital Library at the University of California at Santa Barbara, contains a semiformal abstract model of a gazetteer, depicted in figure 5.9. It specifies the following:

1. A *gazetteer* is a set of gazetteer entries.
2. A *gazetteer entry* describes a single geographic place by an identifier and several key attributes of the place: one or more names, one or more footprints, and zero or more classes. There is no intrinsic structure to a gazetteer in this model beyond

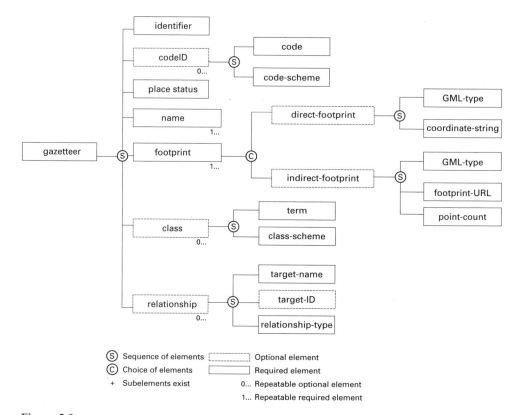

Figure 5.9
Abstract model of a gazetteer as specified by the ADL Gazetteer Protocol, version 1.2

simple containment of gazetteer entries, although relationships between entries may be explicitly represented by the gazetteer.

3. An *identifier* is a string that unambiguously identifies the entry within the gazetteer. The identifier need not be universally unique.

4. A *code* identifies the place within a specified code scheme, namespace, or system for the geographic place. For example, the state of California is identified by FIPS code 06 in the U.S. Federal Information Processing Standard coding scheme for uniquely identifying U.S. administrative units (U.S. National Institute of Standards and Technology, Information Technology Lab, 2005).

5. The *place status* is the temporal status of the place's existence and may be *former*, *current*, or *proposed*.

6. A *name* is a complete, unmodified name for the place. A gazetteer entry can have more than one name, in which case the names denote alternative names for the place.

7. A *footprint* is an approximation, expressed in longitude/latitude coordinates, of the subset of the Earth's surface occupied by the place. Note that a footprint need not be contiguous—that is, a footprint can consist of a set of disjoint areas.

8. A *class* classifies the place with respect to a set of terms. More specifically, a class is the association of the place with a term drawn from a designated vocabulary. A gazetteer entry may belong to multiple classes and even to multiple classes from the same vocabulary.

9. Certain attribute values of a gazetteer entry (namely, each name, each footprint, and each class) are further qualified using two qualifiers. The *primary* qualifier, a Boolean value, indicates if the attribute is the preferred value. For example, a gazetteer entry for the city Köln may mark the name "Köln" as primary but not "Cologne." The *status* qualifier indicates the validity of the attribute value using the same terms (*former, current, proposed*) as the entry's place status attribute. The place status attribute and the status qualifier on attribute values should not be confused; the former refers to the place as a whole, the latter to just the attribute value. For example, a gazetteer entry for the country Thailand may have the place status *current* but qualify the name "Siam" as *former.*

10. For each gazetteer entry, the following conditions on qualifiers must hold:

   a. Exactly one name must be marked as primary.

   b. Exactly one footprint must be marked as primary.

   c. If the entry has been classified, at least one class must be marked as primary.

11. Finally, a gazetteer may be augmented with interentry relationships. A relationship is a named, directed, binary association between gazetteer entries. For example, a gazetteer might support a *capital-of* relationship that relates capital cities and administrative areas: the city of Sacramento is the capital of the state of California, and so on. Note that the *ADL Gazetteer Protocol* defines the necessary structures to support relationships in general, but it does not define any particular relationships, just as it does not define any particular classification scheme (Janée and Hill, 2003).

As the diagram in figure 5.9 shows, only the *identifier, place status, name,* and *footprint* elements are required; all other first-level elements are optional. All first-level elements except *identifier* and *place status* can be repeated. The footprint requirement can be met with either an embedded *direct footprint* or a link to an external *indirect footprint.* Footprints are identified as one of the geometry types included in the Geography Markup Language (GML) standard. Interentry relationships are documented by the primary names of the related features, the gazetteer identifier for the feature (if available), and the type of relationship (e.g., a *part of* relationship).

This gazetteer model supports the search operations and the standard report format of the *ADL Gazetteer Protocol,* which is designed to search across distributed, independent gazetteers whose data can be in various data structures. Since attribution of sources is not required for search operations, such documentation is not included in this model.

ADL Gazetteer Content Standard (GCS)

The complexity of representing the full richness of gazetteer data is covered by the *ADL Gazetteer Content Standard* (GCS), also developed by the Alexandria Digital Library at the University of California at Santa Barbara. The GCS is constructed as an XML schema and is published online both as a schema and as a relational database implementation (see the link in the Sources for Further Information section). It is compatible with the abstract gazetteer model of the *ADL Gazetteer Protocol*, with the exception that in this scheme the classification element is required. The GCS is designed to be the data structure for gazetteers and consequently includes much more detail as well as guidelines for populating gazetteers. In contrast, the abstract model is designed to support interoperability of gazetteers no matter what local data structure is used.

Formally, the GCS bases its gazetteer design on the following premises:

1. An entry in a gazetteer documents a single named geographic feature. Furthermore, a feature is distinct from another feature by virtue of its name, type (class), and footprint (i.e., the tuple of **N,t,g** is distinct). It is possible for a particular location (**g**) to be two separate features with the same name (**N**). This happens when two independent features of different types (**t**) occupy the same space as is true for New Zealand the island and New Zealand the country.

2. A gazetteer is a collection of gazetteer entries each of which has a unique ID in the gazetteer.

3. A full gazetteer entry consists of at least one occurrence of each required element and attribute, zero or more optional elements and attributes, and attribution of the sources of the data. Sources include the identification of classification schemes, contributors, and supporting documents.

4. Where there are multiple occurrences of a required element, one of them is flagged for *primary display*; that occurrence will be used for the main display for online displays and reports.

GCS Top-Level Structure   The top-level structure of the schema is shown in figure 5.10; six of the thirteen top-level elements are required—meaning that at least one subelement of each of these is required. Briefly, these six required elements and subelements are

• A unique feature ID for the gazetteer entry
• An indication whether the feature is *current, former,* or *proposed*—a temporal classification for the feature itself

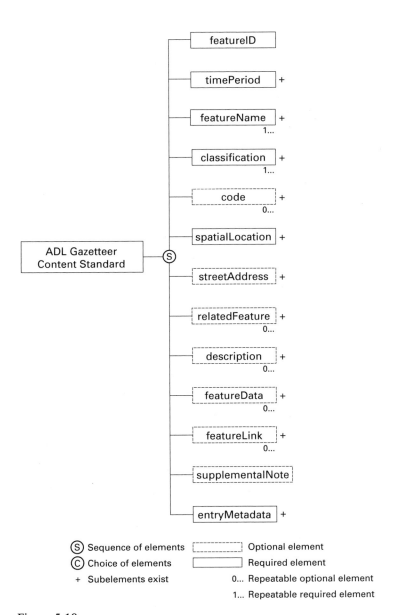

Figure 5.10
Top level of elements in the ADL Gazetteer Content Standard. These elements show the types of information that can be documented about each named geographic feature

• At least one name for the feature and a temporal classification for the name (i.e., *current*, *former*, or *proposed*)

• At least one type term or classification number, identification of the typing scheme used, and a temporal classification for the type (as above)

• At least one spatial footprint expressed both as a *geometry* and as a *bounding box*, with a temporal classification for the *geometry* and additional details explained later

• A couple of administrative bits of data: the date that the gazetteer entry was created and the date(s) it was modified by adding new data or deleting/editing existing data

For illustration, here is a sample brief gazetteer entry with only required elements. It describes Detroit, Michigan; the relationship to the state of Michigan is not explicitly stated in this example because the relationship element is not required.

```
feature ID: 3066491
feature status: current
name: Detroit
    primary display: true
    name status: current
feature class:CT (cities and towns)
    primary display: true
    classification scheme:
        name: ESRI-Type
        version: 2004
    class status: current
spatial location:
    planet: Earth
    bounding box:
        geodetic basis: WGS-84
        west coordinate: -83.2879
        east coordinate: -82.9105
        south coordinate: 42.255
        north coordinate: 42.4504
    how generated: calculated maximum and minimum extent of
    detailed geometry
    source geometry(ies): primary geometry
geometry:
    primary geometry: true
```

```
geometry status: current
reference link to external geometry: false
geometry coding scheme:
     name: Geography Markup Language (OGC)
     version: 2
encoded geometry:
     <gml:coord>
        <gml:X>-83.2879</gml:X>
        <gml:Y>42.255</gml:Y>
     </gml:coord>
     <gml:coord>
        <gml:X>-82.9105</gml:X>
        <gml:Y>42.4504</gml:Y>
     </gml:coord>
entry date: 2000-07-01
modification date: 2001-05-15
```

This example does not show the attribution links that document the source of each piece of information (e.g., for the name, classification scheme, and geometry), which are also required. Such documentation can be handled by having a mirror set of data elements (so-called shadow tables) to hold the attribution information.

A full explanation of all of the elements of the GCS is not appropriate here since the intent is to give an overall view of the structure of the GCS only. The best access to the full scheme is from the ADL Gazetteer Development website, which includes a link to the *Guide to the ADL Gazetteer Content Standard* (Alexandria Digital Library, 2004b). Below is a summary explanation of the elements of the schema. If you are interested in seeing the full spectrum of description related to named geographic places, this is the section to find it.

GCS Time-Period Elements   Time periods are used to add a general temporal status and beginning and ending dates for the feature itself and its names, footprints, relationships, and classes (types). All of these aspects of named geographic features can change through time. For example, the use of a building can change from a religious use to an educational use, thus changing its feature type from *religious facilities* to *educational facilities* (if the typing is based on the *ADL Feature Type Thesaurus*), and administrative relationships change through nation building and dissolution. In this scheme for the documentation of time-periods, only the general time period status is required; the other elements are optional. The same set

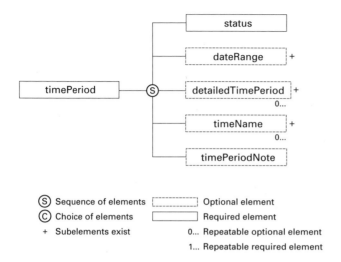

Figure 5.11
Parts of the time-period documentation in the ADL Gazetteer Content Standard, version 3.2

of time-period elements is used throughout the GCS where needed to document time—specifically, for the feature itself, each name, each footprint, each relationship, each classification, and any data associated with the place (e.g., population).

The time period is documented with five top-level data elements; only the first—time-period status—is required (figure 5.11):

1. A time-period status of *former*, *current*, or *proposed*. For example, the place status of the now-nonexistent country of Yugoslavia would be *former*.

2. A date range with beginning and ending dates expressed according to the ISO 8601 standard and with an optional note to explain the date range.

3. A detailed time period expressed as one of the following:

   a. Beginning and ending dates expressed according to a cited standard with the opportunity to record confidence values and notes about each date.

   b. Encoded date string in which different calendar systems and gaps in date expression can be recorded according to a cited standard.

4. A named time period (e.g., the Napoleonic Era, 1799–1815) and, optionally, citation to a scheme that provided the form of the name and beginning and ending dates.

5. A time-period note to add any explanations of unusual circumstances.

GCS Placename Elements   Each gazetteer entry has a name for the feature; this is a toponym unmodified by an administrative parent. For example, the name of the city of Los Angeles is "Los Angeles," not "Los Angeles, California."

There can be multiple names for a feature. For instance, the city known as "Köln" is also known as "Cologne" and the country of "Thailand" was formerly known as "Siam." For display purposes, one of the names is designated as the *primary display name*. This designation does not imply correctness; it means only that in this gazetteer this is the name that will be displayed first, or the one that will be displayed if only one name is shown. This is an important distinction because the preferred or official name for a place is not universal. For example, "Germany" is the name authorized by the U.S. Board on Geographic Names for the country known locally as "Deutschland." A gazetteer that chooses "Germany" as the *primary display name* and "Deutschland" as a variant name is not implying that one name is more correct than the other, but is only indicating which will be used for primary display purposes. Such decisions are made locally usually on the basis of current local or community usage or by adherence to a toponymic authority.

In addition to the primary display name, there can be any number of additional names. The characteristics listed below can be described for each name, as shown in figure 5.12. In each case, only the *time-period* element is required, which can be indicated by the use of *former, current,* or *proposed.*

1. Identification of an official or authoritative toponymic agency that authorizes the use of this name for this feature.

2. Etymology (derivation) of the name.

3. Language of the name in the form of a language code and citation of the code scheme. When the name is the same in several languages, the native language is represented here to avoid listing all languages (e.g., "Paris" is used universally for the capital of France; the language for "Paris" would be cited as "FRA," the three-letter ISO 3166 code for French).

4. Pronunciation of the name in the form of a text string or link to an audiofile and a note about where this pronunciation is used—for example, "in France" or "in southern United States."

5. Transliteration scheme, if one was used, to convert the name from another language to the one used for this version of the name.

6. Expression of the confidence associated with this form of the name (e.g., citing that the name was taken from an archaeological source that could only be partially read).

7. Abbreviated form of the name—for example, "CA" and "Calif" for "California."

8. Time period for the use of the name (using the structure described above).

9. Links or references to further information about the name, such as links to scholarly documents that describe the origins of the name.

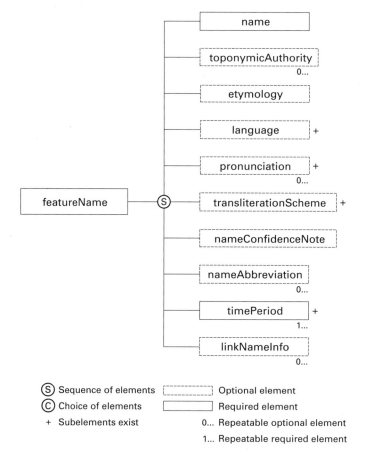

Figure 5.12
Parts of the name documentation in the ADL Gazetteer Content Standard, version 3.2

GCS Feature-Classification Elements   Classification (aka class, category, or type) of features, such as "rivers" or "buildings," is a required element. The classification terms are selected from a primary typing scheme for all of the entries in the gazetteer and, optionally, from other feature-typing schemes. Special schemes can be used—for instance, classification schemes for wetlands or forests. The type of scheme is not limited in any way, but schemes are usually simple vocabularies of terms or hierarchical thesauri (i.e., controlled vocabularies structured with inter-term relationships). Note that if a gazetteer consists of a single class of places, such as a gazetteer of cemeteries, each of its entries must still carry the classification to support interoperable searching and reporting across distributed gazetteers. A time period can be used to show that the type of feature, such as a building, has changed through time (e.g., from a church to a school). In the example from the *Gazetteer of Tibet and the Himalayas* (figure 5.7), the use of classifications from multiple sources is shown; in the example from the *Getty Thesaurus of Geographic Names* (figure 5.15), the use of multiple classifications from the same classification scheme is shown.

GCS Feature-Code Elements   A feature can be known by a code such as a code from a numbering system for dams or by a Federal Information Processing Standards (FIPS) code as used in the United States for administrative units (e.g., "39" is the FIPS code for the state of Ohio and "39-18000" is the code for Columbus, Ohio). The code itself and the scheme associated with it can be documented.

GCS Spatial-Location Elements   Spatial-location elements in the GCS are shown in figure 5.13. There are two ways of representing the spatial footprints for the place: by one or more *geometries* and by one bounding box. One of each representation is required. The bounding box is a generalization of the geometries; it is included with every feature as a base-level footprint that can be used by all information systems, which is especially important for systems without sophisticated spatial processing software.

The *geometry* is a representation of the footprint of the feature; it can be any type of geospatial representation, as described in chapter 4. Note that a *geometry* need not be contiguous. For example, a footprint for the state of Hawaii might consist of a union of disjoint polygons, one per island. A gazetteer entry can have more than one geometry, in which case the geometries represent different interpretations, approximations, or resolutions of the location of the footprint and one of them is designated as the *primary geometry*.

The *geometry* is expressed as an *encoded geometry* that is either included in the gazetteer entry as a string of points plus geodetic basis and geometry type (e.g., point, line, polygon), or a URL reference to a file that contains the coordinate points or other representation of geographic location, such as a grid reference, plus geodetic basis and geometry type. The geometry coding scheme used in either case is documented. *Geometries* have time periods (required) and documentation can be added about how and when the footprint was measured.

Each feature also has a bounding box, which is generated from a single geometry or from the multiple geometries. If the only geometry available is a point, the two longitudes and the two latitudes of the bounding box are the same unless some

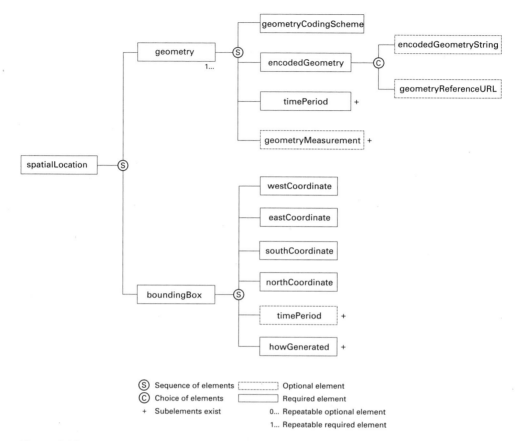

Figure 5.13
Parts of the spatial documentation in the ADL Gazetteer Content Standard, version 3.2

form of buffering has been applied to expand the point to an area. If the only geometry is a box, the bounding box equals the box geometry. If there are several geometries, the bounding box can represent the maximum extent of the set or only the primary geometry. The method used to create the bounding box is documented.

GCS Relationship Elements   Relationships with other named features can be represented and, although this is not a required element of description, such relationships are key to understanding administrative relationships in particular. A relationship is represented by citing the name of the related feature and optionally its unique feature ID when one is available. The type of relationship is documented (e.g., *part of*) as well as the associated scheme of relationship types. This scheme can be a well-known set of such relationships or a local scheme. Currently (in 2005) there are no widely recognized schemes of relationship types for gazetteers. The time period of the relationship is documented since relationships between two features—especially administrative relationships—can change through time.

Other GCS Top-Level Elements

1. If the feature has a street address, this information can be added to the record.

2. Brief descriptions of the feature can be included and these descriptions can be typed to indicate what sort of information they contain. A typing scheme for this purpose might include such terms as *history*, *industry*, *climate*, and *terrain*. Specific time-period documentation is not included with this element since it is a simple text statement that can include reference to a time period.

3. Data such as population and elevation associated with the feature can be included. This data is documented with separate elements for *data value* and *data unit* (and a *data basis*, such as "sea level," when needed). The type of data is represented by a term taken from a typing scheme and the data is referenced to a time period.

4. It is sometimes useful to link the feature to other resources, such as to map sheets that contain the feature, scholarly documents, or web pages. This can be done with the *featureLink* element, which includes a title or brief identification of the resource, the language of the resource, and optionally the type of information involved (and an associated scheme) as well as a URL.

5. An optional supplementary note can be added to the gazetteer entry to explain any unusual circumstances.

6. Administrative details of entry and modification dates are documented.

Documenting Contributors and Sources for GCS Data   The contributor of the information to the gazetteer, the contributor's source for each piece of data, and each classification scheme used in a GCS gazetteer entry is documented according to a separate schema for this purpose that accompanies the GCS. This schema for source documentation is published on the ADL Gazetteer Development website.

ISO TC 211 Gazetteer Standard

A gazetteer model has been developed by the Technical Committee 211 of the International Standards Organization (ISO TC 211) titled *Geographic Information—Spatial Referencing by Geographic Identifiers* (ISO 19112:2003). The intent of the standard is to establish a general model for gazetteer construction and networked gazetteer services within the suite of standards created for GIS data management by this committee. In this standard, a gazetteer is defined as a "directory of geographic identifiers describing location instance … [containing] additional information regarding position of each location instance" (International Organization for Standardization (ISO), Technical Committee 211, 2003b).

This model was developed within the GIS community. Its roots can be traced primarily to an administrative view of gazetteers where an agency has responsibility for a set of named geographic entities, such as countries of the world, the set of population centers in an administrative region, addresses in a town, or a set of hydrographic features in a region. The emphasis is on ownership and responsibility and on administrative management of a set of feature names.

Some distinguishing characteristics of the ISO model are

• Names are unique within a gazetteer (rather than using IDs to create unique entries). That is, the primary placenames serve as the unique identifiers for gazetteer entries. This means that a particular name cannot be used as the primary name for more than one entry. It does not eliminate the possibility of there being a unique ID in addition to the unique name.

• Gazetteers are themselves *typed* as containing specific classes of features. For example, a gazetteer could be documented as containing "towns," as shown in table 5.3.

• Spatial references (e.g., coordinates or grid references), although usually included, are not required for a gazetteer entry if a placename or other type of descriptive reference is sufficient to identify the location within the scope of the application of the gazetteer.

• The ISO model incorporates optional thesaurus-like parent-child relationships between *location instances*.

• A hierarchical feature-typing scheme is embedded in the model itself rather than the scheme being an independent entity apart from the gazetteer.

The ISO model consists of a set of components as shown in figure 5.14:

• The *Spatial Reference System Using Geographic Identifiers* is a type of ISO *Reference System* (RS) and is the overall framework for the model. The RS is documented by a name and, optionally, by a description of its domain of validity.

• The *Spatial Reference System Using Geographic Identifiers* itself is described by its theme (e.g., property ownership) and by its owner or responsible party.

• The *Spatial Reference System Using Geographic Identifiers* is further documented by the *Location Types* it contains. It can contain a single type of location or several types. The types can be structured as a hierarchical set of classes; each class has a name, theme, identifier, definition, territory of use, and an owner who is responsible for creating or maintaining the class. One and only one type from the scheme can be associated with a particular *Location Instance*.

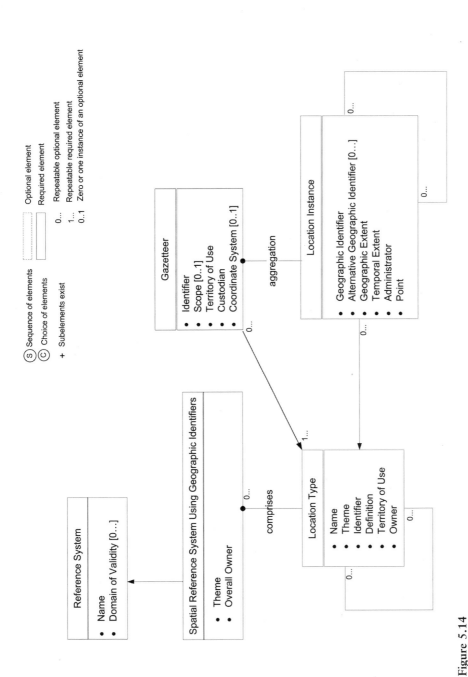

Figure 5.14
ISO Standard 19112:2003, Geographic Information—Spatial Referencing by Geographic Identifiers (a schematic adapted from the ISO standard's document)

Table 5.3
Illustration of the differences in the ADL Gazetteer Content Standard and the ISO 19112 standard

ADL Gazetteer Content Standard	ISO 19112 standard
The ADL GCS structure does not include elements that are the equivalent of the description of the Spatial Reference System in the ISO standard.	**Spatial Reference System Using Geographic Identifiers** **Name** UK property addressing **Overall Owner** Office for National Statistics **Territory of Use** UK **Theme** property **Location Types** administrative area, town, locality, street, property

Gazetteer description

Title ADL Gazetteer **Responsible Party** Alexandria Digital Library, UC Santa Barbara **Scope & Purpose** The ADL Gazetteer combines the US gazetteer entries from the USGS GNIS database and the non-US gazetteer entries from the US NGA gazetteer and other datasets to provide worldwide coverage. . . . **Subject Coverage** All feature types and worldwide **Number of items by type** . . . [more]	**Identifier** towns **Custodian** Ordnance Survey **Scope** large population centres **Territory of Use** UK **Location type** town **Coordinate Reference System** National Grid of Great Britain

Sample gazetteer entries

ID adl-gaz-1-4161415-1a **Feature Name** Cambridge **Name Status** current **Feature Type** populated places **Bounding Box** **West** −2.37 **East** −2.37 **South** 51.73 **North** 51.73 **Geometry** [would be a repeat of the Bounding Box in this case] **Toponymic Authority** U.S. Board on Geographic Names **Related Entity** *part of* Cambridgeshire [more]	**Geographic Identifier** Cambridge **Temporal Extent** 19960401 **Location Type** town **Geographic Extent** 5414 2596, 5440 2532, . . . **Position** 5448 2583 **Administrator** Cambridgeshire County Council **Parent Location Instance** Cambridgeshire

• The *Gazetteer* component is documented with an identifier, the intended territory of use (e.g., an administrative unit), the custodian who maintains the gazetteer, and the types of features and location instances included in the gazetteer. Optionally, a scope statement about the gazetteer can be included and a statement about the coordinate system used for the location instances.

• The *Location Instances* are the gazetteer entries. The elements of the location instances are a geographic identifier (e.g., a placename), alternative geographic identifiers, the geographic extent (e.g., spatial footprint), the temporal extent of the location (i.e., the date of creation for this version of the location instance), the administrator responsible for the particular location instance, and a geographic point (the *position*) that can be used to focus a display map on the location of the feature. Location instances can be structured as a hierarchy with parent and child relationships.

To illustrate the difference between the ISO 19112 model and the ADL GCS model, consider the brief records for Cambridge, UK, in each of the structures shown in table 5.3. Note that the entries are truncated; the intent is to point out the fundamental differences in the two gazetteer models. The ISO example uses UK National Grid references for geospatial location, and the "temporal extent" is the date this location instance record was created. The "Gazetteer Description" for the ADL Gazetteer is not part of the gazetteer itself.

To sum up the models described so far, the ADL models are similar to metadata structures or catalog records with a framework of elements that comprise a record or gazetteer entry. Both of the ADL models include the basic required elements of a name, a type, and a footprint. Both are designed for the general purpose of holding data about all types of named geographic places/features. The ADL GCS is a comprehensive framework of elements for a gazetteer database; the *ADL Gazetteer Protocol* model is a subset of the GCS for the searching of distributed gazetteers. The ISO 19112 standard is designed for the purpose of managing a set of "geographic identifiers" for geographic features in a specified area or for a specified purpose and differs in many ways from the ADL models. Since the ISO standard is part of a suite of GIS standards, it is capable of including complex geospatial referencing. It differs significantly from the ADL models in that the primary placenames must be unique within a particular gazetteer, and a typing scheme is packaged with the gazetteer into a *spatial reference system using geographic identifiers* rather than the typing scheme existing as an independent KOS from which type categories are selected as in the ADL models.

The next model for gazetteer data to be described is the thesaurus model, exemplified by the *Getty Thesaurus of Geographic Names*.

Getty Thesaurus of Geographic Names

The *Getty Thesaurus of Geographic Names* (TGN) (J. Paul Getty Trust, Research Institute, 2005) is a pure thesaurus model for gazetteer data and exemplifies the use of this model for named geographic places. A sample entry is shown in figure 5.15.

The thesaurus model is used extensively for the controlled vocabularies for cataloging and bibliographic indexing. Usually such thesauri are based on genus-species hierarchical relationships. That is, the relationship between a narrower term and its broader term is an *is a* relationship—for example, the concept "oak trees" has an *is a* relationship with the concept "trees," so a possible thesaurus tree could be (indentation indicates a narrower term)

```
trees
    oak trees
```

The other common thesaurus relationship, and the one used by the TGN, is the partitive relationship. In this case, the relationship between a narrower term and its broader term is an *is part of* relationship. An example of this is

```
United States
    Michigan
        Wayne County
        Detroit
```

In comparison to the gazetteer models of ADL and ISO where *is part of* relationships and other types of relationships can be declared optionally within each record, the *is part of* relationship is the basis of the thesaurus framework for gazetteer data. (Note: Some thesauri treat placenames the same way they treat other terms; in those thesauri you will find a hierarchy such that "Detroit" is a child of (a narrower term of) "cities.") You can consider the thesaurus model for gazetteer data to be a model in which at least one *is part of* relationship is required and where multiple *is part of* relationships are optional.

In the TGN model, the following descriptive elements are available for each entry, as shown in figure 5.16:

1. A unique *identifier* for the place/feature in the TGN (internally called the *subject ID*).

2. A *record type*: the type classes are "administrative," "physical," or both.

3. A *descriptive note* covering the history, physical location, or importance of the place.

4. *Coordinates* representing either a point (a longitude/latitude pair) or a bounding box (two longitudes and two latitudes). Elevation of the location can also be documented.

ID: 7009573   **Record Type: <u>administrative</u>**

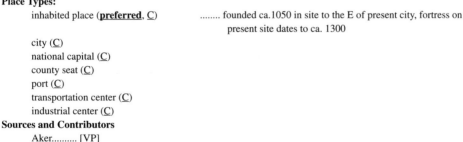   **Oslo (inhabited place)**

Coordinates:

Lat: 59 56 00 N *degrees minutes*   Lat: 59.9333 *decimal degrees*

Long: 010 45 00 E *degrees minutes*   Long:10.7500 *decimal degrees*

Note: Founded by King Harald Hardraade in11th cen.; was destroyed by fire in 1624, & city was rebuilt at the nearby Akershus fortress, which had been built ca. 1300; city grew during 19th cen. & after WW II, & has absorbed several neighboring towns.

Names:

Oslo (**preferred**, <u>C</u>,<u>V</u>, <u>N</u>)   .... name used since 1925

Kristiania (<u>H</u>, <u>V</u>, <u>N</u>)   .... named after Christian IV who rebuilt city after 1624, name used until 1925

Christiania (<u>H</u>, <u>V</u>, <u>N</u>)   .... name used 1624–1877

Aker (<u>H</u>, <u>V</u>, <u>N</u>)   .... name of former town that was absorbed into Oslo in 1948

Ansloa (<u>H</u>, <u>O</u>, <u>N</u>)

Ansloga (<u>H</u>, <u>O</u>, <u>N</u>)

Asloa (<u>H</u>, <u>O</u>, <u>N</u>)

Hierarchical Position:

<u>World</u> (facet)

....   <u>Europe</u> (continent)

....   <u>Norway</u> (nation)

....   <u>Oslo</u> (county)

....   <u>Oslo</u> (inhabited place)

Place Types:

inhabited place (**preferred**, <u>C</u>)   .... founded ca.1050 in site to the E of present city, fortress on present site dates to ca. 1300

city (<u>C</u>)

national capital (<u>C</u>)

county seat (<u>C</u>)

port (<u>C</u>)

transportation center (<u>C</u>)

industrial center (<u>C</u>)

Sources and Contributors

Aker.......... [VP]

.... <u>Encyclopedia Britannica (1988)</u> VII, 1028

.... additional sources listed..........

Figure 5.15

Partial entry from the *Getty Thesaurus of Geographic Names.* © 2005. The J. Paul Getty Trust. All rights reserved. See http://www.getty.edu/research/conducting_research/ vocabularies/tgn/

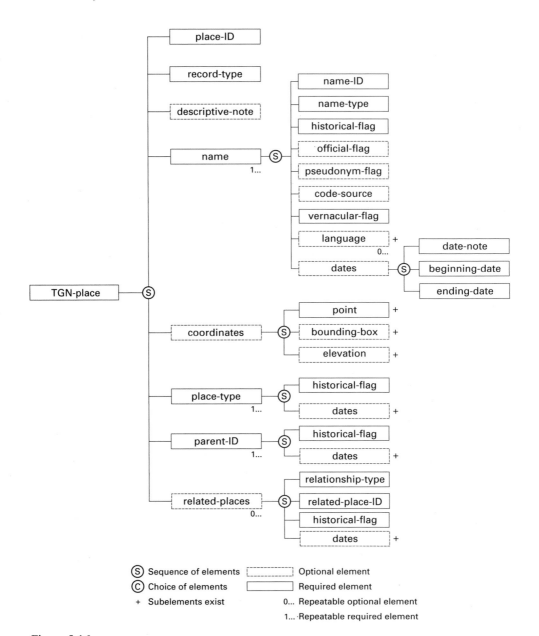

Figure 5.16
Getty Thesaurus of Geographic Names model for the description of named geographic places

5. *Names*, one of which is designated the preferred name for indexing purposes.

    a. A unique *name identifier*.

    b. A *preferred flag* (note: for physical features, the preferred name is often inverted for the purposes of alphabetical lists, as in "Geneva, Lake"). There is also provision for flagging a nonpreferred name as the *display name* or the *index name* when the preferred name is confusing in a term display.

    c. Flags to mark a name as *official* or as a *pseudonym*.

    d. If the name is a code for the place, the source of the code is documented.

    e. A *name type* flag (i.e., whether the name is a noun, an adjective, or both).

    f. A *historical* flag (i.e., whether the name is "current," "historical," or both).

    g. A *vernacular* flag (i.e., whether the name is in a local or some other language).

    h. *Beginning* and *ending dates* for the period that a name was in use.

    i. The *language* of the name; a *preferred* flag can be used to mark a particular name as the preferred name in that language.

6. A *parent ID* to indicate the position of the place in the hierarchy; multiple parents are permitted, with one designated as *preferred*.

    a. A *historical* flag (i.e., whether the parent relationship is "current," "historical," or both).

    b. *Beginning* and *ending dates* for the parent relationship.

7. *Place types*, one of which is *preferred*, using terms from the Getty *Art and Architecture Thesaurus*, where possible, and rules established for political divisions.

    a. A *historical* flag (i.e., whether the place type is "current," "historical," or both).

    b. *Beginning* and *ending dates* for the time period when this place is/was of this type.

8. *Related places* other than the hierarchical relationships, with a *relationship type code* (for a set of relationship types) and a target ID.

    a. A *historical* flag (i.e., whether the relationship is "current," "historical," or both).

    b. *Beginning* and *ending dates* for the relationship.

9. *Contributors and sources*: TGN is a compiled resource, and thus cites the contributors and the published sources of information for the names, descriptive note, and the record overall.

In the TGN, pieces of information about a place can be attributed to contributors and to their sources. Attribution for names, descriptive notes, and the record overall is shown by hyperlinks in the "Sources and Contributors" section in the online version, the beginning of which is shown in figure 5.15.

Gazetteer-Level Metadata

Each gazetteer has a particular scope, both in terms of the purposes that led to its development and the scope of its contents. When this information is formally documented, users can judge the degree to which a particular gazetteer meets their information needs and understand the ownership, purpose, scope, geographic coverage, and potential uses of the information. Such documentation is especially needed in a networked environment for programmatic selection of gazetteers appropriate for particular queries (the *discovery* process). Some gazetteers will cover local areas in depth, some will include only selected types of features (e.g., wetlands or forests in the United States), and others will have worldwide coverage but only of administrative areas. If these gazetteers are registered and documented with gazetteer-level metadata in a formal way, *discovery* processes can be developed to select the gazetteers most likely to contain answers to particular queries. The same level of documentation can be applied to collections (i.e., collection-level metadata).

An outline for a metadata description of a gazetteer includes the following, based on the ADL collection-level metadata model (Hill et al. 1999):

- Name of the gazetteer (e.g., Getty Thesaurus of Geographic Names)
- Short name (e.g., TGN)
- Responsible party
- Scope and purpose statement
- Subject coverage (e.g., worldwide, local, or limited to particular types of features)
- Content type (i.e., gazetteer data)
- Relationship to other collections (e.g., contains data obtained from ...)
- Creation date
- Update frequency
- Collection overview
  - Total item count
  - Count by item types
  - Spatial coverage (graphic representation of density of coverage)
    - Full gazetteer
    - Spatial coverage by item type (graphic representation of density of coverage by type)
- Item metadata scheme (i.e., structure of the data)
- Supported search parameters
- Terms and conditions
- Contact information

For an example of such gazetteer-level metadata, see the metadata for the ADL Gazetteer, which can be located through the ADL Gazetteer Development website (the link to this site is included in the Sources for Further Information at the end of this chapter).

Interoperability of Gazetteer Services

Dictionaries and lists of named locations exist in many guises. Many of them include geospatial referencing, all of them are independent and scattered, and only some of them are presented as formal gazetteers. Today, accessing electronic gazetteer resources requires separate contacts through HTML user interfaces or the use of specialized software (e.g., GIS). There are a couple of efforts to develop and deploy *gazetteer service protocols* to formalize methods of querying independent, distributed digital gazetteers. These protocols define the manner in which queries are sent to and reports returned from gazetteer servers programmatically—that is, from one computer to another.

Such protocols enable several useful functions for information systems. One is to embed a *gazetteer lookup* function in an information retrieval service, so that a placename query can be translated into a geospatial query and thus find maps or aerial photographs for the area as well as text documents. Another is to use gazetteer lookup as a step in a cataloging process so that coordinates can be added to the metadata for an object. A third is to use gazetteers to find the names of other locations in an area so that the placename used as the starting point for a query can be expanded to additional placenames to use in a text-based search. Potentially, when networks of gazetteers are accessible through a gazetteer protocol and the gazetteers are identified through gazetteer-level metadata, queries can be sent to the gazetteers most likely to have relevant entries. For example, a query for Canadian placenames can be sent to a Canadian gazetteer, while one for Russian placenames can be sent to a gazetteer covering Russia.

One gazetteer service protocol has been developed by the Alexandria Digital Library Project, in collaboration with ESRI (Janée and Hill 2003), and another has been developed as an implementation specification by the OGC (Open Geospatial Consortium Inc. 2006). Neither protocol assumes any particular gazetteer model for the data. They work as common search methods for distributed, independent gazetteers because each gazetteer server translates the protocol queries into search statements that work for the local implementation and creates standard reports to send back in return. Gazetteer services can elect to install the protocols and configure them to their gazetteer data structures and access methods in order to provide remote search access through the protocol functions. These protocols are briefly described next.

Protocols for Gazetteer Networks

ADL Gazetteer Protocol   The *ADL Gazetteer Protocol* is a lightweight, *stateless*, XML- and HTTP-based protocol for accessing gazetteers, based on the abstract model of a gazetteer described earlier in this chapter. This protocol provides relatively low level services simple enough to be implemented by all gazetteers, yet powerful enough for combining into higher-level services. For example, a query such as "find Las Vegas, Nevada" cannot be processed in one step. Instead, the protocol supports a multistep process, such as

1. find a place named "Nevada" belonging to class "countries, 1st order divisions" (note: this example uses a feature-type term from the ADL *Feature Type Thesaurus*);
2. user interaction to select the correct listing in the case of multiple returns for this query; and then
3. find places named "Las Vegas" that are spatially contained within the footprint of the place named "Nevada" or which have a *part of* relationship with "Nevada."

The ADL protocol (version 1.2) supports querying gazetteers by

• Identifier (unique identifier within the gazetteer)
• Code (e.g., a FIPS code)
• Status of *current*, *former*, or *proposed* for the feature
• Placename
• Geographic area (footprint)
• Feature class
• Relationship with another gazetteer entry

For each query type, the protocol defines the operations that can be performed. For example, a name query can use the operators *equals*, *contains-all-words*, *contains-any-words*, or *contains-phrase*, and a footprint query can use the operators *within*, *contains*, or *overlaps*.

The response consists of entries matching the query parameters sent in the form of protocol-defined standard reports or as extended reports as defined by the gazetteer owner—both in XML format.

A *capabilities report* can be requested of a gazetteer server to find out which parts of the protocol are supported.

```
ADL Protocol Query Example
<?xml version="1.0" encoding="UTF-8"?>
<gazetteer-service
  xmlns="http://www.alexandria.ucsb.edu/gazetteer"
  version="1.2">
<query-request>
  <gazetteer-query>
    <and>
      <name-query operator="contains-phrase"
        text="las vegas"/>
      <class-query thesaurus="ADL Feature Type Thesaurus"
        term="populated places"/>
    </and>
  </gazetteer-query>
  <report-format>standard</report-format>
</query-request>
</gazetteer-service>
```

Figure 5.17
Example of an ADL Gazetteer Protocol query

An example of a query is shown in figure 5.17. An example of a response to this query is shown in figure 5.18.

The *ADL Gazetteer Protocol* is well documented online. A hands-on web page illustrates the way the protocol works and the server code can be downloaded to facilitate implementation for a particular gazetteer.

Open Geospatial Consortium (OGC) Gazetteer Protocol The other gazetteer service protocol has been developed by members of the Open Geospatial Consortium (OGC). It is based on the gazetteer model of the ISO 19112 standard described earlier in this chapter. It is a specification developed as a specialization of the OGC Web Feature Service (WFS) (see the link from OGC's specification web page, Open Geospatial Consortium Inc. 2005); it is XML/HTTP-based and stateless. This protocol is designed to work within other specifications developed by the OGC and is built on the base of the capabilities of these other standards. This means, among other factors, that the OGC gazetteer protocol inherits the more extensive geospatial querying operations of the WFS (e.g., *crosses* and *touches*) and a higher degree of complexity than the *ADL Gazetteer Protocol* because of the generality of the WFS and GML. Because it follows the ISO 19112 model of gazetteer data, it supports querying for features on the basis of the thesaurus hierarchical properties of broader term (BT), narrower term (NT), and related term (RT). This OGC gazetteer service specification was published as an implementation specification in 2006.

ADL Protocol Query Response Example

```
<?xml version="1.0" encoding="UTF-8"?>
<gazetteer-service
  xmlns="http://www.alexandria.ucsb.edu/gazetteer"
  xmlns:gml="http://www.opengis.net/gml"
  xmlns:xlink="http://www.w3.org/1999/xlink"
  version="1.2">
<query-response>
  <standard-reports>
    <gazetteer-standard-report>
      <identifier>1001652</identifier>
      <codes>
        <codes cheme="FIPS 55-3">40000</code>
      </codes>
      <place-status>current</place-status>
      <display-name>Las Vegas, Nevada</display-name>
      <names>
        <name primary="true">Las Vegas</name>
      </names>
      <bounding-box>
        <gml:coord>
          <gml:X>-115.25</gml:X>
          <gml:Y>36.15</gml:Y>
        </gml:coord>
        <gml:coord>
          <gml:X>-115.12</gml:X>
          <gml:Y>36.25</gml:Y>
        </gml:coord>
      </bounding-box>
      <footprints>
        <footprint-reference xlink:href="http://..."
          geometry-type="Polygon" num-points="4632"
          primary="true"/>
      </footprints>
      <classes>
        <class thesaurus="ADL Feature Type Thesaurus"
          primary="true">populated places</class>
      </classes>
    </gazetteer-standard-report>
  </standard-reports>
</query-response>
```

Figure 5.18
Example of a standard report received in response to the query in figure 5.17 using the ADL Gazetteer Protocol

Conflation of Gazetteer Data

A related interoperability issue is the conflation of gazetteer data from multiple sources, either in the process of building a gazetteer by integrating information from multiple sources or for handling of the results of searching across multiple gazetteers for the same information. It turns out that determining whether two pieces of information pertain to the same place is problematic because no single descriptive element is definitive. Each of the three basic gazetteer elements of description for a feature—name, footprint, and type—can vary. A place can have more than one name, can have more than one representation of its footprint, and can have a different feature-type classification applied to it depending on the classification scheme used. So in order to combine information from multiple sources into one gazetteer entry, some questions have to be answered:

• Are the names the same or is one name a known alternative for the place? If they are different, are they very different or are the differences in the nature of variations in spelling or formatting? Are the names in different languages? Are the names from different historical periods?
• Are the footprints of the same type—that is, both points, both bounding boxes, or both polygons? If one is a point and the other a polygon, is the point within the polygon? If both are polygons, do the polygons overlap substantially? Are the footprints from different historical periods (especially relevant to populated places)?
• Has the same typing scheme (KOS) been used for the various sources of information? Since this is unlikely, are formal mappings between the schemes available, or will customized mappings have to be created so that equivalencies can be recognized?

Figure 5.19 illustrates the nature of the problem. The top example is from a gazetteer with narrative descriptions. The bottom example shows an entry using one of the former names of Lake Tahoe. The feature type varies from "lake" to "reservoir" to the more general "water body." The coordinates are in the same area but not exactly the same. The elevation is given for three of the four entries, and they vary slightly. The issue is whether the four entries represent the same feature (they do). If so, what processes could be used by a computer to correctly judge whether the information can be combined into one entry or whether these gazetteer entries should be grouped together when they appear in a list together—for example, in a results list from a query sent to more than one gazetteer?

To answer these questions, a set of calculations involving textual, geometric, and KOS similarity measures are needed. The result would be a measure of certainty that the information is about the same place based on each element of basic

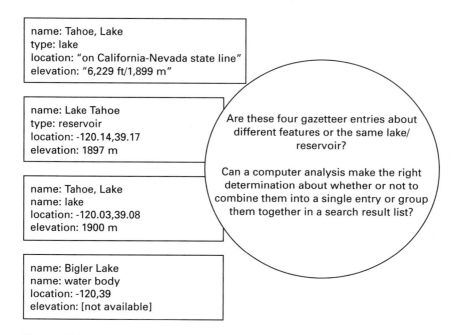

name: Tahoe, Lake
type: lake
location: "on California-Nevada state line"
elevation: "6,229 ft/1,899 m"

name: Lake Tahoe
type: reservoir
location: -120.14,39.17
elevation: 1897 m

name: Tahoe, Lake
name: lake
location: -120.03,39.08
elevation: 1900 m

name: Bigler Lake
name: water body
location: -120,39
elevation: [not available]

Are these four gazetteer entries about different features or the same lake/reservoir?

Can a computer analysis make the right determination about whether or not to combine them into a single entry or group them together in a search result list?

Figure 5.19
Illustration of the difficulty of judging whether multiple gazetteer entries are about the same feature

description; these separate measures could then be combined into an overall similarity measure. This overall measure could be used to make a preliminary decision as to whether the information from two different sources can be combined into one gazetteer entry or grouped together in lists. Such a capability would be particularly valuable in matching the data in gazetteers with the data in GIS databases for the same features, taking advantage of the detailed spatial information in GIS and the extensive placename information in gazetteers (Hastings and Hill 2002).

Summary

Gazetteers have been around for a long time as dictionaries of placenames, compendiums of brief information about named geographic places, indexes for atlases, and placename thesauri. In the last ten years, they have been recognized as key components of georeferenced information systems whose chief function is to translate between formal and informal ways of referencing places—that is, between placenames, coordinate values, and type designations.

Several models of digital gazetteers and gazetteer protocols have emerged. The Alexandria Digital Library (ADL) and the International Standards Organization (ISO) have both developed models for gazetteer data. The Open Geospatial Consortium (OGC) has developed a gazetteer protocol based on the ISO gazetteer model, and ADL has developed a gazetteer protocol based on its abstract model for gazetteer data. These models and protocols differ in their premises and their intended purposes: the ADL models (the *Gazetteer Content Standard* and the abstract model of the *ADL Gazetteer Protocol*) are designed for general use, the ISO model is designed for the administration of sets of "geographic identifiers," and the OGC protocol model is designed to work within the framework of the GIS-based Web Feature Service (WFS). The thesaurus model has also been used for gazetteer data, as exemplified by the *Getty Thesaurus of Geographic Names* (TGN), used extensively for cataloging and bibliographic indexing. While each of these models and protocols incorporates the core elements of the description of named geographic places—names, types, and footprints—there are significant differences in the ways these elements are modeled and in the overall structural designs and additional descriptive elements traceable to their intended purposes.

Sources of data about named geographic places include official toponymic agencies, navigation charts and maps, local governmental activities, projects, and local cultural knowledge about names and places. Increasingly, the availability of GPS units and GPS components of cameras and vehicles is creating the opportunity for on-the-ground collecting of point locations and boundaries for places that could become data for gazetteer entries.

There will never be one gazetteer that comprehensively and deeply covers the entire world. Instead, gazetteers will be built from local and project knowledge to supplement the official gazetteers of the world's toponymic authorities. Interoperability among gazetteers is therefore an issue. One solution is the use of gazetteer-specific protocols to support the searching of distributed, independent gazetteer services, which returns responses in a standard report format and optionally as customized reports developed by the individual gazetteer services. Both ADL and OGC have worked on such protocols. The ADL protocol has been published and implemented and the software is available for download; the OGC protocol is a published implementation specification. A related interoperability issue is the conflation of data about a particular place from multiple sources. Since no single descriptive element of a gazetteer entry is sufficient on its own to uniquely identify a place, an algorithmic solution is needed to combine evidence from the names, types, and footprints to give a degree of certainty that two pieces of information are about the same place.

Gazetteers store information about named places from multiple sources or as a result of original data gathering and their use is not limited to any particular type of activity or to any particular field. They are used to answer questions such as "Where is Cucamonga?", to which a map display is the answer, as well as to support cataloging and indexing functions by providing coordinate values that can be added to metadata and to text documents. For information system user interfaces, the gazetteer is the component that expands a query from a placename to coordinates or to additional placenames, or a footprint to a set of placenames. Gazetteers provide the data to answer questions such as "What schools are in the Detroit area?" and other feature-type queries. Gazetteers are key components of georeferenced information systems in all cases where place-based information is a factor.

Sources for Further Information

Feature-Type Schemes

Alexandria Digital Library. 2004. *Metadata for the ADL Feature Type Thesaurus*. University of California at Santa Barbara. http://www.alexandria.ucsb.edu/gazetteer/Feature-Types/FTT_metadata.htm.

Geoscience Australia. 2004. *Feature Codes Used by the Gazetteer of Australia*. http://www.ga.gov.au/map/names/featurecodes.jsp.

J. Paul Getty Trust, Research Institute. 2004. *Getty Thesaurus of Geographic Names Online: Place Type Lookup*. http://www.getty.edu/research/conducting_research/vocabularies/tgn/ (click Place Type Lookup).

National Geospatial–Intelligence Agency. 2005. *Geonames Feature Designation Code Help*. http://gnswww.nga.mil/geonames/Desig_Code/Desig_Code_Help.jsp.

Natural Resources of Canada. 2003. *Canadian Geographical Names, Geographic Feature Type*. http://geonames.nrcan.gc.ca/info/type_e.php.

U.S. Geological Survey, Geographic Names Information System (GNIS). 2003. *GNIS Data Users Guide 6. Appendix C.—GNIS Feature Class Definitions*. http://geonames.usgs.gov/gnis_users_guide_appendixc.html.

Gazetteers: Models, Protocols, and Workshops

Alexandria Digital Library. 2005. *ADL Gazetteer Development Website*. Alexandria Digital Library Project. www.alexandria.ucsb.edu/gazetteer.

Alexandria Digital Library. 2004. *Guide to the ADL Gazetteer Content Standard*. Version 3.2. University of California at Santa Barbara. http://www.alexandria.ucsb.edu/gazetteer/ContentStandard/version3.2/GCS3.2-guide.htm.

Hill, L. L. 1999. *Digital Gazetteer Information Exchange (DGIE) Workshop*. http://www.alexandria.ucsb.edu/gazetteer/dgie/DGIE_website/DGIE_homepage.htm.

International Organization for Standardization (ISO), Technical Committee 211. 2003b. *Geographic Information—Spatial Referencing by Geographic Identifiers (ISO 19112:2003).* www.iso.org (for purchase information).

Janée, G., and L. L. Hill. 2003. *ADL Gazetteer Protocol.* Version 1.2. Alexandria Digital Library, University of California at Santa Barbara. http://www.alexandria.ucsb.edu/gazetteer/protocol/specification.html.

J. Paul Getty Trust—Research Institute. 2005. *Getty Thesaurus of Geographic Names Online.* http://www.getty.edu/research/conducting_research/vocabularies/tgn/.

Kornai, A., and B. Sundheim. 2003. *Workshop on the Analysis of Geographic References, May 31, 2003, Edmonton, Alberta, as Part of the North American Chapter of the Association for Computational Linguistics and Human Language Technology Conference (NAACL-HLT 2003).* http://people.mokk.bme.hu/~kornai/NAACL/.

Mackay, D., John Bartholomew and Son, and Times Books. 1992. *The New York Times Atlas of the World.* 3rd rev. conciseed, 3rd U.S. ed. New York: Times Books.

National Geospatial-Intelligence Agency. 2005. *GEOnet Names Server (GNS).* http://earth-info.nga.mil/gns/html/.

Networked Knowledge Organization Systems/Services Group. 2002. *Digital Gazetteers—Integration into Distributed Digital Library Services.* http://nkos.slis.kent.edu/DL02workshop.htm.

Open Geospatial Consortium Inc. 2006. *Gazetteer Service Profile of the Web Feature Service Implementation Specification.* Implementation specification OGC 05-035rl, version 0.9.1. https://portal.opengeospatial.org/files/?artifact_id=13593.

U.S. Geological Survey—Geographic Names Information System (GNIS). 2005. *GNIS Website.* http://geonames.usgs.gov/.

Thesaurus Standards

American National Standards Institute, and National Information Standards Organization (U.S.). 2005. *Guidelines for the Construction, Format, and Management of Monolingual Controlled Vocabularies (Z39.19-2005).* NISO Press. http://www.niso.org/standards/index.html (see Z39.19 in the listing).

British Standards. 2005. *Structured Vocabularies for Information Retrieval. Guide. Thesauri. (BS 8723-2:2005).* http://www.bsonline.bsi-global.com/server/index.jsp (search for Standard No. 8723).

Appendix: Understanding the Schema Diagrams

The diagrams are read from left to right. On the left is a box for the root element of the schema with its data element name inside: for example:

> SpatialLocation

From this root element, a connector leads to one of these symbols:

—Ⓢ which links to a *sequence* of sub-elements to be used for description
—Ⓒ which links to a set of sub-elements from which a *choice* can be made for description.

This pattern is repeated across to the right linking elements in each level of the schema tree to sub-elements at the next level.

An element in a box with a solid boundary is *required*; an element in a box with a dashed/dotted boundary is *optional*.

If an element is *required* and it has sub-elements, the requirement is satisfied by using the required sub-element(s) only.

If an element is *optional* and it is used, then the required sub-elements must be used.

If an element has no sub-elements, then it is a *leaf node* and it holds data values.

Boxes for elements are annotated as follows:

• 0 . . . is used with optional elements; it indicates that this element can occur multiple times if it is used at all.
• 1 . . . is used with required elements; it indicates that this element must be used at least one time and that it can be used multiple times.
• 1 . . 1 means that the element must be used, and it can be used only one time.
• 0 . . 1 means that the element is optional, and, if used, it can be used only one time.
• No annotation is the equivalent of 1 . . 1 or 0 . . 1; that is, that the element, whether required or optional, can only be used once.

If an element at the far right of the diagram is followed by a plus sign (+), then it has sub-elements that are not included in the diagram.

6

Georeferencing Elements in Metadata Standards

Metadata is structured descriptive details about an information or data object or a collection of objects. These compact formal descriptions are accessed programmatically or in person for various purposes, in lieu of accessing the information object or collection directly. Purposes include information discovery, browsing, evaluation for fitness for use, and retrieval; information access, conditions of use and guidelines for effective use; and administration and management details. In this chapter, the elements for georeferencing information in object-level metadata standards are reviewed. To the degree that information systems are based on metadata, the georeferencing operations that can be performed are governed by the ways placenames and geospatial references are documented in that metadata.

Metadata standards have been developed for various purposes over time, starting in the 1960s with the development of the MARC standard for "Machine Readable Cataloging" for libraries and the bibliographic indexing standards for the scientific journal literature. The 1990s saw the development of metadata standards for geospatial data. From that time to the present, there have been four trends: (1) the growing maturity of the geospatial data standards and the development of services built on those standards, (2) the development of metadata standards for web-based resources and associated services built on them, (3) the integration of geospatial elements into metadata schemes designed originally for text-based information environments, and (4) the development of digital library technologies, such as in the Alexandria Digital Library at the University of California at Santa Barbara, that are specifically based on georeferencing.

This chapter reviews a selection of metadata standards for the description of information objects that include geospatial referencing. They are presented more or less in historical order since these standards, to some extent, build on one another. The focus is on the current versions of these standards and only on their georeferencing elements. For standards developed specifically for the description of geospatial data, only the core elements for basic georeferencing are discussed. Each of these standards must be considered in relation to the purposes for which it was designed and the time period in which it was developed. The intent is not to point out specific weaknesses or strengths in any particular approach, but to look at the structures anew from the point of view of overall interoperability—discovery, access, and use—of place-based information, on a worldwide basis by communities and for purposes beyond what was originally envisioned. To help understand the differences and commonalities in structuring, hierarchical diagrams of the metadata structures for georeferencing elements are included.

A concluding section introduces a generic georeferencing structure for object-level metadata and the basic principles for a simple geometry language to support geographic information retrieval across all types of information.

Standards Whose Development Started in the 1960s

MARC 21 Format for Bibliographic Data Georeferencing Elements

The *MARC 21 Format for Bibliographic Data* "contains format specifications for encoding data elements needed to describe, retrieve, and control various forms of bibliographic material" (U.S. Library of Congress, Network Development and MARC Standards Office 2005a). MARC has a venerable history and is the backbone of the Anglo-American library-cataloging world, where sharing catalog records created by multiple institutions has been common practice for decades. Inclusion of coordinates and other parameters of spatial location first appeared in the 1970s; in 1981 the *Anglo-American Cataloging Rules* (AACR2) first included a section on coordinates. The new fields were designed by map catalogers and have been most consistently used for the description of maps and geospatial data. These MARC fields, however, are not limited to use for maps; they may be used to represent the spatial coverage of any library object, but this is not widely done.

Figure 6.1 illustrates the MARC fields most often used in library cataloging records for georeferencing the content of the object; for a complete view of these fields, refer to the MARC 21 web pages maintained by the Library of Congress. The numbers in the box labels (e.g., 034) are the identifiers for the MARC fields; the subfields have indicators starting with a dollar sign (e.g., $a).

Briefly, these MARC fields are designed as follows:

• In field 034, the MARC format supports the description of a bounding-box footprint with ddmmss coordinate values, with each side of the box documented. This

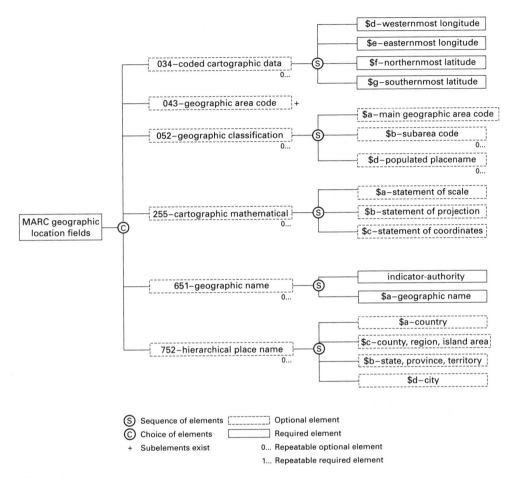

Figure 6.1
Selected MARC georeferencing fields

field also includes subfields for scale that are not shown here. This field is always paired with field 255.

• The 043 field holds geographic codes selected from the *MARC Code List for Geographic Areas* (U.S. Library of Congress, Network Development and MARC Standards Office, 2003) or local codes and is most often used when cataloging non-cartographic items.

• The 052 field contains geographic classification codes derived from the Library of Congress classification schedules.

• Scale and projection are included in the 255 field as well as a statement of the coordinates as a single string of values. This field is always paired with field 034.

• The 651 field contains geographic names from controlled authority lists.

• The 752 field was created to hold hierarchical information about named places; its use was initially intended to document the place of publication, but it has also been used to document the geographic subject of an object. Currently (in November 2005) there is a proposal under discussion within the MARC community to create another field for subject use (field 662) that has the same structure as 752.

In addition to these fields, the MARC general-note fields (the repeatable 500 field) can be used for additional geospatial documentation (e.g., notes about characteristics of a map not documented elsewhere) and the $z subfield is frequently used to add a geographic location to subject headings (the 6xx fields). Here is an illustration of the use of some of these fields for the description of a map; rarely are all of these fields used in a single record:

034: $d W1203000 $e W1191700 $f N0375600 $g N0374330
043: $a n-us-ca
052: 4363 $b M3
255: $a Scale 1:42,240. 1 in. represents 2/3 mile; $b transverse Mercator proj. $c (W120°30′00″–W119°17′00″/N 37°56′00″–N37°43′30″)
500: $a "UTM zone 11."
500: $a "1927 North American datum."
650: $Labor supply $z California $z Mariposa County $v Maps.
651: $a Mariposa County (Calif.) $x Economic conditions $v Maps.
752: $a United States $b California $c Mariposa.

Not shown in the diagram, because they are rarely used in cataloging, are the subfields for *G-rings* in the 034 and 255 fields. A *G-ring* (also known as a *linear ring*) is a set of connected points that forms a boundary—that is, a vector representation of a polygonal boundary (a nonrectangular boundary). An outer ring and an inner ring can be used to represent a donut-shaped area; a single G-ring is used for the boundary of a polygon.

A set of fields was also created in MARC after the publication of the FGDC metadata standard for geospatial data (described in this chapter) so that every element in the FGDC metadata standard could be mapped to an equivalent MARC field. Since this level of description for geospatial objects is beyond this review—beyond the core elements of placenames and basic geospatial location—they are not included here.

Table 6.1 shows the occurrence of some of the georeferencing fields in MARC catalog records from two statistical analyses: (1) a study (Petras 2004) using a set of over five million unique MARC records from 1968 to 2000, and (2) an analysis

Table 6.1
Occurrence of frequently used georeferencing fields in MARC catalog records from two recent studies

MARC georeferencing fields	Petras study	OCLC statistical analysis
Number of records	5,065,574	54,829,227
034 and 255	0.23%	—
043a	46.22%	32.47%
650z	34.9%	26.25%
651a	18.14%	14.54%

of 54,829,227 records from a snapshot of OCLC's WorldCat dataset from early 2005 (D. Vizine-Goetz, personal communication 2005).

In the Petras study, almost half of the records contained either a 650z or 651a subject heading and nearly half contained geographic codes in 043a; few contained the geospatial fields and even fewer a specific geographic classification. The comparable statistics from the OCLC analysis reflect lower figures: 40.8 percent of the records contained either a 650z or 651a and 32.5 percent contained 043a fields. The use of fields 034 and 255 would be much higher for collections of maps and other cartographic objects.

Beyond this georeferencing using MARC fields, there are other ways that MARC catalogers indicate the geographic associations of the objects they catalog. The place of publication is almost always documented, in field 260a as a placename and in field 008 as a publication code. The classification numbers embed number sequences and extension codes that indicate geographic areas and thus support shelf arrangements that bring works together that are about, for example, the history or geography of a particular country.

A general characteristic of MARC cataloging practices is that the georeferencing is at a general level, designed more for bringing together groups of objects that are about the same general topic than for representing the specific geographic area that is the focus of individual objects. Olha Buchel used the following example to illustrate this. The title of the book is *Rannie etapy istorii slavian Dneprovskogo Levoberezh'ia*, which translates into *Early History of the Slavs from the Left Bank of the Dnipro* in English. The Dnipro, aka Dnieper River, she explains, bisects the country into right-bank and left-bank divisions. She adds: "In the history of Ukraine, this division has played an important role. People who live on the left side of Dnieper tend to gravitate to Russia, while Ukrainians who live on the right side are more pro-western" (Buchel 2005). The classification and the subject headings assigned to this book, however, indicate only that the book is about the Dnieper River: a classification of "DK511.D55" for the Dnieper River and subject headings of "Dnieper River Region–History" and "Dnieper River Region–Antiquities." This is sufficient to bring together books about the Dnieper River area and the history of the region but not to differentiate between sections of the river or, in this case, areas with cultural differences located on the left and right banks. Only the MARC geospatial fields currently used primarily for map cataloging (034 and 255) document areas to the specificity of bounding boxes.

GeoRef Bibliographic Format Georeferencing Elements
At about the same time that the MARC format was being developed by the Library of Congress, the Council on Scientific and Technical Information (COSATI) of the Federal Council on Science and Technology was creating a bibliographic description standard that was adopted by the indexing and abstracting services for various scientific disciplines. These services index the world's journal and report literature for their scientific communities. This standard was not used as rigorously as the MARC standard was by the traditional library world, but it provided a starting point for the development of a set of bibliographic indexes such as *Chemical Abstracts* and *Engineering Index*.

One indexing and abstracting service, *GeoRef*, was established to cover the Earth sciences by the American Geological Institute (AGI) in 1966 (American Geological Institute 2005). *GeoRef* has been the only major indexing and abstracting service to incorporate geospatial coordinates in its record format and to have geospatial query capability supported by the online bibliographic services. It started adding coordinates for the geographic coverage of the documents in 1977. The spatial indexing is contained in a *coord* element and the data values are in ddmmss style. This example describes a bounding box for the study area of an article in the journal *Geology*: N331500N343000E0363000E0352000

Approximately 35 percent of the items indexed by *GeoRef* are given coordinates representing the spatial coverage area relevant to the document. For a data-loading project where coordinates were derived from the assigned placenames, *GeoRef* found suitable coordinates for about 75 percent of the records (Sharon Tahirkheli, personal communication, 2005).

GeoRef treats placenames as a type of *descriptor* along with terms for the topics/subjects for the object being described. Figure 3.14 is an example of a GeoRef record that includes placenames. Placenames also appear in the *GeoRef Thesaurus* and often include coordinates in these entries for bounding-box or point representations. An example from the *Thesaurus* is the following ("CO" stands for "coordinates"):

Dogo Island
> Largest of the Oki Islands off W coast of Honshu in Japan Sea . . .
> CO N361000N362000E1332500E1331000
>
> . . .

There are 9,367 terms in the *GeoRef Thesaurus* with coordinates, representing approximately 75 percent of the total of 12,424 terms in the thesaurus (Sharon Tahirkheli, personal communication, 2005).

Standards Whose Development Started in the 1990s and 2000s

FGDC Content Standard for Digital Geospatial Metadata (CSDGM)

The CSDGM was mandated for use by all federal agencies by Executive Order 12906, published in the *Federal Register* on April 12, 1994, for the documentation of all digital geospatial data produced by the federal government. The first version of the CSDGM was released in 1995 and the second version in 1998. Profiles of the standard have been developed for biological and shoreline data, and it has been extended for remote sensing data (U.S. Federal Geographic Data Committee 2003). The objective of the standard is to provide a common set of terminology and definitions for the documentation of digital geospatial data from all sources (not just the U.S. federal government), which will facilitate the sharing and reuse of data and reduce unwarranted duplication of effort in collecting or creating the data. Specifically, the standard document states:

The major uses of metadata are:

• to maintain an organization's internal investment in geospatial data,

• to provide information about an organization's data holdings to data catalogues, clearinghouses, and brokerages, and

• to provide information needed to process and interpret data to be received through a transfer from an external source.

The information included in the standard was selected based on four roles that metadata play:

• availability: data needed to determine the sets of data that exist for a geographic location.

• fitness for use: data needed to determine if a set of data meets a specific need.

• access: data needed to acquire an identified set of data.

• transfer: data needed to process and use a set of data. (U.S. Federal Geographic Data Committee 1998)

Since the CSDGM is designed to describe geospatial data for these purposes, the whole standard pertains to describing such data in exquisite detail. Here only a selection of the structure is highlighted for the purpose of relating its approach to the description of georeferencing as covered in this book.

A location can be represented in the Identification Section of the standard by a bounding box or by a polygon, known in the standard as a *data set g-polygon*. If a polygon is given, an outer polygon around the area is required; exclusionary polygons (i.e., the "hole in the donut") within this area are permitted but not required. Optionally, placename(s) for the area can also be recorded. For placenames, the standard requires that the source of the placename (e.g., the thesaurus or gazetteer) be cited, but "none" is permitted as describing the source and is often used. Placenames are treated in the standard as a type of *keyword*, along with *theme*, *stratum*, and *temporal* descriptors.

The basic georeferencing elements of this standard are diagrammed in figure 6.2. They are

· bounding coordinates for four sides (required)
· data set g-polygon (optional), with the outer ring required and the exclusion ring optional
· place keyword (optional), with each place keyword associated with a "place keyword thesaurus"

Section 4 of the CSDGM is devoted to the documentation of Spatial Reference Information. Details of map projections, scales, coordinate and grid systems, geodetic datum, and additional data are modeled with the specificity needed for programmatic use of geospatial datasets.

The FGDC's CSDGM is now recognized as a standard by the American National Standards Institute (ANSI) under the auspices of the InterNational Committee for Information Technology Standards (INCITS). Technical Committee L1 of INCITS develops standards for GIS and geospatial metadata and serves as the U.S. Technical Advisory Group (TAG) to ISO Technical Committee 211, which is discussed in the next section.

ISO TC 211 Geographic Information—Metadata

In 1995, a new item was proposed by the Geographic Information Technical Committee (TC 211) of the International Standards Organization (ISO) for the development of an ISO metadata standard for "geographic information." This effort, which finally produced a standard in 2003, was able to build on the work of the

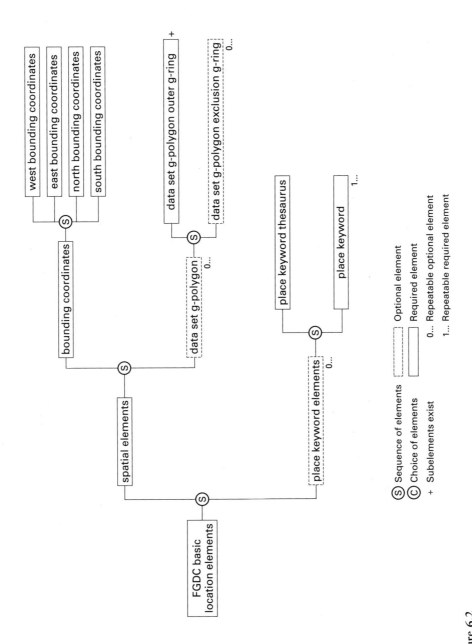

Figure 6.2
Core georeferencing elements of the FGDC Content Standard for Digital Geospatial Metadata (CSDGM)

FGDC. Since the final approval of ISO 19115, titled *Geographic Information—Metadata*, steps are being taken to harmonize the FGDC metadata standard, described above, with the ISO. There are also plans to "collaborate with . . . Canada and Mexico to develop a North American profile [of the ISO TC 211 metadata standard] to achieve metadata consistency among the three countries" (U.S. Federal Geographic Data Committee 2005a).

The ISO 19115 standard is designed for similar purposes to the intended uses of the FGDC's CSDGM. It is applicable to the cataloging of datasets, clearinghouse activities, and the full description of datasets; and to geographic datasets, dataset series, and individual geographic features and feature properties. It defines

• Mandatory and conditional metadata sections, metadata entities, and metadata elements
• The minimum set of metadata required to serve the full range of metadata applications (data discovery, determining data fitness for use, data access, data transfer, and use of digital data)
• Optional metadata elements—to allow for a more extensive standard description of geographic data, if required
• A method for extending metadata to fit specialized needs

Though ISO 19115:2003 is applicable to digital data, its principles can be extended to many other forms of geographic data such as maps, charts, and textual documents as well as to nongeographic data (International Organization for Standardization (ISO), Technical Committee 211, 2003a).

The ISO 19115 standard includes a set of *core elements* suggested for minimum-level description. This is comparable to the Identification Section of the CSDGM. The core spatial elements in the ISO standard are diagrammed in figure 6.3. They include a bounding-box representation, but the standard also permits the location to be represented only by a *geographic identifier*, which in the ISO system includes a placename, address, or other code or text label. *Spatial resolution* is documented by an *equivalent scale* element, which is the "scale of a comparable hardcopy map or chart," and/or by a *distance*, which is the "ground sample distance" (e.g., 30-meter data sampling). The core elements of the ISO standard include the *spatial representation type* element, which documents the "method used to spatially represent geographic information: vector, grid, text table, triangulated irregular network (tin), stereo model, or video." As with the CSDGM, this ISO standard covers in great detail the documentation of geospatial data needed to support data sharing and reuse, beyond this basic set. An XML encoding of the 19115 geographic metadata standard is under development and will be issued as ISO standard 19139

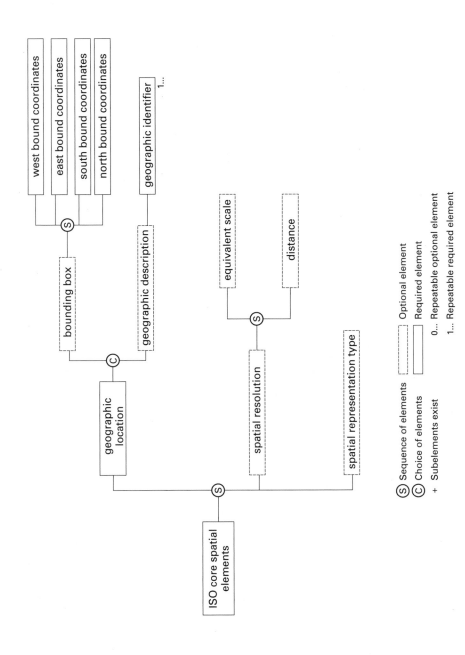

Figure 6.3
ISO TC 211 19115 core spatial elements

(International Organization for Standardization (ISO), Technical Committee 211, 2005).

Dublin Core Metadata Initiative (DCMI) Georeferencing Elements

The Dublin Core Metadata Initiative (DCMI) started with an initial meeting in Dublin, Ohio, in 1995 "to advance the state of the art in the development of resource description (or metadata) records for networked electronic information objects" (Weibel, Godby, and Miller 1995). It has grown into a formal international metadata standard effort with a directorate and board of trustees and a metadata standard established formally as NISO Standard Z39.85-2001 (September 2001) and ISO Standard 15836-2003 (February 2003). The standard consists of only fifteen metadata elements, all of which are optional. One of these elements is *coverage*, which is defined as "the extent or scope of the content of the resource," further explained with this comment:

Typically, *coverage* will include spatial location (a placename or geographic coordinates), temporal period (a period label, date, or date range) or jurisdiction (such as a named administrative entity). Recommended best practice is to select a value from a controlled vocabulary (for example, the *Thesaurus of Geographic Names* (TGN)) and to use, where appropriate, named places or time periods in preference to numeric identifiers such as sets of coordinates or date ranges. (Dublin Core Metadata Initiative 2005)

The *coverage* element is designed to hold a multitude of types of information, which seems to preclude the possibility of searching over the contents of the element in any formal way beyond basic text searching. It is designed more as a high-level category of the metadata content for which more specific refinements can be developed and adopted.

A set of spatial extensions, as shown in table 6.2, for the Dublin Core *coverage* element were proposed by Simon Cox in 2000 for bounding boxes (Cox 2000a) and points (Cox 2000b) and reissued in July 2005 (Cox 2005a, 2005b). The core components include the third vertical dimension of elevation and depth. The documentation of *projection* includes the documentation of datum.

All elements in this proposed spatial extension are "optional but must not be repeated, and the ordering is not significant." Optionality extends to the point of providing for an interpretation of spatial coverage when one or more sides to the bounding box are missing or where a point has only one coordinate value.

The recommendations for point and box extensions for the DCMI *coverage* element include a text string syntax to express the spatial elements according to the

Table 6.2
Proposed extensions to the Dublin Core *coverage* element to represent spatial location

	DCMI box		DCMI point
northlimit	The value of the constant coordinate for the northernmost face or edge	north	The value of the coordinate of the location measured in the north direction
eastlimit	The value of the constant coordinate for the easternmost face or edge	east	The value of the coordinate of the location measured in the east direction
southlimit	The value of the constant coordinate for the southernmost face or edge		
westlimit	The value of the constant coordinate for the westernmost face or edge		
uplimit	The value of the constant coordinate for the uppermost face or edge	elevation	The value of the coordinate of the location measured in the vertical direction
downlimit	The value of the constant coordinate for the lowermost face or edge		
units	The units applying to unlabeled numeric values of northlimit, eastlimit, southlimit, westlimit	units	The units applying to unlabeled numeric values of north, east
zunits	The units applying to unlabeled numeric values of uplimit, downlimit	zunits	The units applying to unlabeled numeric values of elevation
projection	The name of the projection used with any parameters required, such as ellipsoid parameters, datum, standard parallels and meridians, zone, etc.	projection	The name of the projection used with any parameters required, such as ellipsoid parameters, datum, standard parallels and meridians, zone, etc.
name	A name for the place	name	A name for the place

Dublin Core Structured Values (DCSV) encoding method. Using this encoding for the DCMI box, the location of Lake Jindabyne in Australia can be written within a DCMI metadata record (using UTM notation) as: northlimit = 5980000; westlimit = 644000; eastlimit = 647000; southlimit = 5966000; units = m; projection = UTM zone 55 south.

In the 2000 version of the DCMI spatial extension document, an XML encoding for the proposed point and box extensions for the DCMI *coverage* element were included as examples, such as this representation for the same lake:

```
<Box projection="UTM zone 55 south" name="Lake Jindabyne">
    <northlimit units="m">5980000</northlimit>
    <eastlimit units="m">647000</eastlimit>
    <southlimit units="m">5966000</southlimit>
    <westlimit units="m">644000</westlimit>
</BOX>
```

Electronic Cultural Atlas Initiative (ECAI) Metadata Georeferencing Elements

There are other local extensions of the basic DCMI to hold geospatial data. One of these is the Electronic Cultural Atlas Initiative (ECAI), which "uses time and space to enhance understanding and preservation of human culture" (Electronic Cultural Atlas Initiative 2005b). ECAI developers have expanded DCMI metadata to represent both the geospatial and the temporal dimensions of the cultural information their system holds—what they call the "space-time cube" consisting of minimum and maximum longitude (x) and latitude (y) values, and a minimum and maximum time/date (t) (Electronic Cultural Atlas Initiative 2005a; Jarvis, Cross, and Johnson 1999). Here is an example of the use of these and related georeferencing elements in ECAI metadata describing *The McMahon Line, China* (from an ECAI record created by Lawrence Crissman for the China *Time*Map™ Project, University of Sydney):

- dc.coverage.x.min: 69.125000
- dc.coverage.x.max: 140.752000
- dc.coverage.y.min: 18.171
- dc.coverage.y.max: 53.402000
- dc.coverage.t.early: 1950
- dc.coverage.t.late: 2050
- dc.coverage.PlaceName: China
- dc.coverage.PeriodName: Modern

Additional elements are defined to describe "a more precise definition of the nature of the spatial and temporal data in the resource, and the mode of its collection." These include the specification of

- *dc.coverage.spatial.resolution* (ground distance between points or features that can be distinguished)
- *dc.coverage.spatial.aggregation* (geographic units by which the data is aggregated, such as "province" or "census track")
- *dc.coverage.temporal.resolution* (the smallest time interval between events/ features/dates that can be distinguished)
- *dc.coverage.temporal.aggregation* (temporal units in which data is aggregated, such as by years or decades)

Darwin Core Metadata Georeferencing Elements

Like the DCMI and with a name reminiscent of "Dublin Core," the Darwin Core consists of an unordered set of data elements on one level—that is, without nesting. It is the product of the Taxonomic Databases Working Group (TDWG), an international association affiliated with the International Union of Biological Sciences, which was formed to "establish collaboration among biological database projects so as to promote the wider and more effective dissemination of information about the World's heritage of biological organisms for the benefit of the world at large" (Taxonomic Databases Working Group (TDWG) 2005b). The composition and structure of Darwin Core continues to be a discussion topic among TDWG participants as of November 2005.

The application scope includes

databases about natural history collections, living collections (i.e., zoological and botanical gardens), germplasm and genetic resource collections, and data sets produced from biodiversity survey and monitoring programs. These data resources support a wide variety of purposes and consequently they have different structures, but all can contribute to documenting the distributions of organisms. A secondary function of the Darwin Core is to enable the discovery of the contents of biological collections. Because biological collections are diverse, however, the Darwin Core supports the search and retrieval of descriptive information in relatively simple ways. (Taxonomic Databases Working Group (TDWG) 2005a)

The metadata elements reflect the core elements of the descriptions of collection sites for natural history museum specimens.

The draft set of element definitions for Darwin Core 2 v1.4, as of August 2005, includes two sets of elements for georeferencing, one set of Locality Elements and an extension set of Geospatial Elements to represent the georeferencing for a particular specimen (all elements are optional):

- Locality Elements
  - Higher Geography: holding a concatenation of all of the next seven elements to support searching
  - Continent
  - WaterBody
  - IslandGroup
  - Island
  - Country
  - StateProvince
  - County
  - Locality (description of the collection site for the organism)
  - ElevationInMeters
  - ElevationRangeInMeters
  - DepthInMeters
  - DepthRangeInMeters
- Geospatial Elements
  - DecimalLatitude
  - DecimalLongitude
  - GeodeticDatum
  - CoordinateUncertaintyInMeters
  - VerbatimCoordinates
  - OriginalCoordinateSystem
  - GeoreferenceProtocol
  - GeoreferenceSources
  - GeoreferenceVerificationStatus
  - GeoreferenceRemarks

Definitions for these elements are included in the Darwin Core documentation online; see the reference in Sources for Further Information at the end of this chapter. Some examples of locality descriptions and the calculation and representation of coordinate uncertainty from the MaNIS project are included in chapter 3.

Records using the Darwin Core metadata have been made available through the Global Biodiversity Information Facility (GBIF), which on March 6, 2005, included 107 data providers, 408 collections, and over 64 million records. Only some of them include geospatial elements, but this number will grow as projects such as MaNIS and BioGeomancer continue to develop the systems to enable the assignment of geospatial footprints from the information contained in locality descriptions (Global

Biodiversity Information Facility (GBIF) 2005; Mammal Networked Information System (MaNIS) 2005).

Digital Library for Earth System Education (DLESE) Metadata Georeferencing Elements

The ADN Metadata Framework supports the cataloging of objects in the Digital Library for Earth System Education (DLESE). The name ADN derives from the three organizations that participated in its initial development: the Alexandria Digital Library, DLESE, and NASA's Earth Science Enterprise (now called the Science Mission Directorate, Earth-Sun System Mission); the Colorado School of Mines also contributed. ADN is a highly structured XML schema and well-documented metadata structure designed to be used by individuals and organizations contributing collections to the DLESE—a distributed community effort involving educators, students, and scientists working together to improve the quality, quantity, and efficiency of teaching and learning about the Earth system at all levels (DLESE Metadata Working Group 2005).

The *geospatial* element set in ADN includes (figure 6.4):

- bounding box (required and represented by four sides)
- detailed geometries (polygons, points, and lines)
- elevation (vertical minimum and maximum of the bounding box and detailed geometries
- coordinate system (i.e., longitude and latitude in decimal degrees)
- vertical and horizontal datum projection (for visualizations)
- placename or event name tied to coordinates (i.e., a placename associated with the footprint)
- planet or body (planet, moon, or other body in our solar system)
- objects in space (location of objects (e.g., nebulas) that are not within the solar system, described using the convention of right ascension, declination, and epoch)
- source documentation for data

The purpose of the geospatial section of the ADN metadata framework is to describe the geospatial and placename characteristics of resources associated with locations on the Earth or in space and to do so in a way that meets the needs of basic and more complex representations within DLESE. It differs from the other metadata structures described in this chapter by adding elements to describe *named events* such as hurricanes and to describe objects in astronomical space.

As of March 1, 2005, 10 percent of the records in DLESE include bounding boxes (910 out of 9,736) and 8 percent contain at least one placename. Far more of the

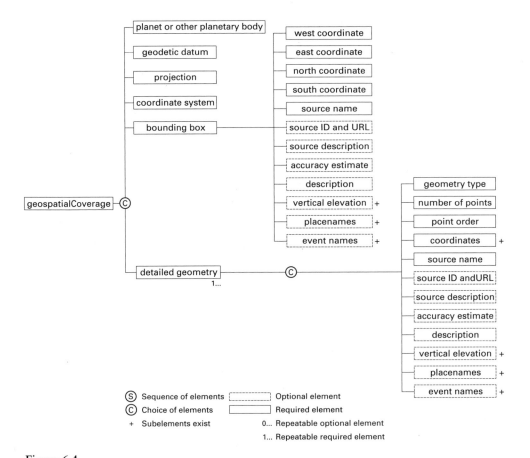

Figure 6.4
Georeferencing element structure in the ADN metadata framework used by the Digital Library for Earth System Education (DLESE)

records in DLESE would benefit from having geospatial referencing (Kathryn Ginger, personal communication, 2005).

Metadata Object Description Schema (MODS) Georeferencing Elements
The Library of Congress released version 3 of its Metadata Object Description Schema (MODS) in December 2003. MODS is an XML schema that "is intended to be able to carry selected data from existing MARC 21 records as well as to enable the creation of original resource description records. It includes a subset of MARC fields and uses language-based tags rather than numeric ones, in some cases regrouping elements from the MARC 21 bibliographic format" (U.S. Library of Congress, Network

Development and MARC Standards Office, 2005b). Georeferencing in MODS is covered by elements of the *subjectType*, as shown in figure 6.5. It includes a *geographic* element for placenames, a *geographicCode* element for MARC and ISO country or area codes, a set of subelements for *hierarchialGeographic* units, and a *cartographics* element for *scale*, *projection*, and one or more *coordinates*. These elements have the same semantics as the equivalent MARC elements with some extensions.

Here is an example showing the georeferencing elements for a map record using the MODS schema, shown in XML style:

```
<subject authority="lcsh">
      <geographic>Goleta (Calif.)</geographic>
      <geographicCode authority = MARC Code List for
Geographic Areas>n-us-ca</geographicCode>
      <hierarchicalGeographic>
            <continent>North America</continent>
            <country>United States</country>
            <state>California</state>
            <county>Santa Barbara County</county>
            <city>Goleta<\city>
      </hierarchicalGeographic>
      <cartographic>
            <scale>1:16,500</scale>
            <projection>Lambert conformal conic proj.
            </projection>
            <coordinates>W1194936/N342609</coordinates>
      </cartographic>
</subject>
```

When looking at MARC and MODS as members of a set of standards that include georeferencing elements, rather than from strictly within the traditional library cataloging world, one is struck by the use of terminology that is at odds with the way the same terms are used in other standards. Since these differences may be part of the problem of working out interoperability and understanding between traditional library practices and various other communities, it is important to recognize the way some terms are used in library cataloging standards. In MODS,

• *place* is used for the place of publication and not for place in the general sense of a geographic location; the term *geographic* is used to designate the element that holds placenames.

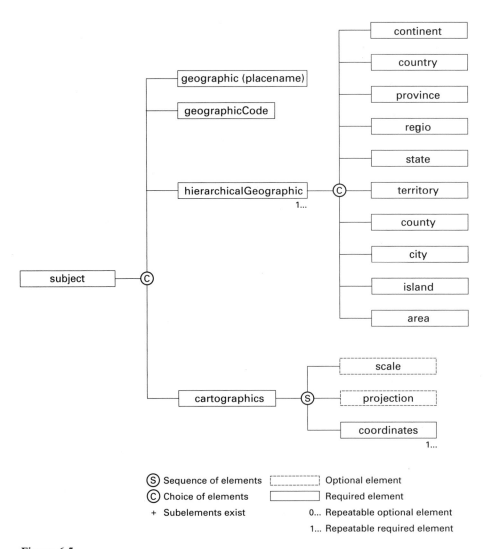

Figure 6.5
Georeferencing element structure in MODS. The diagram omits other subelements of "subjects" unrelated to georeferencing

• *location* is used for the repository or physical location with or without a shelf location of the book or other object—that is, it is used for the call number, not in the general sense of a geographic location.

• *cartographics* is used for geospatial representation, which, in library cataloging, is most closely associated with maps and other geospatial object types; unfortunately, the label reinforces the notion that geospatial representation is associated only with cartographic products.

Other Metadata Frameworks with Geospatial Elements

In addition to the metadata frameworks just described, there are other extant metadata structures that include basic geospatial descriptive elements. For example:

• The Global Information Locator Service (formerly, Government Information Locator Service), known as GILS, is built on the Z39.50 standard and its GEO Profile (Moen 1996).

• The Spatial Information Council of the Australia New Zealand Land Information Council (ANZLIC) developed a metadata framework for the description of geospatial data, based on the FGDC's CSDGM and drafts of the ISO TC 211 metadata standard. It contains forty-one elements (Australia New Zealand Land Information Council, Spatial Information Council, 2001).

• NASA's Global Change Master Directory (GCMD) describes spatial coverage in its Directory Interchange Format (DIF) as a bounding box, with all four sides documented, and with minimum and maximum values for both altitude and depth:

```
Group: Spatial_Coverage
       Southernmost_Latitude
       Northernmost_Latitude
       Westernmost_Longitude
       Easternmost_Longitude
       Minimum_Altitude
       Maximum_Altitude
       Minimum_Depth
       Maximum_Depth
End_Group
```

The DIF guidelines specify the use of decimal degrees with E,W,N,S letter designations. It provides this example of the spatial metadata elements for an oceanic dataset in the Pacific Ocean crossing the equator and the International Date Line:

```
Group: Spatial_Coverage
```

```
       Southernmost_Latitude: 40S
       Northernmost_Latitude: 50N
       Westernmost_Longitude: 160E
       Easternmost_Longitude: 130W
       Minimum_Depth: surface
       Maximum_Depth: 1500 m
End_Group
```

Generic Structures for Georeferencing in Object-Level Metadata

In this chapter, the focus has been on a selection of object-level metadata standards that include the representation of footprints and placenames, ranging from the MARC standard used for library cataloging to the FGDC and ISO standards for the documentation of geospatial datasets. The metadata applications reviewed span across the Earth sciences, biological sciences, cultural history, general GIS, and library cataloging systems. Each of the metadata structures described in this chapter is the result of designing for a particular purpose and at a particular time.

Object-level metadata is used to describe an information object to a level sufficient for purposes such as information retrieval, evaluation of fitness for use, visualization, and information access (e.g., downloading the data and understanding the

Panel 9
Georeferencing Paradigm

The georeferencing paradigm where geospatial knowledge can be used as an access point to information stored in a collection is one of the unique features of digital libraries that can't be easily replicated by traditional libraries. This unique feature will make georeferenced digital libraries increasingly popular if people learn to solve problems within the spatial paradigm of thinking. Everything happens in time and space. There will be a golden age for georeferenced digital libraries if people learn to solve problems in the spatial paradigm and if they are aided by georeferenced digital libraries and georeferenced collections that are publicly available and easy to comprehend and use. Making the process of installing the software and adding collections to georeferenced digital libraries easier is therefore very important to further the distribution and thus the availability of georeferenced digital libraries.

Kai Dragland
Department of Computer and Information Science
Norwegian University of Science and Technology
Trondheim, Norway

---

intellectual property rights associated with it). The georeferencing elements are nested within a more comprehensive metadata structure that includes creators, titles, dates of coverage and publication, format, and so on. As such, the georeferencing elements are representing the geographic associations of the information object as a component of the whole metadata record. This is an important distinction to make: georeferencing in the object-level metadata is about the information object, not about the places themselves as found in gazetteers.

This review of the geospatial elements from a set of object-level metadata structures illustrates the great variety of approaches to representing core elements of georeferencing. Although there are similarities as well, it is the variety that is remarkable. The influence of the standard that seeks to establish a common way to represent geospatial referencing, the Open Geospatial Consortium's *Geography Markup Language* (GML) (Open Geospatial Consortium Inc. 2003)—briefly described in chapter 4—is not evident in the majority of these structures. This is partly because the GML is a new standard and most of these metadata structures predate it. But it is also because the GML is a complex standard that only a few specialists will ever understand. This is also true of the FGDC and the ISO metadata standards to some degree; although both of these standards include a core set of elements that can be used for minimal representation of georeferenced information, they also require an understanding of other parts of the standard and its terminology. To achieve a high level of interoperability across all types of information on the basis of georeferencing—that is, be able to find all types of information associated with a geographic location either through formal or informal georeferencing—some common use of basic metadata elements for georeferencing is needed.

Generic Georeferencing Structure for Object-Level Metadata

If we were to create a generalized framework for georeferencing in object-level metadata for the purpose of information retrieval, what would it look like? Figure 6.6 is a possible model for discussion purposes. This model takes as a starting point the two forms of georeferencing: informal and formal. From there, it identifies the core elements and the structure needed for object-level description for geographic information retrieval at a basic level. The assumption is that a model like this is useful for understanding the metadata structures reviewed in this chapter, and for designing future georeferencing metadata modules for interoperability across all forms of information. The idea of having such a model is that the core elements of a more complex geospatial metadata structure could be mapped to such a structure for interoperability, and a less complex set of georeferencing elements could be evaluated to determine the degree to which it satisfies the basic requirements.

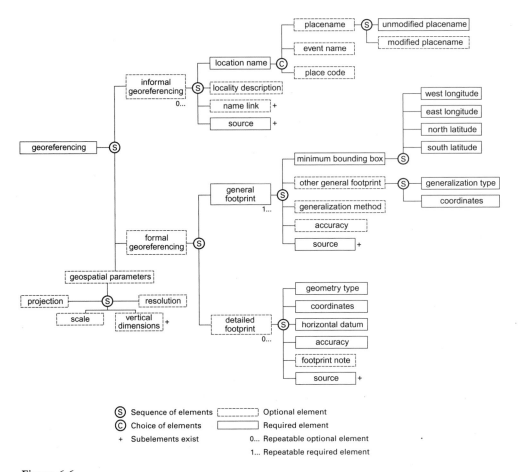

Figure 6.6
Generic model of georeferencing elements for object-level metadata to support geographic information retrieval

This model includes the basic division between informal and formal georeferencing. It does not imply relationships between multiple names or codes nor between specific names and specific footprints when there are multiples of each. Each georeferencing element adds separate descriptive information to the object-level metadata for the purpose of information retrieval and selection by the end user. This model assumes the integration of free-standing information sources within the information system, in particular one or more gazetteers; with such integration some information does not have to be in the object-level metadata itself (e.g., the administrative hierarchy of a named place). A georeferencing module built to this model could be plugged into various metadata structures to provide georeferencing inter-operability at the description level.

The components of the generic model for object-level metadata are

- *informal georeferencing* (optional; repeatable)
  - *location name*
    - Subelements are *placename, event name,* and *place code.* Events in this context are named activities that take place in a geographic and temporal framework, such as hurricanes (e.g., Hurricane Katrina). Place codes can be FIPS codes, zip codes, telephone calling areas, and so on. For any instance of *location name,* one of these subelements can be used
    - The *placename* element has two subelements: for *unmodified placename* and *modified placename* (e.g., either as "Detroit" or as "Detroit–Wayne County–Michigan–United States"). The unmodified form is required when a placename is included. The modified placename element was added to satisfy the need to display placenames in an unambiguous way. This is a way to include the administrative hierarchy of a place without formalizing a set of elements for the parts of the hierarchy and without duplicating the data elements of the gazetteer
  - *locality description* (optional) for a text description of the geographic location associated with the information object; this might be a snippet of text from a document or the narrative description about the collection site for a biological specimen
  - *name link* (optional) for a URI to an individual entry in a gazetteer or to a whole gazetteer; individual links would be required to link to additional information about the named location
  - *source* (required) to document the resource that provided the informal georeferencing (e.g., identification of the gazetteer or authority file and its version)
  - Possible additional details needed for information retrieval are the language of the name and an indication of which of the names are the most indicative of what the information object is about (i.e., a flag to mark whether a name is peripheral or central to the object's geographic coverage)
- *formal georeferencing* (optional; repeatability is available at the subelement level)
  - *general footprint* (required; repeatable)
    - *minimum bounding box* (required)
      - Subelements: *west longitude, east longitude, north latitude, south latitude*; all required
      - In decimal degrees
      - Possible additions: degree-minute-second coordinates could be added in addition to the decimal degrees
    - *other general footprint* elements (optional)
      - Subelements: *generalization type* (e.g., convex hull; point and radius) and *coordinates*

(a coordinate string as specified by GML, using commas to separate the longitude/latitude coordinates of points and a space to separate the points in a convex hull or other generalization)

- *generalization method* (optional)
  - A statement of how the *minimum bounding box* or *other general footprint* was created
- *accuracy* (optional)
  - Statement of the certainty or confidence in the general footprint
  - Possible additions: subelements for quantitative measures of accuracy (e.g., ±5 miles) and descriptive notes
- *source* (required)
  - Subelements to describe the source of the *general footprint*, such as resource name, version, and date
- Each instance of the *general-footprint* set of elements must have a minimum bounding box and can also have another form of general footprint
- This *general-footprint* section does not include a *horizontal-datum* element based on the assumption that a common geodetic basis will be used for all general footprints within a system
- Possible additions: indication of which *general footprint* is the primary one for display and searching where more than one is used
- *detailed footprint* (optional; repeatable)
- *geometry type* (required)
  - GML name for the type of footprint (e.g., point, linestring, box, or polygon)
- *coordinates* (required)
  - Coordinate string as specified by GML, using commas to separate the longitude/latitude coordinates of points and a space to separate the points of a line, box, or polygon
  - Optionally, the coordinate representation could be detailed in subelements such as the structure of the ADL spatial bucket structure described in chapter 7
- *horizontal datum* (required)
  - Name of datum should be drawn from a controlled vocabulary of datum names
- *accuracy* (optional)
  - Statement of the certainty or confidence in the general footprint
  - Possible additions: subelements for quantitative measures of accuracy (e.g., ±5 miles) and descriptive notes
- *footprint note* (optional)
  - Explanatory note
- *source* (required)
  - Subelements to describe the source of the *detailed footprint*, such as resource name, version, and date
- *geospatial parameters* (optional)

- *projection* (optional)
  - Name of the projection for visualizations of geospatial data (e.g., a map) from a controlled vocabulary
- *resolution* (optional)
  - Smallest resolvable object (e.g., house or city) or expressed as a matrix of dots (e.g., 640 × 480)
- *scale* (optional)
  - Denominator of the representative fraction (e.g., 1/25,000)
- *vertical dimensions* (optional)
  - Subelements for elevation/depth range and the data basis (e.g., "sea level")

An accepted generic set of georeferencing elements that could be—would be—adopted as plug-in modules for metadata structures would be a significant advance. It would greatly improve our chances of having operational interoperability between the text-based and GIS communities and their rich collections of place-based information, and between the information systems with low-level support for geospatial operations and sophisticated services with GIS software.

Simple Geometry Language for Generic Georeferencing

Another aspect of interoperability for georeferenced information is to reach agreement on a simplified standard way of representing footprints. A geospatial *footprint* represents the location on the surface of the Earth associated with the object being described (e.g., a named place, a photograph, a map, a book). This footprint can be generalized (e.g., as a point, a box, or a convex hull) or it can be detailed as a line, a polygon, or a more complex shape. The easiest generalizations to create and to process are points and bounding boxes. These generalizations are the predominant form of geometry used outside of formal GIS processing environments. It makes sense then to always include one of these generalizations in the metadata standards for georeferencing elements, so that even the most complex geometry can still be used for information retrieval purposes by the most basic information system. In particular, data held in a GIS and represented by a geospatial metadata standard would be more useful outside of the GIS environment in a more general form with fewer descriptive requirements (Janée and Frew 2004).

A generic method of footprint representation to satisfy the requirements of interoperability across all types of information has been addressed by Greg Janée and James Frew as part of the Alexandria Digital Library Project, in the form of a proposal for a *simple geometry language* and a presentation at a workshop on Geographic Information Retrieval (Janée 2004; Janée and Frew 2004). In developing the *simple geometry language*, Janée (2004) stated the following basic principles:

A geometry language defines a set of possible shapes and standard representations and encodings of those shapes, and also addresses the handling of cartographic quantities (Earth datums, projections, and coordinate systems), either by mandating standard quantities or by providing standard declaration mechanisms.

The motivation for a standard geometry language is rooted in the observation that every system/service/effort that has had to deal with geographic regions has ended up defining its own geometry language. All these languages have broadly similar capabilities to varying degrees, yet all have enough idiosyncrasies to bedevil easy interoperability. . . .

From the perspective of distributed geospatial digital libraries and distributed gazetteer services, which use geometry only for the limited purposes of representing object footprints and query regions and performing spatial comparisons between the two, a geometry language must satisfy three requirements:

1. The language must support enough possible shapes—and complex enough shapes—so that spatial matching over those shapes yields acceptable search precision. . . . [A] sufficient set of shapes is not known, but necessary shapes include points for point features such as water wells, polylines [linestrings] for linear features such as rivers, and at least simple polygons for areal features.

2. The spatial reference system (SRS) in which shapes are defined (i.e., the Earth datum and coordinate system) must not be mandated by the language, but must be declarable in a standard way. Mandating a particular SRS forces language users to translate SRSs, which can be mathematically complex and can introduce unintended consequences. . . .

3. The language must provide a lingua franca that virtually all geometry producers and consumers can operate on; in practice, due to simplicity of implementation, ease of mappability, and general widespread support, the lingua franca is latitude/longitude-aligned minimum bounding rectangles, or *bounding boxes* for short.

   i. Notwithstanding requirement 2 above, to support interoperability, bounding boxes must be defined in a standard SRS, e.g., WGS84 latitude/longitude coordinates. (It is reasonably easy to compute such bounding boxes from commonly-used cylindrical and polar projections.)

   ii. In principle, bounding boxes are deterministically computable from primary shapes; nevertheless, bounding boxes must explicitly accompany all primary shapes in instance [e.g., metadata] documents. To fail in this regard is to place the burden of computing bounding boxes on the very geometry consumers that are incapable of doing so: those that rely on bounding boxes because they're incapable of operating on more complex shapes.

   iii. Bounding boxes must be defined in a manner that supports geodetic continuity—that is, in a manner that recognizes that the Earth is, topologically, a sphere. In particular, there must be no discontinuity that bounding boxes are not allowed to cross such as, in many geometry languages, the ±180° meridian.

Summary

It seems clear that interoperability of georeferencing and georeferenced objects would be enhanced if a common understanding of and descriptive structures for georeferencing could be developed and adopted. The metadata standard efforts of the GIS community have contributed greatly to this goal by the development of the FGDC and ISO metadata standards and the Geography Markup Language (GML) by the OGC. These standards, however, are complex and therefore inaccessible for general cataloging and indexing purposes—even at the level of the core element sets of the FGDC and ISO standards.

Informal and formal georeferencing can be associated with all types of information—a fundamental premise for this book—and we should be designing systems so that geospatial access (i.e., spatial search and retrieval) and visualization at a basic level can be applied to all information resources. We are a long way from a common vocabulary for referencing the components of geospatial referencing (e.g., "northlimit," "northbound latitude," "north-bounding coordinate," and "northernmost latitude" have all been used to label the same metadata element). We have, however, come to the point where there are emerging and merging standards and practices that are building the foundations of interoperability.

In some of the examples reviewed here, information about the placenames, such as an administrative hierarchy, has been embedded in the object-level metadata. This practice results in the repetition of such information in multiple records when it could be stored instead in a separate gazetteer that is integrated into the information system and that can be updated as necessary.

A generic structure for georeferencing and the requirements of a simple geometry language are proposed in this chapter to meet the needs of widespread interoperability—that is, to support the retrieval of all types of place-based information with a single placename- or coordinate-based query. Each metadata structure is designed for its own purposes, and the generic structure will not be the answer to all of the community-based requirements. But to reach the goal of being able to find and benefit from all types of place-based information, movement toward a common georeferencing structure in metadata—or agreement on an intermediary structure to which other structures can be mapped—as well as toward a simple geometry language would be useful.

Sources for Further Information

American Geological Institute. 2005. *GeoRef Information Services*. http://www.agiweb.org/georef/index.html.

Australia New Zealand Land Information Council, Spatial Information Council. 2001. *ANZLIC Metadata Guidelines* Version 2. http://www.anzlic.org.au/download.html?oid=2358011755.

Cox, S. 2005a. *DCMI Box Encoding Scheme: Specification of the Spatial Limits of a Place, and Methods for Encoding this in a Text String.* Dublin Core Metadata Initiative. http://dublincore.org/documents/dcmi-box/#dcsv.

Cox, S. 2005b. *DCMI Point Encoding Scheme: A Point Location in Space, and Methods for Encoding This in a Text String.* Dublin Core Metadata Initiative. http://dublincore.org/documents/dcmi-point/#dcsv.

DLESE Metadata Working Group. 2005. *ADN Metadata Framework.* http://www.dlese.org/Metadata/adn-item/index.htm.

Dublin Core Metadata Initiative. 2005. *Dublin Core Metadata Initiative (DCMI) Website.* http://www.dublincore.org/.

Electronic Cultural Atlas Initiative. 2005. *Metadata Tags.* http://ecaimaps.berkeley.edu/clearinghouse/html/list_md_elements.php.

Global Change Master Directory. 2005. *Directory Interchange Format (DIF) Writer's Guide, Version 9.4.* NASA Aeronautics and Space Administration. http://gcmd.nasa.gov/User/difguide/.

Global Information Locator Service (GILS) Website. http://www.gils.net/.

International Organization for Standardization (ISO), Technical Committee 211. 2003a. *Geographic Information—Metadata (ISO 19115:2003).* http://www.iso.org/iso/en/prods-services/ISOstore/store.html (search for "19115" for ordering information).

Janée, G. 2004. *Simple Geometry Language.* Alexandria Digital Library Project, University of California, Santa Barbara. http://www.alexandria.ucsb.edu/~gjanee/archive/2004/geometry/writeup.html.

Mammal Networked Information System (MaNIS). 2005. *Georeferencing Guidelines.* http://elib.cs.berkeley.edu/manis/GeorefGuide.html.

Open Geospatial Consortium Inc. 2003. *Geography Markup Language (GML) Implementation Specification.* Version 3. https://portal.opengeospatial.org/files/?artifact_id=7174.

Taxonomic Databases Working Group (TDWG). 2005. *Darwin Core 2 Documentation.* http://darwincore.calacademy.org/Documentation/.

U.S. Federal Geographic Data Committee. 1998. *Content Standard for Digital Geospatial Metadata.* Version 2. http://fgdc.er.usgs.gov/metadata/contstan.html.

U.S. Library of Congress, Network Development and MARC Standards Office. 2003. *MARC Code List for Geographic Areas.* http://www.loc.gov/marc/geoareas/.

U.S. Library of Congress, Network Development and MARC Standards Office. 2005a. *MARC Standards.* http://lcweb.loc.gov/marc/.

U.S. Library of Congress, Network Development and MARC Standards Office. 2005b. *MODS: Metadata Object Description Schema: Official Web Site.* http://www.loc.gov/standards/mods/.

7

Geographic Information Retrieval

Picture a user interface to an information service (e.g., a digital library or a consortium of museum catalogs and data archives) where the user can pose a question like "tell me what you know about this place" where "place" is a geographic location. The user identifies the place by circling it on a map, giving it a placename that is translated to coordinates, or uploading coordinates from a GPS for the user's current location. The answer might be something like "I know about these things":

- 500 websites and here is the most popular one . . .
- 20 maps and here is the one that matches your area the best . . .
- 15 books: the latest one is . . .
- 35 journal articles from these publications: . . .
- 12 photographs: click here to see thumbnails
- 10 remote sensing images and here is the one that matches your area the best . . .
- 100 placenames in the area: 20 populated places, 12 hydrographic features . . .
- 75 species reported to be in the area: . . .
- More, including census data, neighborhood characteristics . . .

The user can display the footprints for any of these items on the map and ask for thumbnails of the most interesting photographs, images and maps, and summaries of the textual items. The user can sort the results by spatial similarity to the query area or by date. For any items of interest, the user can store away the metadata, the actual objects or data, or the gazetteer entries in local databases where they can be searched by place in the future (of course, within the limits of intellectual property rights). Maybe all the user wants to know is a more specific question like "What birds have been reported in this area where I am now?" With a GPS and the ability to send the current location to a *spatially aware* natural history museum catalog (as well as the user's own personal library of observations), the answer could be a list of all that the museum knows about birds sighted in or collected from the area and any previous information about birds in the area the user has collected. If the query was sent to a digital library as well, the user could find out about books and articles about birds specific to the area.

Behind the user interface for this to happen, there have to be many components. There have to be cyberinfrastructures and available collections that can adequately handle and respond to georeferenced queries. In other chapters, the basics of geospatial referencing, gazetteers and gazetteer services, and the georeferencing elements of object-level and collection-level metadata have been the topics of discussion. This chapter explains the basics of geographic information retrieval (GIR)—the methods by which georeferenced queries are matched to relevant information about areas of interest and returned to the user in useful ways. In short, it is about place-based information retrieval.

Techniques of information retrieval (IR) have grown along with the implementation of electronic databases that store enormous collections of information objects, first as metadata and more recently also as full text, images, datasets, and so on. Having the information in electronic form has opened up new possibilities for both *indexing* the information and *searching* over it to find information *relevant* to particular user information needs. The IR field has been primarily text-based, focusing on methods of matching controlled vocabularies and *free text* (i.e., uncontrolled text) in information objects with text-based queries to achieve results that satisfy the user. Extending IR to GIR adds a new dimension to both the capability and uncertainty of information retrieval (Frontiera 2004). Users need to learn to express their information needs in terms of a spatial location in concert with other query parameters (e.g., author, subject, and time period). User interfaces need to present the spatial query option and the geographic associations of relevant documents in new ways, using map displays. System designers need to understand spatial matching operations and the storage of spatial footprints. There is an overall challenge of making it clear to users why they get the results they do from spatial queries.

Geographic information retrieval is a new field, first described and named by Ray Larson (1996). It is based on comparing a query spatial footprint to the footprints of objects in a collection and identifying the objects with *matching* footprints. A match is usually not exact but rather a match based on some degree of overlap of the footprints of the query and the object—that is, matching footprints have some area in common. Simplistically, any object whose footprint overlaps the query footprint is a match, with the strength of the match based on the degree of spatial overlap and the relative sizes of the query and object footprints. Since it is fairly straightforward to identify objects with overlapping footprints in response to spatial queries, GIR researchers focus on developing algorithms to rank responses to queries so that the most spatially relevant objects are at the top of the list of results. This is similar in intent to the way Google and other search engines analyze text and other clues to rank text-based search results.

Consider, for example, a spatial search for the region around Lake Tahoe. A simple *overlaps* comparison of the query box with a large collection of information objects will retrieve a set that includes items that are highly spatially relevant to the Lake Tahoe region, as well as global and national maps and datasets that are not of particular interest even though their footprints do overlap the Lake Tahoe region. If the results are not ranked to move the global and national items to the bottom and those most specifically about the Lake Tahoe region to the top of the list, the user is faced with having to wade through a large set to find them (Frontiera 2004). The use of a more restrictive spatial matching method (e.g., *is contained* to find objects with footprints totally within the query area) will retrieve a smaller set and those specifically relevant to the Lake Tahoe region, but it will not find items whose footprints extend slightly beyond the query box that are likely to be relevant also. Spatial ranking methods compensate for coverage-area differences by ordering the retrieved set from most spatially relevant to least.

The clickable geographic-area devices found in some user interfaces are also a type of geographic searching but, in this case, selection is limited to a set of divisions of the world, such as nations, counties, provinces, and the like. Items in the collections are usually indexed to a limited set of geographic areas directly by name or code rather than by geospatial coordinates. This type of GIR, therefore, does not depend on the matching of spatial footprints and is not described further in this chapter.

GIR and text-based IR can be used independently or together, as in a georeferenced digital library system. For example, in the ECAI-*Time*Map™ project (figure 3.15) and the Alexandria Digital Library (ADL) (figure 7.6), the spatial search parameters can be combined with other parameters such as text and date. Using such interfaces, a user can search for collection items that are about a designated spatial area and also add such parameters as "maps published in the 1990s." A user searching a catalog that contains geospatially referenced text documents or data files might want to add some controlled vocabulary or free text to the spatial search, such as "population growth" or "fires." This capability raises issues of how to measure retrieval effectiveness when spatial and textual retrieval is combined. It will probably develop that users are given some options about how to rank search results when both factors are used together, and that choice of ranking method will be investigated to determine its effect on the usefulness of results. This chapter does not go into this issue; it is just mentioned here for consideration.

As further introduction to GIR for those familiar with text-based searching:

• For text searching, the user is often given a choice of the type of text string matching to apply; basic choices are usually some version of *equals, contains all words, contains any words,* or *phrase.* For spatial searching, the basic choices are *contains, is contained,* and *overlaps*—all forms of topological relations.

• For text searching, a variety of words and phrases can be used to represent a concept, plus there are problems with differences in spelling, word form, and syntax. There are IR techniques that extend text matching to text where there is some difference with the query text but where, presumably, the meaning is the same. For example, if the query contains the word *woman,* the retrieval process can be extended to recognize *women* as a match also. For spatial searching, the representation of the query footprint is more straightforward and less problematic as a search statement. Still, there are some issues with unexpected variations in the object footprints and their boundaries and in the way that the spatial matching operators work that cause some problems with finding all relevant—and only relevant—information.

Topological and Geometric Spatial Relationships

The relationship between two geospatial locations can be represented as either a topological or a geometric relationship. These relationships are complementary and overlapping in the sense that some comparisons can be treated with either approach. However, they do have fundamentally different bases. In a topological relationship, measurable distance and absolute direction *are not* factors; in a geometric relationship, distance and direction *are* factors. Topological relationships include *overlap, containment, in the neighborhood of,* and *connectedness* and point-of-view relationships like left and right. Geometric relations are based on direction and distance (e.g., "5 miles south of") and calculations within a *spatial referencing system* (SRS) that includes a geodetic datum. Topological relationships have "no particular relationship to any coordinate system" (Larson 1996). Topological relationships are the basis of GIR.

In chapter 2 on spatial cognition, the point was made that our spatial knowledge is more qualitative than quantitative. That is, our spatial knowledge is more topological than geometric. Distance, direction, sizes, and shapes are less distinctly known and play less of a role in the ways we ask for and transmit spatial information and the ways we reason about spatial relationships (Egenhofer and Mark 1995).

In chapter 5 on gazetteers, types of declared relationships between named geographic features are discussed, such as that one feature (e.g., Paris) can be declared to be *part of* another feature (e.g., France). These declared types of relationships are distinct from the topological relationships discussed in this chapter; declared relationships are based on a vocabulary of relationship types, while topological relationships are based on spatial location.

Spatial Matching

Spatial Relationships

When a query can be expressed in terms of a spatial footprint (i.e., a spatial coverage area) using longitude and latitude coordinates and the information objects are also represented by spatial footprints, a match can be made to retrieve the items from collections whose spatial coverage is relevant to the query area. Note that both query and object footprints can be obtained in a two-step process by looking up placenames in a gazetteer and translating them into footprints.

The basic spatial matching operations are illustrated in figure 7.1 by showing the query region and its relationship to three object footprints. The footprints are represented as boxes.

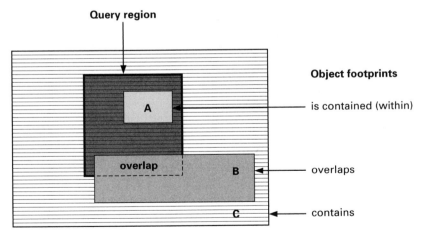

Figure 7.1
Relationships between a query area and three object footprints (A, B, and C)

For GIR, the basic spatial relationships are

- *overlaps* (*intersects*): objects whose footprints overlap the query footprint
- *is contained* (*within*): objects whose footprints are contained within the query footprint
- *contains*: objects whose footprints completely enclose the query footprint

Or expressed another way, let **df** stand for document (object) footprint and **qf** stand for query footprint; the relationships can then be expressed as

- **df** *overlaps* **qf** (all of the examples in figure 7.1)
- **df** *is contained* in **qf** (A in figure 7.1)
- **df** *contains* **qf** (C in figure 7.1)

All of the footprints in figure 7.1 *overlap* the query footprint; *overlap* is the most inclusive spatial relationship. Only object A has a footprint that falls within the query region—that is, *is contained* by the query region. Note that if object A's footprint fell even a little bit outside the query footprint, it would not be retrieved when using the *is contained* operator. Only object C has a footprint that completely *contains* the query region.

The definition of spatial relevance includes, at its broadest, any item with a footprint that overlaps the query footprint. All of the object footprints illustrated in figure 7.1 are relevant to the query footprint on this basis. If you ignore the relative sizes and placements of the boxes in figure 7.1 and focus just on the spatial relationships, the query region could be the country of Spain. Object A could be about the Madrid area and thus *is contained* in Spain. Object B could be about the Mediterranean region and thus *overlaps* Spain. Object C could be a map of the world. For a more extreme case of relative sizes, object A could be the footprint of a city block in Madrid; a map of Spain and a map of the world would still be considered relevant on the basis of an *overlap* comparison. I return to the subject of spatial ranking later in this chapter, elaborating on these issues of comparative size of the query and object footprints and the degree of overlap.

This illustration of spatial relationships is a type of *region* query that includes cases where both the query and the object footprints enclose a region (i.e., all footprints have spatial extent). The other common case for GIR is spatial matches involving *points*. When the query is a *region* and the object footprints are *points*, the matching process is called *point-in-polygon*; points that are *contained* in the query box are matches. When the query is a *point*, the spatial matching can return footprints that *contain* the point.

Because spatial matching using boxes can be implemented with simple mathematical expressions for small collections, GIR based on the use of boxes is the most common approach outside of specialized software. All types of spatial matching can be expressed as box comparisons, including the *point-in-polygon* type query where both the point and the polygon can be treated as bounding boxes; the point simply repeats its longitude and latitude values for the four boundaries (sometimes called a *degenerated box*). A point and radius footprint can be generalized to a bounding box, as can linear footprints, which can be extended to a box containing the line. A bounding box can also be drawn around the maximum extent of an irregular polygon.

A fuller set of spatial relationships used as the basis for mathematical pairwise comparisons of geometric shapes (footprints) in GIS software contains nine relationships—an extension of the three basic relationships already described. They have been defined as

• *Equals*: the interiors intersect and no part of the interior or boundary of either geometry extends outside of the other
• *Disjoint*: the geometries do not intersect one another in any way
• *Intersects*: the interiors or the boundaries of both geometries intersect
• *Touch*: the boundary of one geometry intersects the boundary of the other but the interiors do not intersect
• *Overlaps*: an intersection between geometries of the same type (e.g., polygon-polygon) where the overlapping space is of the same type (e.g., linestrings can overlap along the linestring they have in common)
• *Cross*: applicable to specified types of intersections, such as a line crossing the interior of a polygon
• *Within*: the first geometry (object) is completely within the second geometry (query)
• *Contains*: the second geometry (query) is completely contained by the first geometry (object)
• *Minimum distance*: the minimum distance separating two disjoint features

This description of spatial relationships is paraphrased from an ESRI website (Environmental Systems Research Institute Inc. 2005) that provides technical descriptions of the spatial matching functions. These relationships are based on the *Dimensionally Extended Nine-Intersection Model* (DE-9IM) (Clementini and Di Felice 1996), which is in turn based on the *9 Intersection Model* of Egenhofer and Herring 1990. For GIR, *equals*, *disjoint*, *touch*, and *cross* relationships are rarely useful. *Equals* is a very restrictive requirement; footprints that are nearly the same or occupy the same space (i.e., *overlap*) are just as likely to be relevant. *Disjoint* is the negative of *overlaps* and rarely would anyone want to retrieve everything that does not overlap the query area. *Touch* is a problematic relationship when the boundaries of areas are inexact. The *cross* relationship is useful when working with linear footprints for features such as rivers, but computing the relationship requires a GIS environment. In this set of definitions, *overlaps* and *intersects* are two different concepts; *overlaps* is restricted to the intersection of footprints of the same type. In GIR, this distinction is not made; the GIR use of *overlaps* is the same as this definition of *intersects*, which includes the concepts of *equals*, *cross*, *within*, and *contains*.

Spatial Footprints

Geographic information retrieval operations are greatly influenced by the types of geographic footprints associated with the information objects. There are significant differences in the information content of a point location compared to a footprint representing the general extent of the geographic location (e.g., a minimum bounding box) or to a detailed boundary (polygon) of the area. As the complexity of the footprint increases from a single point to a complex polygon, the uncertainty about the area of coverage decreases. A more detailed footprint, in other words, is more informative (more expressive) and more useful for determining spatial relationships (e.g., whether one footprint overlaps or is contained in another footprint). Consider possible footprints for the city of San Jose, California, as shown in figure 7.2. This progression from a point to an aggregation of multipolygons and the inclusion of holes illustrates the extremes and the options in between.

A key consideration for GIR is to determine the level of footprint detail that is most useful for information retrieval implementation, and for this the costs of creating the representations, storing them, and performing spatial matching operations with them must be taken into account. There is an enormous difference in the burden of creation and computation between the base-level point and MBB representations and all of the other footprint representations, getting progressively more expensive as the footprints become more expressive. The common practice for footprint representation outside of GIS environments has been to use points and MBBs. A growing body of research and expert opinion supports this practice, most notably Frontiera 2004 and Janée and Frew 2004. The cost of using anything more complex than the basic footprints for information retrieval is one persuasive argument for not doing so; the other is that, despite their limitations, spatial retrieval and spatial ranking based on points and MBBs perform remarkably well. Improvement in the performance of spatial retrieval seems more likely to result from more sophisticated spatial ranking methods than from requiring the use of footprints that are more faithful to the shape and extent of the geographic location.

A possible future model for GIR is a multistep process. First a search is performed using basic footprints and basic spatial matching operations designed

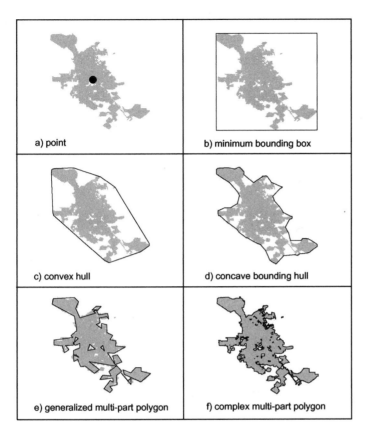

Figure 7.2
A set of possible geographic footprints for the city of San Jose, California. (Figure 3.1 in Frontiera 2004.)

to result in high recall. Second, this set is ranked by spatial similarity (spatial relevance) to the query footprint. Optionally, a third step would use more detailed footprints of the most highly ranked objects (if available) to display on a base map where the spatial relationships will be visually evident or to perform a subsequent filtering process supported by sophisticated spatial matching software.

Implementations of Spatial Matching

Implementations of GIR have advanced along two lines of development: as extensions of text searching and as spatial extensions for relational database management systems (RDMSs), which include geometric functionality:

• Spatial extensions of text matching are essentially equals or range matching operations on each of the boundaries of a longitude/latitude aligned box to determine whether any of the object's boundaries are the same as or fall within the query boundaries or if the object's boundaries surround the query boundaries.

• Spatial extensions for RDMS employ geometric operations and support sophisticated indexing techniques that enable the storage and efficient processing of large sets of spatial data. They support some or all of the following:

  • SQL-based system commands containing spatial data types and functions
  • Implementation of the OGC *Simple Features Specification for SQL* (Open Geospatial Consortium Inc. 1999)
  • Multidimensional indexing for spatial and temporal query performance
  • Support for global space queries without limitations inherent in map projections
  • Spatial functions on a planar or spherical basis
  • Testing of the relationship between two bounding boxes (minimum bounding rectangles)
  • Spatial visualization tools
  • Integration with GIS software

Links to current spatial extensions for RDMS software, as of November 2005, are included in the Sources for Further Information section of this chapter. The following are brief descriptions of six example GIR implementations starting with an implementation of spatial searching of the *GeoRef* bibliographic file.

GeoRef   When user interfaces require the user to enter coordinates in query statements (i.e., text strings), spatial searches become complex and difficult for users to understand and enter correctly. An early implementation of spatial searching is an example of this—the Dialog implementation of spatial searching for *GeoRef.*

GeoRef has been adding coordinates to some of its records since 1977. A Dialog guide for searching the *GeoRef* file (*Dialog Search Aids: File 89, GeoRef: Geographic Coordinate Fields,* 2003) explains how to express a spatial query using coordinate values to retrieve those records. To make this type of searching work at all, special codes had to be created. For exact matches, searchers can use codes for each side of the bounding box. This query statement

SELECT N1 = N54(S)N2 = N61(S)W1 = W135(S)W2 = W163

defines a query box with the latitudes north of the equator (N54 and N61) and the longitudes west of the prime meridian (W135 and W163), following the order of

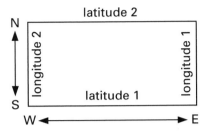

Dialog/GeoRef order of expressing coordinates:
  latitude 1, latitude 2, longitude 1, longitude 2

Figure 7.3
Specification of the order of expressing coordinates in indexing and querying for the Dialog implementation of *GeoRef* searching

coordinates shown in figure 7.3: N1 = latitude 1, N2 = latitude 2, W1 = longitude 1, W2 = longitude 2. The query expresses an exact match where matching documents will have the same set of coordinates *to the extent of the degrees only.* That is, this query will match any set of coordinates where the degrees match for all four parameters, ignoring any further specification of the coordinates to minutes and seconds. The (S) operator specifies that pairs of coordinates must appear in the same coordinate string in order for a match to be made between a query and an object's footprint.

This exact match search at the level of degrees can be extended to a search on a range of degrees for the boundary coordinates, as illustrated by this query statement:

SELECT N1 = N50:N55(S)N2 = N60:N65(S)W1 = W130:W135(S)W2 = W160:W165

For this search statement, the set of matching documents includes a larger set of possible matches, but still only those with coordinates that match the range of degrees in the query statement. This will not retrieve smaller footprints that are *contained* in the smallest query box nor *overlapping* or *containing* footprints.

To support retrieval of documents with areas of coverage that *contain* the search area, Dialog created another set of codes (LN, LS, LE, and LW) and an indexing and searching method based on including all "intermediate" longitude and latitude values within the query and the document footprints. For a box with longitudes of 135 and 145 West and latitudes of 54 and 61 North, the boundary and intermediate values are

Longitudes: 135, 136, 137, 138, 139, 140, 141, 142, 143, 144, 145
Latitudes: 54, 55, 56, 57, 58, 59, 60, 61

A query box expressed with these intermediate-inclusive codes will match documents with footprints that *contain* all of these intermediate values, which includes exact matches and footprints that are larger and include all of these values (like box C in figure 7.1). An example search statement looks like this:

SELECT LN = N54(S)LN = N61(S)LW = W135(S)LW = W145

The most general spatial search method supported by Dialog on the *GeoRef* file is to use ranges of values with the intermediate search codes. This method matches footprints that include any of the set of intermediate values: *overlapping* footprints, *containing* footprints, and footprints that share a common boundary with the query box. An example search statement looks like this:

SELECT LN = N54:N61(S)LW = W135:W163

Anyone who has not studied the Dialog user's guide for *GeoRef* and used it often—that is, who is not a seasoned searcher of the *GeoRef* bibliographic file—will not find these text-based methods easy to understand. The reason for including them here is to illustrate that

• Spatial searching has been available for more than 20 years in a bibliographic file where expert searchers can construct search statements to locate documents about geographic areas using coordinates, but only a few are proficient at it.
• Expressing a spatial query as a text string query is complicated and unforgiving in syntax.
• Spatial query statements similar to these are created by today's GIR systems but out of the view of the user. The user can work directly with a map interface to draw or zoom into the query area or enter coordinates for boundaries and ignore the details of matching operations behind the scenes.

GEO Profile of Z39.50   Implementation of a GEO server is one method of providing standardized access to geospatial metadata across distributed collections. The GEO profile is a specification of the Z39.50 standard (Nebert 2000; U.S. Library of Congress, Network Development and MARC Standards Office, 2005c). Z39.50 specifies a client/server-based protocol for searching and retrieving information from remote databases. It was first published as a NISO standard in 1995 and is now maintained by the U.S. Library of Congress. The GEO profile adds elements from the FGDC *Content Standard for Digital Geospatial Metadata* (CSDGM) and spatial matching functions to the Z39.50 text-based search-and-retrieval specification.

Five spatial relationships are specified in the GEO profile:

• *overlaps* where the object footprint has a geometric area in common with the search region

• *fully enclosed within* where the object footprint is fully enclosed within the search region

• *encloses* where the object footprint fully encloses the search region

• *fully outside of* where the object footprint has no geometric area in common with the search region

• *near* where the object footprint falls within a default distance (defined by the server) of the search region

The *overlaps* function is explained as a mathematical comparison using *greater than or equal* (>=) and *less than or equal* (<=) operators on the four sides of a box within a Boolean search statement (figure 7.4):

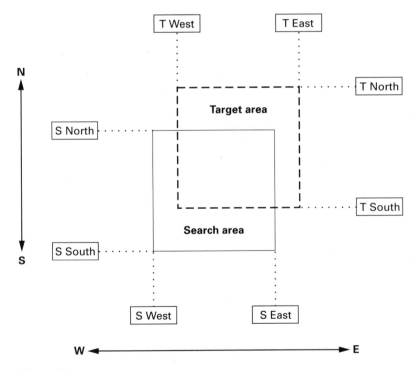

Figure 7.4
Illustration of the overlaps function for the GEO profile of the Z39.50 standard as described in the text

Given a search area of **S** and an object (target) footprint of **T**, the following algebra expresses the conditions required to satisfy an *overlaps* relationship:

{S(North) >= T(South)} and
{S(South) <= T(North)} and
{S(East) >= T(West)} and
{S(West) <= T(East)}.

Implementations of the other spatial relationships presumably use similar mathematical comparisons that do not require the use of specialized spatial matching software.

C-Squares   In chapter 4, the *Concise Spatial Query and Representation System (c-squares)* was briefly described. A spatial location in c-squares notation is a string of grid notations, such as "7311:249:248" to describe a single grid square or the syntax of "7311:248|7311:249" to describe a set of c-squares. Searching c-square data is a text-search operation, matching the query parameter c-square string against the c-square notations for the objects. For example, a query for location "7311:249" would match objects with the locations of "7311:249:248" and "7311:248|7311:249" on the basis of text string matching. A strength of this approach is its ability to support spatial searching by *geographic identifier* without the requirement for any underlying specialized spatial software. Alternatively, any c-square string can be converted into a minimum bounding box, which can be used for coordinate-based spatial matching (Rees 2003a, 2003b).

Endeavor   In 2000, Endeavor Information Systems, Inc. released its *Geospatial Search Module*, "a first for the library automation market" (Endeavor Information Systems Inc. 2000). It is designed for the retrieval of cartographic objects, geospatially referenced imagery, charts, and other georeferenced documents. Endeavor is a MARC-based system and uses the 034 field as the source for coordinates (*minimum bounding rectangle* or *g-ring* footprints) and scale (see chapter 6 for more explanation of the MARC georeferencing elements). The user interface presents boxes for the entry of longitude and latitude coordinates for the query and a range of choices for the type of spatial search the user would like to do:

• Choice of geospatial representation for the query area
    • Rectangle (two points for the "lower-left" and "upper-right" corners of the minimum bounding rectangle (MBR))
    • Polygon (a closed sequence of points describing the boundary of an area)

- Point and radius (a point plus, optionally, a radius distance in one of a choice of units of length)
- Corridor (an open sequence of points describing a line plus a buffer around the line)
- Range (four sides of the MBR boundary to retrieve items *contained in* the box)
- Choice of "format type"
  - Degrees/min/sec
  - Degrees/decimal minutes
  - Decimal degrees
  - UTM meters
  - Military Grid Reference System (MGRS)
  - Universal Polar Stereograph (UPS)

The user is not given a choice of type of spatial matching to perform (e.g., *overlaps*). Instead each choice of geospatial representation includes a default matching operator. Because the matching operators are primarily *overlaps* and *contains* and because this type of search returns global and national maps, Endeavor includes the option to limit the search to maps with scales within a specified range. For example, the user can specify a range of $1:1$ to $1:25,000$ to limit the retrieval to *large-scale* maps covering a small area and eliminate *small-scale* maps that cover a lot of area.

Alexandria Digital Library (ADL) Spatial Search Bucket   The ADL search buckets are designed to provide a common set of search parameters for search of and retrieval from a network of distributed library collections. The ADL architecture calls for the native object-level metadata to be mapped to the ADL search buckets for search interoperability. These search buckets are similar to the Dublin Core (DCMI) elements but, unlike the DCMI elements, they are *typed* so that remote search functions can operate on them—that is, the types are clearly defined and each has associated search operations that are permitted for that type of data. For example, the DCMI has a *coverage* data element that can be used for placenames and coordinates as well as other values, while the corresponding ADL search bucket is the *geographic-location* bucket, which is limited to coordinate values by virtue of its *spatial* data type. The seven search-bucket types are called *spatial*, *temporal*, *hierarchical*, *textual*, *identification*, *numeric*, and *relationship*. (For more information about the ADL search-bucket architecture, see Janée and Frew 2002.)

The *spatial type* is defined as

Name: spatial

Value type: any of several types of geometric regions defined in WGS84 longitude/latitude coordinates, expressed in an ADL-defined syntax

Search constraints: overlaps, contains, within

The schema for the ADL spatial data type is diagrammed in figure 7.5 (Alexandria Digital Library 2004a). It is based on the Geography Markup Language (GML) version 2. The specification includes the types of footprints that can be used in a spatial query and the number of expected points (vertices) for each type of footprint—for example, a polygon must have at least three vertices but can have more. Geospatial values from object-level metadata would be mapped to this generalized schema in order to be accessible to ADL software for search and retrieval from distributed digital library collections.

In the ADL system implementation at UC Santa Barbara the spatial components of queries are created by users through an HTML user interface by using a map browser component where the query area can be drawn as a box and the coordinates for the four sides of that box define the query area. The user is given the choice of finding items that are *inside*, *overlap*, *contain*, or *are excluded from* the specified query area. This query footprint is compared with the object-level footprints stored in the *geographic-location* search bucket, which has its data stored according to the schema in figure 7.5. A sample spatial query that could be sent to this search bucket (in XML) is

```
<spatial-constraint
      bucket="geographic-location"
      operator="overlaps">
            <box   north="37.5"   south="30.0"   east="-110"
            west="-140"/>
</spatial-constraint>
```

ADL processes such queries using a spatial extension for a database management system.

Users can add other search parameters and can also choose to sort the results "by similarity to the query region." When sorting is requested, all of the matching results must be retrieved before any of the results are shown; otherwise, matching items are shown as they are found and in the order found. Results are presented as a list of brief metadata descriptions and the footprint of any of these items can be displayed on the map browser (figure 1.6). The ADL search interface also facilitates the use of the ADL Gazetteer to locate the area of interest. The first step for a search

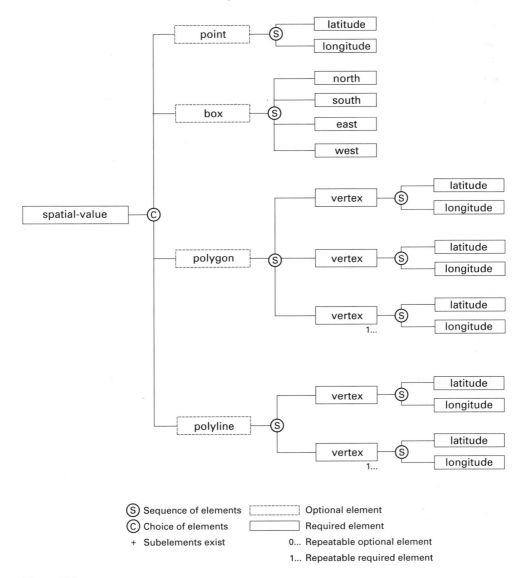

Figure 7.5
Alexandria Digital Library structure for the spatial data type

Panel 10
Implementing a Georeferenced Digital Library

I joined the Alexandria Digital Library (ADL) Project in its midlife, at a point when the project had succeeded in building a succession of prototypes for a single georeferenced digital library and was just starting to think about how federations of such libraries might interoperate and what a global digital library infrastructure might look like. This broader focus parallels that of other groups such as the Open Geospatial Consortium, except that ADL approached the problem from a more inclusive, more library-like perspective. Specifically, we looked at defining geospatial interoperability standards that are sufficiently lightweight as to allow groups and systems that would not ordinarily be thought of as spatial data providers (traditional library catalogs, for example), nor capable of being spatial data providers (small digital library implementations lacking spatial software, for instance), to in fact participate in a spatial system.

One of the surprising lessons to come out of this effort is the sensitivity of implementation difficulty on the exact specification of the problem. It came as little surprise that polygons, especially polygons defined on a spherical surface, are impossible to support without access to sophisticated mathematical software. But even bounding boxes can pose difficulties in some circumstances—for example, when they cross a discontinuity at the edges of a projection or in polar regions. So far, we have specified that an object will be represented by a single bounding box indicating the extent of the associated geographic coverage, but there are circumstances where a set of boxes would be decidedly better (for the United States, for example). Should the standards for geospatial operations in digital libraries address these issues, or are these complexities beyond what can be expected of geospatial operations outside of GIS? Other issues we have dealt with are choosing the basic set of spatial searching operators (e.g., is *overlap* alone sufficient?) and the ranking methods that best serve the end user. The difficulty (and even possibility) of providing lightweight geospatial search hinges greatly on the answers to such questions.

Greg Janée
Lead Software Developer
Alexandria Digital Library Project

can be to start with a placename, pick out the entry for the place from the list returned by the gazetteer, display this place on the map browser, and then draw the query area around this location. The description here covers the functionality of the ADL client as of November 2005.

ADL Gazetteer Protocol Spatial Searching   Spatial searching is specified in the ADL Gazetteer Protocol (Janée and Hill 2003) as a *footprint query* where an operator and a footprint are the components of the query. There is a choice of three operators: *within*, *contains*, and *overlaps*. Only the *within* operator is required for each server implementation of the protocol. There are three choices for the form of the footprint:

• *polygon*, which is "a simple polygon with geodesic edges, defined in WGS84 latitude/longitude coordinates"

• *box*, which is "a rectangle whose edges are aligned with the WGS84 latitude/longitude graticule"

• *identifier*, which is "one of the footprints of the gazetteer entry identified by *identifier*"

The *identifier* option for the footprint is a way to specify a footprint via a placename in a series of steps. For example, if the query is something like "Where is the Paris that is in Texas?" the steps would be

1. Find the gazetteer entry for "Texas" with the feature type of "countries, 1st order divisions" (this feature-type term is from the ADL *Feature Type Thesaurus* (Alexandria Digital Library 2004c)

2. Use the primary footprint associated with the identifier for this entry as the footprint for a spatial query: find entries with the placename of "Paris" that have footprints *within* the footprint associated with the query identifier.

The processing steps for such a query consist of looking up the identifier and then using the footprint (the primary footprint if there is more than one) of that entry as the query region.

An ADL Protocol query that includes a spatial footprint component looks like this (this is a full query record that can be sent to the ADL Gazetteer through the protocol server):

```
<?xml version="1.0" encoding="UTF-8"?>
<gazetteer-service
       xmlns="http://www.alexandria.ucsb.edu/gazetteer"
       xmlns:gml="http://www.opengis.net/gml"
       version="1.2">
<query-request>
      <gazetteer-query>
           <and>
                     <name-query operator="contains-phrase"
                     text="las vegas"/>
                     <footprint-query operator="overlaps">
                          <gml:Box>
                               <gml:coordinates>-120.35,34.65
```

```
                              -113.69,42.34</gml:
                              coordinates>
                        </gml:Box>
                  </footprint-query>
            </and>
      </gazetteer-query>
      <report-format>standard</report-format>
</query-request>
</gazetteer-service>
```

This query asks for standard reports for entries about "las vegas" whose footprints *overlap* a query box defined by two points as specified by the GML standard.

Calculating Spatial Similarity and Ranking Results

For spatial searching and the ranking of result sets, the degree of spatial match between a query footprint and the footprint of an information object is significant. We can say, for example, that if an object's footprint exactly equals the query footprint, then the *spatial similarity* of the two spatial areas equals 1. Where the area of overlap is less than 1, the degree of overlap is expressed by a number between 0 and 1 that can be calculated using one of a set of possible methods. Inherent in this reasoning is that when two areas touch at the boundary but do not overlap and when they are some distance from one another, they are not spatially similar and thus not geographically relevant to one another (Frontiera 2004).

One measure of the spatial similarity of two areas is based on the degree to which the two areas overlap and the relative size of the two areas. A widely used similarity measure is

$$2 \times (\text{area of overlap of } X \text{ \& } Y) / (\text{area of } X + \text{area of } Y)$$

where X and Y represent the spatial extent of two locations. This formula describes a ratio where the numerator is two times the extent of the area where X and Y overlap and the denominator is the combined total area of X and Y.

For illustration, we can assign coverage areas (in square miles, for example) to the boxes in figure 7.1 as follows (shown in figure 7.6 but not to scale):

Query region = 4
Box A = 2
Box B = 5
Box C = 20
Overlap of the query area and Box B = 2

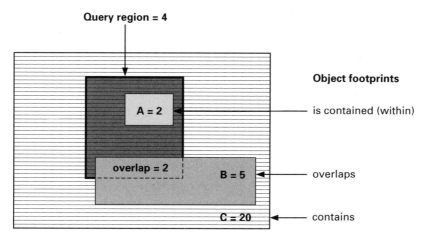

Figure 7.6
Spatial relationships illustration showing relative sizes between query area and object footprints (sizes are not to scale)

The similarities can then be calculated for the relationship of each box to the query area:

Box A: 2(2)/2 + 4 = 4/6 = 0.67
Box B: 2(2)/5 + 4 = 4/9 = 0.44
Box C: 2(4)/20 + 4 = 8/24 = 0.33

Based on this calculation, footprint A is most relevant to the query area, B is next, and C is the least relevant. This is based only on the degree of overlap and relative sizes of the footprints. This method reduces the significance of the area of overlap by taking into account the size of the areas, assuming that a footprint that is much larger or much smaller than the query footprint is less likely to be geographically relevant to the query. A related assumption is that the difference in the area of coverage is likely to indicate a difference in the density or spatial resolution of the data that may not meet the user's expectations (Frontiera 2004).

There has been experimentation with other spatial similarity calculations for GIR applications. One known as the Hausdorff distance method is used widely to locate or match objects within digital images and has been investigated by the Alexandria Digital Library Project for spatial comparison calculations within GIR. The calculation is based on the Euclidean distance between points in the point sets of two footprints (Frontiera 2004; Janée 2003; Janée and Frew 2004).

In her dissertation, Frontiera (2004) reviews these two methods of calculating spatial similarity and others that have appeared in the literature and proposes a new method based on the basic probability model for general information retrieval. The probabilistic approach estimates the probability that the information content of a particular object is relevant to a particular query statement and ranks the object set on the basis of the strength of this probability. This approach has been shown to be both theoretically sound and practically effective for information retrieval where there is inherent uncertainty in both query statements and object content. Frontiera compares the performance of each of the methods for GIR to reach the conclusion that the probabilistic method achieves superior results overall. This work has been described in Larson and Frontiera 2004.

Similarity measures are very useful for ranking retrieval sets from the most spatially relevant to the least spatially relevant to the query. Such a ranked order ensures that a map of the world will be at the bottom of the list for a city-block-sized query area. Coupled with visualization of the object footprints on a map display and user options to rerun the query with a modified search area, spatial similarity ranking provides an effective approach to useful GIR services.

Effectiveness of Geographic Information Retrieval

The ideal result of GIR is for the user to find all of the items in a collection that provide information specific to the geographic area of interest and also provide information relevant to the time and topic of interest. Here the focus is on the geo-referenced part of this process, but always with the assumption that the whole query and response framework will include the use of textual, temporal, and quantitative query parameters as well.

Relevance is a central concept of information retrieval; it refers to the degree to which an information object is an appropriate and useful response to a user's information need. IR systems are evaluated on the basis of how well they can process a user's query and return a set of potentially relevant information in a useful way. The measures of *recall* and *precision* are used to evaluate the effectiveness of IR methods: *recall* measures the percentage of relevant items retrieved from the estimated number of relevant items actually in a collection and *precision* measures the percentage of relevant items among the items retrieved. In other words, there are two ways to fail in IR: one is to miss relevant items in the collection and the other is to find items that are not relevant to the query. These two measures of IR effectiveness, recall and precision, are at odds with one another. To reach high recall so that everything in the collection that is relevant to some degree is returned, precision will drop; to reach high precision so that every item retrieved is on target, recall will suffer. To deal with this, systems such as Google are designed for high recall with the use of relevance ranking algorithms to move the most relevant items to the top of the list. Measurement of the effectiveness of ranking algorithms is based on how successfully this is done—for example, measurement of how far down the list of retrieved items a user has to go to find all of (or a percentage of) the most relevant items, and how many of the most relevant items are among the first ten items in the list (or above some other cutoff level).

What constitutes *relevance* ultimately depends on the judgment of the user. The information system can be designed to do its best in matching the user's query to the information content of objects in the collection. For spatial searching, it can

• Give the user a choice of spatial matching methods (e.g., *contains*, *is contained*, and *overlaps*) to control the type of matching made
• Provide spatial similarity computation to move the most spatially similar objects to the top of the results list
• Display the footprints of the items returned to show how these items are spatially related to the query and to one another

Little work has been done to date to test effectiveness of GIR in returning spatially relevant information in response to user queries. Perhaps the earliest investigation was my dissertation in library science in the School of Library and Information Science at the University of Pittsburgh (Hill 1990). The research involved a test of the effectiveness of using placenames and textual IR techniques for the retrieval of geoscience documents about locations within the same general region. The test collection was ninety-nine geoscience articles, each of which included a sketch map showing the location discussed in the text (such as the sketch map in figure 7.7, depicting an area in the southwestern United States). Each article had been indexed by two indexing and abstracting services: the American Geological Institute's *GeoRef* Information Services and the Petroleum Abstracts Service at the University of Tulsa (American Geological Institute 2005; University of Tulsa 2005). The sketch maps were converted to polygonal representations using GIS software so that each of the ninety-nine articles was represented not only by the bibliographic record including abstracts but also by a footprint. These polygons were used to determine the spatial overlap, containment, or distance-away relationships for each document pair in the set.

Documents were considered spatially relevant to one another if their footprints overlapped; the shortest distance between the boundaries of nonoverlapping

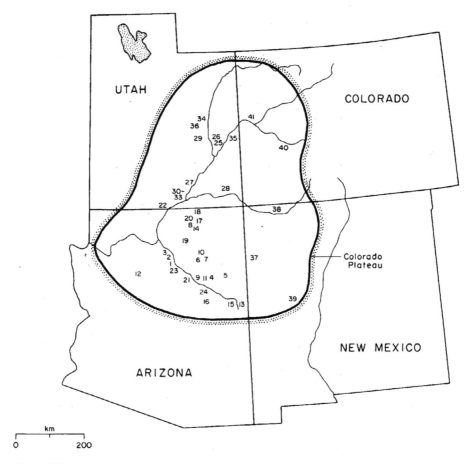

Figure 7.7
Example of a sketch map showing the location of the area of study in a scientific document. (From Agenbroad and Mead 1989.)

document pairs was also measured. A calculation of *spatial similarity* between documents was used to rank documents relative to one another, so that for each article all other articles could be ranked from the most spatially similar to the most distant and nonoverlapping. This ranking was taken to represent the *true* spatial relationships among the set of articles—the documents at the top of each listing were most spatially similar to a particular target document. This ranking was then compared to the rankings that could be obtained when using the placenames in the bibliographic records for each article with the application of various IR techniques. Basically, this was a test of how well a text-based representation of geographic location performs for GIR compared to the use of spatial footprints. The results provided evidence that using placenames to search for documents relevant to a particular location is an ineffective method compared to spatial methods.

Placename problems identified in this research included

1. The study areas were not always associated with particular placenames, particularly in the open sea and coastal areas. For example, a study area off the west coast of Italy did not have a familiar name; words to describe the area referred to adjacent places such as "Italy" and "Mediterranean Sea," which were nonspecific to the study area. Even if a name was created and used for a particular study area (e.g., a drilling-site identification number), it was unlikely to be used in other documents about the same general region.

2. Placenames relevant to the study area were not used as index terms. In some cases, placenames were used to describe a large area but not the places inside the boundaries of that area. Another study area might be identified with a placename for a more local area and a match could be made only if the indexing for this article included the name of the parent area.

3. One variation of a placename was used but not an equally valid one for the area—for example, Tyrrhenian Basin but not Tyrrhenian Sea. In some cases, the use of a particular form of placename reflected the scientific focus of the article; this type of difference is a barrier to gathering together place-based information from different points of view.

4. Inconsistencies in spelling and syntax were evident.

5. Placenames in titles and abstracts that did not appear in the indexing were discoverable only by careful analysis.

More recently, Frontiera (2004) evaluated the effectiveness of different spatial similarity methods for information retrieval, comparing the probabilistic approach to five published spatial similarity measures. The test collection was composed of 2,527 information objects selected from the California Environmental Information Catalog (CEIC) and included a wide variety of resources: geospatial datasets, digital and hardcopy maps, database files, documents, websites, and so on. Each object was represented by metadata prepared in accordance with the FGDC metadata standard (described in chapter 6); each contained a minimum bounding box (MBB) footprint and a placename. The placenames were either well-known administrative districts within California or they were user-defined areas specific to a particular resource. For the administrative districts, detailed footprints were available and were used to generate convex-hull footprints and to perform spatial similarity and ranking tests, which were compared to the tests based on the MBB generalizations. The user-defined areas were used as contained in the metadata. Query areas were created from eighty of the test-collection footprints: forty from the administrative districts and forty from the user-defined areas.

The probabilistic model permits the inclusion of a number of variables to be used and weighted to arrive at an estimate of relevancy. For this research, Frontiera included the

- Area of overlap divided by the query region
- Area of overlap divided by the object footprint
- Hausdorff distance
- Fraction of the query region that is onshore minus the fraction of the object footprint that is onshore

These variables were tested to evaluate which led to the best results for the test conditions.

The research compared the probabilistic and the published spatial similarity and ranking methods to one another and evaluated the use of MBBs and convex hulls as footprint generalizations for GIR. Some of the conclusions are

1. All of the spatial ranking methods tested resulted in practical improvements to spatial retrieval performance where spatial similarity ranking was not applied.
2. The probabilistic methods tested outperformed the five spatial similarity methods tested.
3. Convex hulls as footprint generalizations produced better retrieval results than MBBs when using the five published spatial similarity methods tested. Significantly, however, use of the probabilistic methods and MBBs together achieved better retrieval results than the spatial similarity methods with convex hulls, which "suggests that probabilistic geographic information retrieval offers an alternative to the use of higher quality spatial representations that may be more difficult to implement" (Frontiera 2004, 2).

These early GIR evaluation studies are significant because they provide evidence for the superiority of spatial over text-based georeferencing for information retrieval, as well as evidence for the effectiveness of minimum bounding boxes combined with sophisticated spatial ranking methods in lieu of using more computationally demanding convex-hull or polygonal footprints. Related to the second point, Janée and Frew (2004) propose the adoption of the most basic level of spatial representation and spatial matching for interoperable GIR services: (1) using four-sided minimum bounding boxes for the spatial footprints of information objects, and (2) using the most basic spatial comparison of *intersects* (*overlaps*) as the basis for distributed spatial searching across dissimilar collections.

Spatial Browsing

User interfaces can support spatial browsing of georeferenced collections by visualizing the geographic coverage of a whole collection or by displaying the spatial footprints of items in a subset of a collection. Subsets can be precomputed or created on the fly for the results of queries. Because of the computation required to create spatial overviews of large sets of geospatially referenced objects, overviews are more likely to be available as precomputed tables and visualizations.

The Alexandria Digital Library describes its collections with collection-level metadata (Alexandria Digital Library 2003). One component of this metadata, created by a piece of software that gathers the statistics and creates the images, is a visualization of the spatial coverage of the collection and the density of coverage, as shown in figure 7.8. The Electronic Cultural Atlas Initiative does something similar in its user interface; see figure 3.15.

Spatial distribution and density are also provided for maps and images in the collection. The coverage image for maps is shown in figure 7.9 and clearly illustrates that the collection's maps are concentrated in the United States, with some coverage for the rest of the world.

The Alexandria Digital Library also experimented with a user interface that displayed the footprints of a retrieved set. An example is shown in figure 7.10; foot-

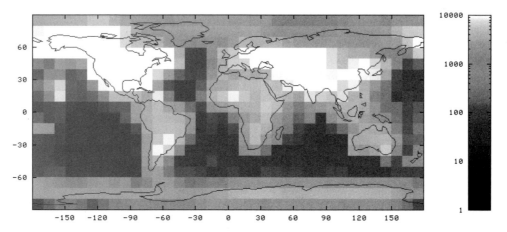

Figure 7.8
Spatial coverage and density image from the collection-level metadata for the 2,339,675 items in the ADL Catalog as of March 5, 2000. (http://collections.alexandria.ucsb.edu/adl_catalog/coverage/spatial/overall.html.)

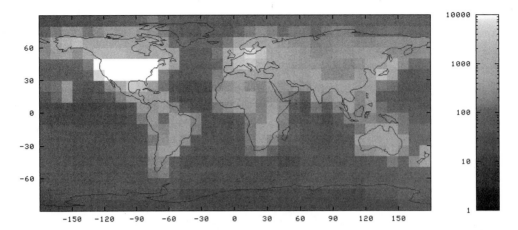

Figure 7.9
Spatial coverage and density for the 324,876 maps in the ADL Catalog as of March 5, 2000. (http://collections.alexandria.ucsb.edu/adl_catalog/coverage/spatial/cartographic-works. html.)

prints for 100 images retrieved from the ADL collection are shown displayed on a base map depicting the coastline. When a particular image was selected in the search results list, its footprint was highlighted in red, showing its spatial coverage and its relationship to the other images in the context of the general location of the search. The interface allowed the user to select a footprint and review its metadata and also to zoom into dense areas of footprints to see more detail. This ability to browse through a set of collection items in several different ways was effective because it highlighted the spatial coverage of each item and the user could choose which ones were more likely to be useful based on spatial coverage. Unfortunately, this interface design has not been reimplemented with the current software environment.

Summary

Information retrieval based on geographic relationships (GIR) is a new field of research, development, and standardization that draws on both text-based IR techniques and geospatial matching operations. The basic spatial relationships used for GIR are *overlaps* (*intersects*), *is contained* (*within*), and *contains*. The basic spatial footprint used is the longitude/latitude aligned minimum bounding box, a generalization of a more specific boundary, or point location. To a limited extent, ordinary text string and mathematical operations can be used to make spatial matches in GIR

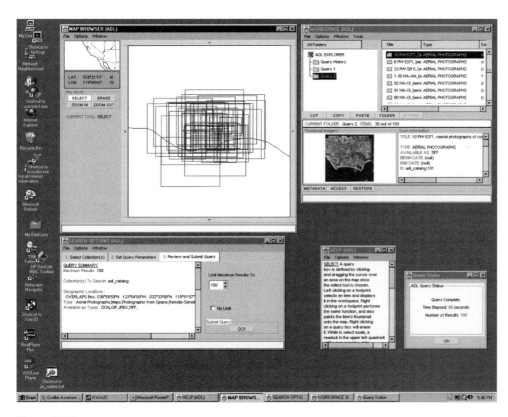

Figure 7.10
User-interface component of the ADL JIGI system showing the footprints of a set of 100
images retrieved from the ADL Catalog

systems. More specialized software is needed for collections holding many items and
for the use of more types of spatial footprints and additional spatial comparisons.
GIS software supports GIR operations as one component of its analysis environment;
the complexity of GIS software, however, is more than a basic GIR system needs.

In GIR, any object with a footprint that *overlaps* a query region is considered to
be geographically relevant to the query unless a more specific matching function is
used (e.g., *contains* or *is contained*). To measure the degree of spatial relevance to
the query, spatial similarity methods are used. These spatial similarity methods are
based on the degree of overlap and the relative sizes of the query and the object
footprints or on other methods such as the Hausdorff distance method. The spatial
similarity values can be used to sort the most relevant items to the top of the set of
retrieved items, especially when the *overlaps* matching operation is used.

Little work has been done to evaluate the effectiveness of GIR. One research project compared the effectiveness of retrieval based on placenames to retrieval based on spatial footprints for a set of geoscience articles and found the text-based retrieval to be less effective. When placenames are used for queries, the retrieval is sensitive to language, spelling, and syntax issues, and placenames are not available for every spatial location on Earth. Footprints avoid these problems. A recent research project compared various methods of calculating spatial similarity and ranking information retrieval results by spatial relevance to the query. It found that all spatial similarity and ranking methods improved the quality of the GIR results, and the probabilistic methods achieved superior results even when using basic minimum bounding boxes (MBBs) as the footprints for the resources.

Sources for Further Information

Links to spatial extensions for Relational Database Management Systems (listed from the inexpensive options to modules for large RDMS products):

• PostgreSQL http://www.postgresql.org/, optionally with PostGIS http://postgis. refractions.net/ (freeware)

• MySQL, version 4.1 or higher http://dev.mysql.com/doc/mysql/en/Spatial_extensions_in_ MySQL.html

• DB2 Spatial Extender http://www-306.ibm.com/software/data/informix/blades/spatial/

• MapInfo SpatialWare http://extranet.mapinfo.com/products//Overview.cfm?productid= 1141

• Informix Spatial DataBlade Module http://www-3.ibm.com/software/data/informix/blades/ spatial/

• Informix Geodetic DataBlade Module   http://www-3.ibm.com/software/data/informix/ blades/geodetic/ (for a globe, not a flat projection)

• Oracle 10g Spatial & Oracle Locator: Location Features http://www.oracle.com/technology/ products/spatial/index.html

Larson, R. 1996. Geographic information retrieval and spatial browsing. In L. C. Smith and M. Gluck, eds., *Geographic Information Systems and Libraries*: *Patrons, Maps, and Spatial Information*, 81–123. Urbana-Champaign: Graduate School of Library and Information Science, University of Illinois at Urbana-Champaign. http://sherlock.berkeley.edu/geo_ir/ PART1.html.

Purves, R., and C. Jones, eds. Forthcoming. Special issue of *Computers, Environment and Urban Systems* based on the papers given at the 2004 SIGIR Workshop on Geographical Information Retrieval.

Sparck Jones, K., and P. Willett. 1997. *Readings in Information Retrieval*. Morgan Kaufmann series in multimedia information and systems. San Francisco: Morgan Kaufmann.

8
Future of Georeferencing

Many users of information systems and services have needs for information that are best approached from a geographic perspective. These users include scientists who research global climate modeling and ocean dynamics and those who characterize and track the ecological and geological characteristics of a region; historians who require information on specific geographic areas at particular times; students learning about particular urban areas and countries or working on class projects where geographic distribution patterns and their changes through time are key to understanding; developers and city planners who must prepare environmental impact reports for a proposed development site; managers of community resources and infrastructure; those with responsibility for emergency management and national security; and citizen advocates who will use geographic presentations to make their points. Successful international and local commerce requires close attention to the management of distributed supplies, processes, and customers. The exploration for, exploitation of, and management for sustainability of natural resources are examples of activities highly dependent on georeferenced information; these activities require knowledge of the locations of exploitable mineral and petroleum deposits, ocean fisheries, stands of trees suitable for harvesting, and other resources. The list of activities with crucial geographic components goes on: public health, genealogy, tourism, and the coverage of events in the public media. The fact is that the geographic associations of information are widespread through most of the activities of our lives.

This is a period of rapid change in any field that benefits from advances in cyber-infrastructures and associated computer and information science technologies, including all information system development and management in libraries, museums, online searching and browsing services, data centers, and scientific data services. In the past few years, geographic information systems (GISs) have advanced rapidly from an original set of simple ideas and inefficient software to a mainstream technology for the management of geographic information. GIS, global positioning system (GPS) technologies, and spacecraft imaging have combined to revolutionize our daily lives and our understanding of our world (Clarke 2001). Our technical infrastructure now exposes us to place-based information on a global scale to a much greater degree than just a few years ago. We have a global economy, world-wide news coverage of major events in the world, and access to local news and information resources anywhere in the world through Internet connections. Barriers to understanding the import of this information flow given multiple languages and cultural contexts are now moving to the forefront of our concerns.

We live in a time where place-based information is becoming ever more important in our thinking, analyses, planning, and activities, whether it involves our local areas or the world at large. The use of GIS, for example, is expanding beyond the scientific community to the general public to support positions on a community planning process, plan an election campaign, educate our children, and avoid traffic jams (Clarke 2001). The availability of geospatial information in the form of digital maps, remote sensing images, climate and vegetation data, gazetteer data, and so on makes many new insights possible.

We are only beginning to consider this new emphasis on and use of place-based information when it comes to integrating the organization and retrieval of all forms of information based on geographic location, not just geospatial information objects but also the vast stores of information that are informally georeferenced with place-names but not currently accessible through geospatial searches or capable of being displayed on maps. There is also a looming problem of the archiving of digital geospatial information for future use. Historical maps have proven to be very important for historical research and they have been cataloged and made accessible through map libraries; will current digital maps and datasets be preserved and remain accessible for future generations (Clarke 2001)?

We in the information and library science community—academics, researchers, managers, practitioners, vendors—should be concerned with the impact of these trends on our information systems so that we are not caught flat-footed and unprepared to meet the needs and expectations of end users. Although we cannot predict the future with certainty, some trends are obvious, and they are the subject of this chapter.

This chapter revisits the topics and discussions of the preceding chapters, but this time the focus is on looking forward and identifying potential impacts of the major trends on the future development of information systems and services and profes-

Panel 11
Promise of Georeferencing

One of the first academic papers I published, in the late 1960s, was with Kate Donkin, the map librarian at McMaster University where I was a graduate student. We devised a way to describe each map in the collection on punched cards, and to compile them into a computerized catalog. The computer was in a different building from the map library, and the catalog could only be used by library staff. But it planted an idea in my mind that later blossomed into the Alexandria Digital Library, and the idea of providing remote access via the Internet both to the catalog and to the contents of the library, and allowing users to search for information about geographic locations. Georeferencing has become far easier with GPS, massive databases of already georeferenced material, gazetteers, and geocoding services. Today, it is almost trivial to convert street addresses or placenames into geographic coordinates, and to integrate such data with other similarly georeferenced information. But it is still difficult in some areas, particularly indoors beyond the reach of GPS, where it is possible to imagine a vast array of interesting applications if the technical problems of high-resolution indoor location measurement can be solved.

Michael Goodchild
Alexandria Digital Library Project co-PI
UCSB Geography Department

sional education. This development will happen within a society that will be increasingly aware of the geographic associations of information through ubiquitous georeferencing embedded in cars, cameras, and cell phones, frequent use of customized map displays online and in print, the three-dimensional spaces of augmented reality in games and "virtual tours," common use of datasets with geocoding based on street addresses, and a rich technological environment bringing us streams of remote sensing data views and GIS analyses.

Linking Spatial Cognition to Georeferenced Information Systems

Understanding human spatial and temporal cognition as it relates to information system design, both within and outside of GIS, will be an important area of research in the coming years. It is clear that humans think rather vaguely (and sometimes erroneously) about geographic spaces and that our knowledge of and ability to understand geographic relationships and use maps effectively varies widely. But it is also clear that georeferencing is very common and is a natural way to think about and use information. There is much left to learn about how humans link geographic space to information when they are using information systems: How do we express the geo-referencing part of a question to an information service? What do we mean to say with such queries? What do we expect the system's response to be? How can information systems best support the use of space and time in problem-solving activities?

A favored method of thinking about worldwide geographic locations is with administrative units (e.g., countries and their subdivisions) and nested hierarchies of administrative organization. But administrative units are only one type of named geographic features. There are also natural features such as rivers and mountains, biogeographic regions such as forests and climate zones, human-made or cultural features such as buildings and highways, and local neighborhoods; although these overlap with the administrative units, an administrative hierarchy is not a natural way of organizing them. Instead we think in terms of topological relationships (e.g., near, within, along, a distance away), inexact locations and boundaries, and names/labels for places. How should our information systems best integrate these hierarchies and relationships between various types of geographic features to emulate the norm for georeferencing in ordinary discourse and to support spatial reasoning?

Designing effective user interfaces to describe, find, and visualize the geographic associations of information will be informed by continuing research into human spatial cognition. If the interfaces include a map display (the best way to show the spatial context of geographic information), there are issues of how to make the map understandable and useful—applying the best practices of cartography and accommodating what we know about human processing of geographic information. One thing we know is that individuals have different styles of georeferencing, influenced by preferences for formal or informal georeferencing and other cultural, linguistic, and disciplinary contexts. To some extent, user interfaces to georeferenced information systems need to accommodate these preferences by providing multimodal methods of interacting.

Spatial cognition research will help in other ways, such as in designing interfaces to take full advantage of the human mind's ability to recognize what it cannot recall completely, and studying the roles of map displays, labeling of georeferenced images, and administrative hierarchies in the recognition process. We know that we frequently think about geographic space in vague terms, but can an information system let a user know how vagueness has been implemented in the system (e.g., in footprints and in interpretations of topological relationships) in a meaningful way?

It will be interesting to note the effect of increased exposure to maps and depictions of geographic space on information system design. Will georeferencing become more central—more common—in information systems? Will there be a noticeable enhancement of human geographic knowledge and movement toward shared vocabularies for referring unambiguously to places and categorizing types of geographic features?

Future of Georeferenced Information Objects in Information Systems

The segmentation of geospatial object types (e.g., maps, remote sensing images, and digital elevation data) and other georeferenced information object types into distinct and independent information domains is coming to an end. End users will increasingly expect to be able to consult maps and georeferenced images at the same time they are reading about political and cultural histories, art and music, earthquakes, ecology, geology, geography, and so on and enjoying or studying fiction and prose. A search for a suitable travel guide should simultaneously (or at least through the same interface) search for maps, photographs, *National Geographic* articles, and movies and fiction set in the region and will be successful because the search can be based on coordinates in addition to text. Place-based research will benefit from collecting data from otherwise noninteracting subject specialties and untranslated languages because geospatial access can be used as a common search method.

Where national and regional geospatial datasets, remote sensing images, aerial photography, and gazetteers of the government agencies are freely available, as they are in the United States, these resources are available for many applications and services and are directly available to individuals through online services. Where there are intellectual property rights attached to such data that restrict use or require payments for use, this will hamper the integration of such data into general information systems.

Digitization and scanning projects will continue to make large collections of historical geospatial information objects available. For example, the U.S. Library of Congress has digitized a set of U.S. railroad maps and Civil War maps, and the David Rumsey Map Collection, a private collection available via the Internet, has over 11,000 maps online (Cartography Associates 2005). At the same time, streams of images will be added to our information stores from remote sensing activities, scientific exploration and monitoring, social science research, GIS analyses, and so forth.

The issue of archiving geospatial data and products for their historical value is being addressed by the U.S. Library of Congress through the National Digital Information Infrastructure and Preservation Program (NDIIPP), funded by Congress with

$100 million. The Library of Congress is the lead agency for a collaborative project involving "other federal, research and private libraries and institutions with expertise in the collection and maintenance of archives of digital materials" (U.S. Library of Congress 2005). As part of the action plan for the first year, the libraries of the University of California at Santa Barbara (UCSB) and Stanford University are partnering to design an infrastructure for a National Geospatial Digital Archive (NGDA), a collecting network for the archiving of geospatial images and data (University of California at Santa Barbara and Stanford University 2005).

In the next few years, advances in geoparsing methods will turn ordinary text into geospatially referenced information. Imagine, for example, being able to submit novels that are in the public domain (e.g., Jack London's *Call of the Wild* or Tolstoy's *War and Peace*) to a geoparsing process and create a geographic timeline for the narrative of the places where action takes place and to be able to find books and sections of books that describe a particular place. Imagine back-of-the-book indexes, bibliographic indexes for journal literature, and full-text news archives that augment named places with their geospatial footprints.

Future Developments in the Representation of Geospatial Locations

Currently we have a set of mature and evolving standards and practices for the representation of geospatial locations—some designed to support the exchange and use of geospatial data and some designed as part of library and bibliographic metadata structures. To support integrated use of georeferenced information, we need to have a set of standards and practices that establishes baseline representations for non-GIS applications that retains compatibility with geospatial data standards and that contains the basic elements needed for actual use of the georeferenced information beyond the uses initially contemplated—uses such as georeferenced information retrieval across all types of information; networks and federations of georeferenced information involving data centers, libraries, and museums; and gazetteer development. These standards need to deal with the representation of uncertainties so that the level of confidence in the footprints or the placement of their boundaries can be conveyed to the end users and incorporated in information retrieval and use practices.

Once it is recognized that the geographic associations of all types of information are fundamental elements of metadata description and retrieval services, the concepts of coordinates and other spatial referencing systems, geodesy, projections, scale, resolution, accuracy, and precision will be incorporated into library and information science curricula, supplementing the learning of these concepts from earlier education—not as exclusively associated with maps, but as a key descriptor for any kind of information.

Future of Gazetteers and Gazetteer Services

Gazetteers will be increasingly integrated into information systems as translation devices between formal and informal georeferencing. They will continue to be available as reference sources to look up where a place is, what kind of place it is, and which names have been authorized by toponymic authorities, but there will be more of them in more languages and created for different purposes. In a word, gazetteers will be *discovered* anew and put to new purposes. As a result, new demands will be made of them: that they be up to date; have better footprints; include the time dimensions for names, footprints, and relationships; accommodate multiple languages and scripts; are well documented; and are accessible programmatically so that they can be accessed from other software. As with other georeferenced information resources, some attention should be given to archiving versions of gazetteers for historical research; a complementary activity would be making digital copies of historical printed gazetteers.

Networks of gazetteers will be established with registered gazetteer servers and ways of discovering which gazetteers to access for particular queries. We will be able to download gazetteer data and add it to local gazetteers for personal or project use. Software will be built for the express purpose of building gazetteer data, either by direct entry or by downloading information from other gazetteers—like the citation-building software available now. These networks will develop *middleware* services such as crosswalks between feature-typing schemes and *duplicate-detection* services to indicate when two gazetteer entries may be about the same place and therefore can be combined into one entry.

Practices such as geoparsing, dynamic labeling of the features in aerial photographs or remote sensing images, and translation of placenames to footprints in information systems will drive the need for gazetteer services.

Another direction of gazetteer development will be to use the structural gazetteer model for related purposes. One natural extension is to develop *event gazetteers* where the temporal and geographic elements are both primary attributes. Event gazetteers would describe named events such as hurricanes; the *name* is the hurricane's given name (e.g., Katrina) and the footprint is the path of the hurricane plus a bounding box to indicate the extent of the geographic area covered. Any named event with a strong geographic component could be documented in terms of its

Panel 12
Spatial Alignment of Information

In 1969, Ian McHarg's book titled *Design with Nature* greatly influenced landscape architecture, my chosen profession. Maps with different layers of information became primary tools, and the analysis of a landscape or an environment for a project consisted of manually overlaying transparent map layers that represented the local terrain, geology, soils, hydrography, and so on. On each layer, reference points were depicted and the sheets were adjusted to align these reference points as accurately as possible and then secured with punch pens to hold the layers in position. Some of these layers were photo transfers to Mylar sheeting; others were hand traced from the original maps onto semitransparent paper. By the early 1980s, computer processing became available for such tasks, and some of the early leaders in the development of GIS and early adopters of the technology were landscape architects (for example, Jack Dangermond (ESRI), David Sinton (Intergraph), Dana Tomlin (Map Analysis Package)). From this early orientation, I have always been interested in the use of maps in different spaces and by extension in the broader concepts of georeferencing to meet the needs of scientific users in specific environments. This interest extends to the ways in which users classify and structure spatial information and the scale of environments in which they work and increasingly in the need for cross-disciplinary information exchange. Alignment of information by location—whether location in the human brain, location within genomes, or geographic location—becomes a powerful concept for knowledge discovery within and across disciplines.

Kate Beard
Professor of Spatial Information Science and Engineering
University of Maine

---

name, time, geographic association, and type of event (e.g., explorations like the Lewis and Clark expedition). Another extension that has already been investigated is for *named time periods*, such as the period known as the Italian Renaissance (Feinburg 2003). In a gazetteer of named time periods, the *name* is for the time period and the equivalent of the *footprint* is a date range. With such a knowledge organization system (KOS), a named time period in a text document, subject indexing, or other labeling could be translated into a date range and, as with geographic footprints, this transformation would provide a common temporal base for information retrieval, where named time periods and actual dates could be accessed interchangeably. There are interesting issues with the naming of time periods that are explored in the Feinburg paper. For example, the date ranges of named time periods can vary from one part of the world to another (e.g., the Bronze Age occurred at different times in various parts of the world), and often an event like "World War II" is also used as a time period. The structure developed for gazetteer data, where formal and informal means of representation are interchangeable, provides a good basis for the organization of both named events and named time periods into digital KOS resources that can be integrated into information systems.

Future of Georeferencing in Metadata Standards

Convergence on a georeferencing module for object-level metadata description, along the lines of the georeferencing structure proposed in chapter 6, would be an effective way to extend geospatial information retrieval to all types of information. This would encourage a common vocabulary and common practices of representing both formal and informal georeferencing. If such a module is developed collaboratively among the GIS community, the library community, and related information system application developers, and if it is accompanied by best practices for populating the elements, we could achieve the goal of *unified georeferencing*.

It should become common practice to link placenames in object-level metadata to gazetteers, either locally or remotely, so that the details of placenames do not have to be duplicated in the metadata. For example, the object-level metadata can indicate that the object is about "Chicago" and "Lake Michigan," but it does not have to carry the footprints for these places because the footprints can be obtained from a linked gazetteer database. To put it another way, if the metadata is georeferenced using placenames and if the placenames are linked to gazetteers that provide the footprints and the feature types, then the information system can use the integrated gazetteer and catalog to perform georeferenced information retrieval on placenames, footprints, and feature types.

Increased awareness of the value and use of georeferencing should lead to more specific identification of associated geographic locations for information objects in addition to (or in lieu of) the more general georeferencing practice in some fields. A book about how the boundary between the United States and Canada was established, for example, should have a footprint identifying that boundary in addition to identifying the two countries as the political entities involved—preferably in a way that does not falsely imply that the book's geographic coverage extends to the whole of the two countries.

Future of Georeferenced Information Retrieval

In the information retrieval research community, geographic information retrieval (GIR) is a new focus, with the first workshop on the topic held in 2004. Out of that workshop came a collaborative effort to establish test collections to use for trials of various geoparsing methods. This focus and other GIR applications in online search services, digital libraries, and other information services will advance the sophistication and effectiveness of GIR services in the coming years. Formal GIR test conditions will provide the means to test various forms of footprint generalizations for information retrieval, ways of implementing topological relationships, and spatial similarity methods for ranking results. Test conditions including real users will provide needed information about how effective GIR implementations and user interfaces are in meeting their expectations.

Evaluating Future Georeferenced Information Systems

As new place-based information systems develop and become options for finding information, and as we invest limited resources in information system development, we need some criteria for the characterization and evaluation of georeferenced information systems. Here are some factors to consider:

• What georeferenced resources are being accessed in terms of their formats, their variety, and their spatial and temporal distribution?

• What georeferenced services are provided (e.g., answering "where is," "what's there," "what information is associated with," and "how do I get there" type questions)?

• What audiences or activities are supported by the system?

  • What can be accomplished by use of this system that cannot be done at all or as well by a similar system in terms of georeferencing?

  • What georeferenced information gaps are filled by this system?

• How is georeferencing integrated into the user interface?

  • How is the query area defined—by drawing on a basemap, by entering coordinates, by placename, by an administrative hierarchy of placenames, or by a choice of several methods?

  • What spatial relationships are offered for queries (e.g., *overlaps, contains, is contained, near*)?

  • What geospatial ranking options are supported for items returned in answer to a query?

  • Can the footprints of individual objects be viewed in a map window? Can all of the footprints in a retrieval set (or a subset) be viewed at the same time?

  • Does the interface provide sufficient geographic context and thumbnail views of objects for the user to evaluate the resources without having to consult each item in a result set individually?

  • Is there support for geographic browsing of the whole collection?

- How are the complexities of georeferencing in information services handled?
  - Are footprints generalized to points, bounding boxes, convex hulls, or a simple grid system of geocoding?
  - What is the level of resolution in terms of the detail for metadata elements and geospatial description?
  - How are geospatially complex information objects described and made available for use?
- Are gazetteer services an integral part of the system for translating between informal and formal ways of georeferencing? (See chapter 5 for additional criteria to judge the quality of gazetteers.)
  - Does gazetteer access include the ability to search across distributed or remote gazetteers?
  - If a local gazetteer is used, how is it populated and updated?
  - What is the density of toponyms in your area of interest (both primary and alternate names for places)?
  - How extensive is the scheme of feature types? For multiple gazetteers, is there a harmonization or mapping between different feature-type schemes?
  - What types of relationships between geographic features are supported (e.g., *part of*)?
- If the system is accessed through Internet web browsers, has it been designed for rapid response to geospatial queries, or do you notice a substantial delay?
- Does the system require the use of complex software to handle geospatial object storage and spatial queries?
- Does the system use established georeferencing standards for information representation and retrieval?
- How is the time dimension integrated into the system (i.e., can georeferenced information be viewed on a time scale to track, for example, a series of photographs from a trip or changes through time in the footprint of a city)?

Conclusion

The biggest change in the coming years will be the recognition that georeferencing is a key element of description, retrieval, evaluation, visualization, and use in information systems of all types—not just in geographic information systems and not just associated with maps and geospatial datasets. It will be the realization that when informal georeferencing with placenames is linked to formal georeferencing with coordinates or other spatial referencing systems, the result is new and powerful capabilities for information retrieval and analysis. It will be realizing that formal georeferencing overcomes language barriers, bridges community contexts, and is, after all, doable and necessary in our increasingly global information universe.

This new understanding of the role and potential of georeferencing in information systems will have to be supported by changes in our educational systems and in our mainstream information environments. Professional practice and education in librarianship and related information science domains will have to include formal and informal georeferencing as standard components of all information description and analysis, not a focus for specializations only. Professional practice and education in GIS will have to include the understanding and teaching of the relationships between formal and informal georeferencing and the need for generalized, accessible methods for integrating information across the divides between analysis environments and other georeferenced information resources. Web-based information retrieval systems, benefiting from advances in geoparsing processes, will then be able to perfect methods of browsing the world's electronic information with a place-based orientation that integrates placenames, topological references, and coordinate footprints. Desktop computer programs that now help us create and organize text, citations, data, genealogies, photographs, and directories will have new software enabling us to add space-time indexing to our information, create personal gazetteers, add maps to our travel reports (not as imported images but generated from the space-time indexing), and browse our information stores geographically and temporally.

Libraries will adjust by integrating formal georeferencing into their metadata creation for all sorts of resources and will do so by adapting software and user interfaces to process geospatial referencing and to link informal and formal georeferencing. This means, ultimately, adding map views to user interfaces for the creation of place-based queries in concert with other search parameters, as well as for the geographic visualization of information objects and collections. Local collections of geospatial information objects will need to be integrated into mainstream catalog searching methods rather than remaining in largely self-contained specialized collections.

A unified approach to georeferencing—across all types of information objects, professional practices, and user groups—is the key to a greater understanding of and use of the geographic associations of information. It is up to you who design and implement the information systems and user services, who manage information resources, and who teach information science to apply the georeferencing concepts and methods presented in this book to make this happen.

Glossary

accuracy   refers to conformity to fact, or the degree to which the recorded value represents the "correct" value.

aerial photography   is the process of taking photographs from the air, such as with a camera mounted in an aircraft; usually taken in strips of overlapping prints for mapping purposes. (Adapted from Jackson 1997.)

bounding box   *See* minimum bounding box.

buffering   is spatially expanding a point, line, or polygonal footprint by a zone of adjacent area.

cadastre   is an official registry of the real property of a political subdivision, maintained for the purposes of taxing land. Parcels of land in a cadastre are often uniquely identified, by number or by code, and are reasonably persistent through time, thus satisfying the requirements of a georeferencing system. (Adapted from Longley et al. 2001.)

Cartesian coordinates   refers to the use of two- or three-dimensional coordinates representing the location of a point in relation to an x, y, z set of axes that are at right angles to one another; also called *rectangular coordinates*. This representation is based on René Descartes' conception of geometry and is the basis of the familiar x, y graphs used for print displays of data points. (Adapted from Weisstein 1999.)

cartography   is the art and technique of making maps and charts. (*American Heritage Dictionary of the English Language* 2003.) *See also* map.

centesimal coordinates   are decimal coordinates (relating to or divided into hundredths). *See also* sexagesimal coordinates.

centroid   is a point location at the center of a feature used to represent that feature. (Clarke 2001.)

chloropleth map   is a thematic map in which areas are colored or shaded to represent the density of a particular phenomenon or to symbolize classes within it. (ESRI 2004.)

conflation   is a process by which geospatial data from various sources is matched and merged into one composite and consistent dataset. (Adapted from Jackson 1997.)

contour   refers to an imaginary line, or a line on a map or chart, that connects points of equal elevation of the land surface above or below some reference value or datum plane, generally sea level. (Jackson 1997.)

convex hull   is the smallest set of points forming a convex boundary around a set of points; informally described as a rubber band wrapped around the "outside" points. (Hausner 1996.)

coordinate systems are (a) local or global systems for use in precise positioning, navigation, and geographic information systems for the location of points in space. The most commonly used Earth coordinate system today is the longitude and latitude system. Others include the Universal Transverse Mercator (UTM) system and national grid systems such as the British National Grid (BNG) (adapted from Hausner 1996); (b) systems with all the necessary components to locate a position in two- or three-dimensional space—that is, an origin, a type of unit distance, and two axes (Clarke 2001); (c) two- and three-dimensional coordinate systems used in analytic geometry are often referred to as Cartesian systems (Dana 1999a). *See also* latitude; longitude; centesimal coordinates; sexagesimal coordinates; Cartesian coordinates.

cyberinfrastructure is the use of high-end computation networks for the academic research and education community, including supercomputers; high-capacity mass-storage systems; system software suites and programming environments; productivity software libraries and tools; large-scale data repositories; and the experts and support staff that create and maintain these research environments (National Science Foundation, Computer and Information Science and Engineering (CISE), 2005). The foundation of this infrastructure consists of the libraries, archives, and museums that preserve information; the bibliographies, finding aids, citation systems, and concordances that make that information retrievable; the journals and university presses that distribute the information; and the editors, librarians, archivists, and curators who link the operation of this structure to the scholars who use it (American Council of Learned Societies (ACLS), Commission on Cyberinfrastructure for the Humanities and Social Sciences, 2005).

datum *See* geodetic datum.

digital libraries consist of (a) organized collections of digital resources; (b) data of any type (e.g., text, maps, sounds, scientific data, and static or dynamic images), format (e.g., digital and nondigital, image formats, text formats, dataset formats), and at multiple levels of granularity (e.g., collections and collection objects that can be decomposed and recomposed); (c) metadata that describes collections and objects and supports collection management, searching, retrieval, evaluation of lineage, and "fitness of use"; (d) technologies to support integrated use of distributed networks of digital collections and knowledge organization systems (e.g., thesauri, gazetteers, dictionaries); and (e) services (e.g., discovery and browsing, searching and ranking, visualization, translation, annotation, and peer review).

Euclidian distance is the straight-line distance, or distance "as the crow flies," between two points, normally on a plane. It can be calculated using the Pythagorean theorem. (Adapted from ESRI 2004.)

feature (geographic) is used to mean any distinct element (object) in the landscape; an element that is represented on a map or included in a gazetteer. *See also* placename.

feature type is a category of feature from a system of categorization (e.g., water body, city, building, administrative area). *See also* placename.

footprint is a representation of the spatial location or extent of a geographic object or feature represented in terms of a geospatial reference system, such as longitude and latitude coordinates or grid references. Also known as a *geometric shape*.

formal georeferencing *See* geospatial referencing.

gazetteer is a dictionary or list of geographic names (placenames), together with their geographic locations, their feature types (e.g., lakes), and other descriptive information.

geocoding is a term that is applied in various ways: (a) assigning a data value to a spatial object that provides information on the geographic location of the object and that is used as a key to access data relating to the object (Jackson 1997); (b) the conversion of analog maps into computer-readable form by scanning or digitizing (Clarke 2001); (c) the process of matching a particular street address with a spatial location by use of a street network database (e.g., TIGER/Line files) (Wikimedia Foundation Inc. 2005).

geodesy is (a) the science concerned with the determination of the size and shape of the Earth and the precise location of points on its surface; (b) the determination of the gravitational field of the Earth and the study of temporal variations such as Earth tides, polar motion, and rotation of the Earth. (Jackson 1997.)

geodetic box *See* minimum bounding box.

geodetic datum is a system of measurement and representation that defines the size and shape of the Earth and the origin and orientation of an Earth coordinate system. (Dana 1999b.)

geographic information retrieval (GIR) is an expansion of information retrieval (IR) that adds geospatial indexing, topological relationships, and spatial matching operations to the core functionality of text-based indexing and query processing. It also includes research into geoparsing technologies.

geographic knowledge is an individual's mental store of geographic facts, spatial environments, and geographic relationships obtained from observation, from personal navigation, and from secondary sources such as verbal descriptions, maps, and texts; often classified into declarative, procedural, and configurational geographic knowledge.

geometric relations are calculated within a geometric framework, where distance and direction can be measured on a continuous scale. For example, given the geographic coordinates in longitude and latitude of Chicago (4152′N 8737′W) and New York (4040′N 7358′W), a fairly simple calculation can give the direct distance between the two cities. (Larson 1996.) *See also* topological relations.

geometric shape *See* footprint.

geometry is used in geographic information systems to mean a point or an aggregate of points representing the spatial location of a geographic feature; aka a footprint. (Adapted from *MySQL AB* 2005.)

geoparsing is the process of identifying geographic references in text and assigning geospatial coordinates to these references.

georectification *See* georegistration.

georeferenced information objects are information objects that are either explicitly or implicitly associated with geographic locations. Explicit georeferencing is formal referencing of location with longitude and latitude coordinates or with grid references; implicit georeferencing is informal referencing with placenames and place codes. *See also* geospatial information objects.

georeferencing is establishing a relationship between information (e.g., documents, datasets, maps, images, biographical information) and geographic locations through placenames (i.e., toponyms) or place codes (e.g., postal codes) or through geospatial referencing (e.g., longitude and latitude coordinates).

georegistration   is the process used to bring together or maintain in perfect alignment a number of separate components that, when combined, form a single image or map. The careful use of a registering system during map production helps to ensure the accurate fit of overlays and avoid misplaced or overlapping features on the final map. ("Registration" in Natural Resources of Canada 2004.) Also known as *georectification. See also* rubber sheeting.

geospatial information objects   are information objects that are geometrically (mathematically) referenced to geographic locations—that is, with longitude and latitude coordinates or grid references.

geospatial referencing   (formal georeferencing) is the use of mathematical values to describe locations on the Earth and to place them within a framework that covers the globe (e.g., longitude and latitude coordinates, UTM grids) or a local area (national grid systems, township and range systems).

GIR   *See* geographic information retrieval.

global positioning system (GPS)   is a system of satellites, computers, and receivers that is able to determine the latitude and longitude of a receiver on Earth by calculating the time difference for signals from different satellites to reach the receiver. (*American Heritage Dictionary of the English Language* 2003.)

GPS   *See* global positioning system.

granularity   refers to the level of detail of the organizational unit in information systems and is used to explain the difference between a system that, for example, treats a map as the information object and another system that treats the features within the datasets of the map as the information objects (i.e., at a more detailed level of granularity).

graticule   is a longitude and latitude grid drawn on a map. The angle at which the graticule meets is an indicator of the projection used to create the map. (Adapted from Clarke 2001.) *See also* grid.

grid   refers to (a) a network composed of two sets of uniformly spaced parallel lines, usually intersecting at right angles and forming squares, which is superimposed on a map to provide a coordinate system more convenient than that provided by the graticule. The term is frequently used to designate a plane-rectangular coordinate system super-imposed on a map projection, and usually carries the name of the projection; e.g. "Lambert grid." A grid differs from a coordinate system in being composed of only a finite number of lines and differs from a graticule in not necessarily representing lines of longitude and latitude; (b) commonly, a raster data structure. (Adapted from Jackson 1997.) *See also* graticule; raster.

G-ring   is a string of longitude-latitude points that represents a closed boundary around an area. The term *outer g-ring* is used to mean the outside boundary, while the term *inner g-ring* or *exclusion g-ring* is used to mean a boundary within an outer g-ring that represents an area of exclusion (like a donut).

indirect georeferencing   when used in this book means the georeferencing of locations with placenames, codes, and other labels (i.e., informal georeferencing).

informal georeferencing   is referencing locations by placenames, place codes (e.g., postal codes), street addresses, and topological references (e.g., in, near, within, to the left or right). *See also* geospatial referencing; placename; topological relations.

information systems   are systems, whether automated or manual, that comprise people, machines, and/or methods organized to collect, process, transmit, and disseminate data for delivery to a destination user. (Wikimedia Foundation Inc. 2005.) *See also* digital libraries.

latitude   is the angular distance north or south of the Earth's equator, measured in degrees along a meridian, expressed in degrees, minutes, seconds (ddmmss), or in decimal degrees (negative decimal degrees are used to represent south). Latitude lines are parallel to the equator. The range of values is 90° to −90°.

longitude   is the angular distance on the Earth's surface, measured east or west along the equator from the prime meridian at Greenwich, England, to the meridian passing through a position, expressed in degrees, minutes, and seconds (ddmmss) or in decimal degrees (negative decimal degrees are used to represent west). The range of values is 180° to −180°. Meridians of longitude converge at the poles.

map   is a representation (usually two-dimensional) of geographic data (e.g., the Earth's surface) or data about some other spatial domain (e.g., the heavens). It is the end product of a cartographic process. *See also* cartography.

map layer   is a set of digital map features collectively (points, lines, and areas) with a common theme in coregistration with other layers. (Ellis 2001.)

map projection   is an attempt to portray the surface of the Earth or a portion of the Earth (or another spherical body) on a flat surface. Some distortions of shape, distance, direction, scale, and area always result from this process. Some projections minimize distortions in some of these properties at the expense of maximizing errors in others, while others attempt to only moderately distort all of these properties. (Adapted from Dana 2000.)

map scale   is the ratio between linear distance on a map, chart, globe, model, or photograph and the corresponding distance on the surface being mapped. It may be expressed in the form of a direct statement using different units (e.g., 1 inch to 1 mile) or a representative fraction or numerical ratio (e.g., 1/24,000 or 1:24,000) indicating that one unit on the map represents 24,000 identical units on the ground. A *large-scale map* refers to one that shows greater detail because the representative fraction (i.e., 1/25,000 or 1 inch on the map to 25,000 inches on the ground) is a larger fraction than in the case of a *small-scale* map, with a representation fraction of 1/250,000 to 1/7,500,000. Large-scale maps have a scale of 1:50,000 or greater (i.e., 1:10,000). Maps with scales between 1:50,000 and 1:250,000 are of intermediate scale. Maps of the world that fit on two 8 1/2 by 11 inch pages are very small scale, about 1 to 100 million. (Adapted from Rosenberg 2004.) *See also* resolution.

meridian   is an imaginary great circle on the Earth's surface passing through the North and South geographic poles. All points on the same meridian have the same longitude. (*American Heritage Dictionary of the English Language* 2003.)

metadata   is structured descriptive details about an information or data object or a collection of objects that is accessed programmatically or in person for various purposes in lieu of accessing the information object or collection directly or as supporting information for the use of the information, data, or collection. Purposes include information discovery, browsing, evaluation for fitness for use, and retrieval; information access and conditions of use; and administration and management of the information objects and collections.

minimum bounding box (MBB)   is the smallest longitude/latitude aligned box that completely encloses a set of points. Also known as a *bounding box* and as a *minimum* *bounding rectangle (MBR).* It represents the minimum and maximum longitudes and the minimum and maximum latitudes of the set of points. It can be represented by two points at diagonal corners of the box (e.g., −120,34 −119,35) or by four distinct coordinate values (west boundary = −120, east boundary = −119, north boundary = 35, and south boundary = 34). The latter expression is less ambiguous and is known as a *geodetic box.*

partition member   is a part or section of a spatial unit that has been divided; a division of a country or other administrative unit.

place   is a geographic location.

placename   is a label for a geographic place in the form of a formally established toponym, a colloquial name, a code (such as a postal code), or a street address. *See also* feature, feature type.

planar   refers to features lying or arranged as a plane or in planes, usually implying more or less parallelism; it is a two-dimensional arrangement, in contrast to the one-dimensional linear arrangement. (Jackson 1997.)

planimetric map   is a map that represents only the horizontal positions of geographic features, as opposed to a topographic map, which also shows vertical data or relief. Features usually shown on a planimetric map include roads, railways, rivers, populated places, and boundaries. (Natural Resources of Canada 2004.)

precision   is the specificity (or exactness) of a value; typically, the number of decimal points used to express the fractional part of a number.

precision (information retrieval)   is one of a pair of measurements of the performance or effectiveness of information retrieval methods. It measures the proportion of retrieved information objects that are relevant. For example, if 100 items are retrieved in response to a query and 30 of them are judged to be relevant to the query, then the precision ratio is 0.3 or 30 percent. *See also* recall (information retrieval); relevance (information retrieval).

projection   *See* map projection.

raster   refers to a data structure for geospatial data based on grid cells—that is, on cells in a rectangular grid. (Clarke 2001.) *See also* grid.

recall (information retrieval)   is one of a pair of measurements of the performance or effectiveness of information retrieval methods. It measures the proportion of relevant information objects in the collection being searched that is retrieved. For example, if there are 100 items in a collection that are judged relevant to a query and only 20 of these are retrieved, the recall ratio is 0.2 or 20 percent. *See also* precision (information retrieval); relevance (information retrieval).

recall (thought process)   is the ability to remember or the act of remembering information or experiences. (Adapted from *American Heritage Dictionary of the English Language* 2003.)

recognition (thought process)   is the process of seeing something in a recurring event, process, pattern, or thing that is familiar and thus understood to some degree. (Adapted from Wikimedia Foundation Inc. 2005.)

rectification   *See* georegistration.

relevance (information retrieval)   can be measured in terms of system performance or from the point of view of the user: the system view of relevance is that it is a measure of how well an information object matches a query, given the representation of the object and the system capabilities; a user view of relevance takes into account a deeper knowledge of the user's needs beyond what is stated in the query. *See also* recall (information retrieval); precision (information retrieval).

remote sensing is the collection of data by a sensor that is not in direct contact with the area being investigated. Active remote sensing involves transmitting a beam that is detected after reflection; passive remote sensing simply measures light from the sun being reflected by objects being sensed. Instruments for remote sensing can operate from aircraft or satellites. (Adapted from Clarke 2001.)

resolution is (a) a measure of the ability to distinguish detail or to define closely spaced targets; (b) the minimum size of a feature that can be detected; (c) the measure of detail of a graphic display expressed as dots per inch, pixels per line, and so on. (Adapted from Jackson 1997.)

rubber sheeting is a statistical process for adjusting the coordinates of all the data points in a dataset to allow a more accurate match between known locations and a few data points within the dataset. Rubber sheeting preserves the interconnectivity, or topology, between points and objects through stretching, shrinking, or reorienting their interconnecting lines. The process in useful when matching the edges of adjacent data layers. (Adapted from ESRI 2004.) *See also* georegistration; topology.

scale *See* map scale.

sexagesimal coordinates are coordinates expressed in degrees, minutes, and seconds (ddmmss) (of, relating to, or based on the number 60). *See also* centesimal coordinates.

spatial cognition deals with human perception, memory, reasoning, and communication involving the spatiotemporal and thematic attributes of objects and events, both in the real world and in digital representations. (Adapted from University Consortium for Geographic Information Science 1998.)

spatial reference system (SRS) specifies a position on or near the Earth's surface. Within the OpenGIS frame of reference, it can mean either a specification using coordinates or one based on "geographic identifiers (e.g., postal addresses, administrative areas)." When used for coordinate-based representation, the SRS includes a specification of the geodetic datum and the coordinate system employed. (Adapted from Open Geospatial Consortium Inc. 2004.)

spatial relevance *See* spatial similarity.

spatial similarity is a measure of the degree to which two spatial footprints (e.g., a query footprint and the footprint of an information object) occupy the same geographic space and the degree to which they cover additional space that they do not share. The strength of the spatial similarity between two footprints is a measure of their *spatial relevance* to one another.

stateless describes computer software and protocols that do not retain information about a user between contacts or a history of transactions for a series of contacts; the HTTP protocol used by the World Wide Web is a stateless protocol. The opposite condition is "stateful," where information is maintained about a user from session to session by the software or protocol.

terrain refers to the surface features of an area of land. (*American Heritage Dictionary of the English Language* 2003.)

thematic layer is a map layer containing information about a special subject, such as geology, rainfall, or population. (Adapted from Jackson 1997.)

thesaurus   is, for writers, a tool like *Roget's Thesaurus* with words grouped and classified to help select the best word to convey a specific nuance of meaning. For the information storage and retrieval functions, it is a set of controlled vocabulary (preferred terms) for representing concepts (topics, subjects) that includes hierarchical, equivalent, and associated relationships among the terms. Hierarchical relationships are based on generic (*is a*) or partitive (*is part of*) relationships. Equivalent relationships are between synonymous or "near-synonymous" terms for the same concept (i.e., between preferred and nonpreferred terms). Associative relationships are between preferred terms that do not have a hierarchical relationship—for example, between *art* and *artist*. Thesaurus construction for information storage and retrieval is guided by the ANSI/NISO standard Z39.19, *Guidelines for the Construction, Format, and Management of Monolingual Thesauri* (http://www.niso.org/standards/resources/Z39-19.html), and by ISO standard 2788, *Guidelines for the Establishment and Development of Monolingual Thesauri* (http://www.nlc-bnc.ca/iso/tc46sc9/standard/2788e.htm).

topographic map   is a type of map usually showing a suite of features including terrain, streams, boundaries, roads, and towns, which are commonly used as reference maps and as reference information behind GIS map layers. (Adapted from Clarke 2001.)

topography   is (a) the general configuration of a land surface or any part of the Earth's surface, including its relief and the position of its natural and human-made features; (b) the natural or physical surface features of a region; (c) the art and practice of accurately and graphically delineating in detail, as on a map or chart or by a model, selected natural and human-made surface features of a region. (Adapted from Jackson 1997.)

topological relations   refer to relations between features that are spatially related without regard to measurable distance or absolute direction. Examples of topological relations include such properties as overlap, adjacency, connectivity, and containment. For example, whether some building is inside or outside of the city limits of Chicago has to do with the building's relationship to an arbitrary boundary, but the distance or direction between the two is not an issue. Topological directions may have no particular relationship to the coordinate system in which they are embedded. "Left" and "right" are valid topological directions only in relation to the observer's frame of reference and have no absolute relationship with, for example, "north" or "west." (Larson 1996.) *See also* geometric relations.

topology   is (a) the property that describes adjacency and connectivity of features—in other words, the numerical description of the relationships among geographic features, as encoded by adjacency, linkage, inclusion, or proximity (Clarke 2001); (b) a branch of mathematics that studies patterns of geometric figures involving position and relative position without regard to size. Topology is sometimes referred to as "rubber-sheet geometry" because a figure can be changed to that of an equivalent figure by bending, stretching, twisting, and the like, but not by tearing or cutting. (*Columbia Electronic Encyclopedia* 2003.) *See also* rubber sheeting.

toponym   is a placename, a geographic name, or a proper name of a locality, region, or some other part of Earth's surface or its natural or artificial feature. In some cultures, most or all such placenames have a definite meaning in the language; this is not the case, generally, for native English-language speakers. (Wikimedia Foundation Inc. 2005.)

tuple   is a set of values passed from one programming language to another application program or to a system program such as the operating system. Typically separated by commas, the values may be parameters for a function call or a set of data values for a database. (Computer Language Company Inc. 2004.)

Unicode   is an international standard whose goal is to provide the means to encode the text of every document people want to store in computers. This includes all scripts in active use, many scripts known only by scholars, and symbols (e.g., mathematical) that do not strictly represent scripts. It is considered to be the most complete character set available and has become the dominant encoding scheme in the internationalization of software and for multilingual environments. Unicode's role in text processing is to provide a unique code for each character in an abstract way, leaving the visual rendering (size, shape, or style) to another program, such as a web browser or word processor. There are several established Unicode Transformation Formats (UTFs) that map to the actual internal storage method for data processing. UTF-8 is the de facto standard encoding for interchange of Unicode text, with UTF-16 and UTF-32 being used mainly for internal processing. (Adapted from Wikimedia Foundation Inc. 2005.)

vector   is a structure for geospatial data using the point or node and the connecting segment as the basic building block for representing geographic features. (Adapted from Clarke 2001.)

vertex   is one of a set of ordered x, y coordinate pairs that defines a line or polygon feature. Plural form: *vertices*. (ESRI 2004.)

References

Aerial Arts. 2004. *History of Aerial Photography: The Aerial Perspective.* http://www. aerialarts.com/History/history.htm.

Agenbroad, L. D., and J. I. Mead. 1989. Quaternary geochronology and distribution of *Mammuthus* on the Colorado Plateau. *Geology, 17,* 861–864.

Alexandria Digital Library. 2003. *ADL Collection Metadata.* University of California at Santa Barbara. http://www.alexandria.ucsb.edu/~gjanee/collection-metadata/.

Alexandria Digital Library. 2004a. *ADL Bucket Report DTD.* (Revision 2004/02/22). University of California at Santa Barbara. http://www.alexandria.ucsb.edu/middleware/dtds/ ADL-bucket-report.dtd.

Alexandria Digital Library. 2004b. *Guide to the ADL Gazetteer Content Standard.* Version 3.2. University of California at Santa Barbara. http://www.alexandria.ucsb.edu/gazetteer/ ContentStandard/version3.2/GCS3.2-guide.htm.

Alexandria Digital Library. 2004c. *Metadata for the ADL Feature Type Thesaurus.* University of California at Santa Barbara. http://www.alexandria.ucsb.edu/gazetteer/FeatureTypes/ FTT_metadata.htm.

Alexandria Digital Library. 2005. *Website.* University of California at Santa Barbara. http://www.alexandria.ucsb.edu/.

American Council of Learned Societies (ACLS), Commission on Cyberinfrastructure for the Humanities and Social Sciences. 2005. *What Is Cyberinfrastructure?* http://www.acls.org/ cyberinfrastructure/cyber_what_is.htm.

American Geological Institute. 2005. *GeoRef Information Services.* http://www.agiweb.org/ georef/index.html.

American Heritage Dictionary of the English Language. 2003. 4th ed. Boston: Houghton Mifflin. Accessed through GuruNet: http://www.gurunet.com/.

Ancient World Mapping Center. 2004. *The Inscription on the "Moorlands Patera."* http://www.unc.edu/awmc/moorlandspatera.html.

Australia New Zealand Land Information Council, Spatial Information Council. 2001. *ANZLIC Metadata Guidelines.* Version 2. http://www.anzlic.org.au/download.html?oid= 2358011755.

Baker, D. J. 1990. *Planet Earth: The View from Space.* Frontiers of Space Series. Cambridge, MA: Harvard University Press.

Ball, M. 2005. Biodiversity building blocks—BioGeomancer unlocks historical observations. *GeoWorld.* http://www.geoplace.com/uploads/featurearticle/0508em.asp.

Barkowsky, T. 2002. *Mental Representation and Processing of Geographic Knowledge: A Computational Approach.* New York: Springer.

Beaman, R., J. Wieczorek, and S. Blum. 2004. Determining space from place for natural history collections. *D-Lib Magazine, 10* (5). http://www.dlib.org/dlib/may04/beaman/05beaman.html.

Bosco, A., A. Longoni, and T. Vecchi. 2004. Gender effects in spatial orientation: Cognitive profiles and mental strategies. *Applied Cognitive Psychology, 18,* 519–532.

Buchel, O. 2005. *Geographic Information Retrieval of Non-cartographic Materials from Library Catalogs.* Independent Reading Final. Professor Timothy Craven, Faculty of Information and Media Studies, University of Western Ontario.

Buckland, M. K., F. C. Gey, and R. R. Larson. 2002. *Going Places in the Catalog: Improved Geographic Access.* Electronic Cultural Atlas Initiative, University of California at Berkeley. http://ecai.org/imls2002/.

Buckland, M. K., and L. Lancaster. 2004. Combining place, time, and topic. *D-Lib Magazine, 10* (5). http://www.dlib.org/dlib/may04/buckland/05buckland.html.

Canadian Permanent Committee on Geographical Names. 1992. *Guide to the Field Collection of Native Geographical Names.* Provisional ed. Geomatics Canada. http://geonames.nrcan.gc.ca/pdf/native_field_guide_e.pdf.

Cartography Associates. 2005. *David Rumsey Map Collection.* http://www.davidrumsey.com/.

Center for Spatially Integrated Social Science. 2005. *Spatial Resources for the Social Sciences.* University of California at Santa Barbara. http://www.csiss.org/.

Clarke, K. C. 2001. *Getting Started with Geographic Information Systems.* 3rd ed. Upper Saddle River, NJ: Prentice Hall.

Clementini, E., and P. Di Felice. 1996. A model for representing topological relationships between complex geometric features in spatial databases. *Information Sciences, 90* (1–4), 121–136.

Columbia Electronic Encyclopedia. 2003. 6th ed. Boston: Houghton Mifflin. Accessed through GuruNet: http://www.gurunet.com/.

Computer Language Company Inc. 2004. *Computer Desktop Encyclopedia.* Accessed through GuruNet: http://www.gurunet.com/.

Council of Geographic Names Authorities in the United States (COGNA). 2005. *COGNA Website.* http://www.cogna50usa.org/.

Cox, S. 2000a. *DCMI Box Encoding Scheme: Specification of the Spatial Limits of a Place, and Methods for Encoding This in a Text String.* Dublin Core Metadata Initiative. http://dublincore.org/documents/2000/07/28/dcmi-box/.

Cox, S. 2000b. *DCMI Point Encoding Scheme: A Point Location in Space, and Methods for Encoding This in a Text String.* Dublin Core Metadata Initiative. http://dublincore.org/documents/dcmi-point/.

Cox, S. 2005a. *DCMI Box Encoding Scheme: Specification of the Spatial Limits of a Place, and Methods for Encoding This in a Text String.* Dublin Core Metadata Initiative. http://dublincore.org/documents/dcmi-box/#dcsv.

Cox, S. 2005b. *DCMI Point Encoding Scheme: A Point Location in Space, and Methods for Encoding This in a Text String.* Dublin Core Metadata Initiative. http://dublincore.org/documents/dcmi-point/#dcsv.

Crane, G. 2004. *Georeferencing in Historical Collections.* Perseus Project, Tufts University. http://www.dlib.org/dlib/may04/crane/05crane.html.

Dana, P. H. 1999a. *Coordinate Systems Overview.* Geographer's Craft Project, University of Colorado at Boulder. http://www.colorado.edu/geography/gcraft/notes/coordsys/coordsys.html.

Dana, P. H. 1999b. *Geodetic Datum Overview.* Geographer's Craft Project, University of Colorado at Boulder. http://www.colorado.edu/geography/gcraft/notes/datum/datum.html.

Dana, P. H. 2000. *Map Projection Overview.* Geographer's Craft Project, University of Colorado at Boulder. http://www.colorado.edu/geography/gcraft/notes/mapproj/mapproj.html.

Dialog Search Aids: File 89, GeoRef: Geographic Coordinate Fields. 2003. Thomson Dialog. http://support.dialog.com/searchaids/dialog/f89_geo.shtml.

Digital Data Services. 2004. *USGS Quads: Digital Ortho Quarter Quads.* http://www.usgsquads.com/prod_doqq.htm.

DLESE Metadata Working Group. 2005. *ADN Metadata Framework.* http://www.dlese.org/Metadata/adn-item/index.htm.

Dublin Core Metadata Initiative. 2005. *Dublin Core Metadata Initiative (DCMI) Website.* http://www.dublincore.org/.

Dutton, G. 1999. *A Hierarchical Coordinate System for Geoprocessing and Cartography.* Lecture Notes in Earth Science, no. 79. Berlin: Springer-Verlag.

EDINA. 2005. *Map and Data Place.* http://edina.ac.uk/maps/.

Egenhofer, M. J., and J. Herring. 1990. *Categorizing Binary Topological Relationships between Regions, Lines, and Points in Geographic Databases.* Technical report. Department of Surveying Engineering, University of Maine. http://www.spatial.maine.edu/~max/9intReport.pdf.

Egenhofer, M. J., and D. M. Mark. 1995. Naive geography. In A. Frank and W. Kuhn, eds., *Spatial Information Theory: A Theoretical Basis for GIS (COSIT '95)*, 1–15. Lecture Notes in Computer Science, no. 988. Berlin: Springer-Verlag.

Electronic Cultural Atlas Initiative. 2005a. *Metadata Tags.* http://ecaimaps.berkeley.edu/clearinghouse/html/list_md_elements.php.

Electronic Cultural Atlas Initiative. 2005b. *Website.* http://www.ecai.org/.

Ellis, F. 2001. *GIS Self Learning Tool: Glossary.* Department of Geomatics, University of Melbourne. http://www.sli.unimelb.edu.au/gisweb/glossary.htm.

Endeavor Information Systems Inc. 2000. *Voyager Geospatial Search Module.* http://www.endinfosys.com/prods/geo.pdf.

ESRI (Environmental Systems Research Institute Inc.). 2004. *GIS Dictionary.* http://support.esri.com/index.cfm?fa=knowledgebase.gisDictionary.gateway.

ESRI (Environmental Systems Research Institute Inc.). 2005. *ArcSDE Developer Help: Understanding Spatial Relationships.* http://edndoc.esri.com/arcsde/9.1/.

Feinburg, M. 2003. *Application of Geographic Gazetteer Standards to Named Time Periods*. Student paper, School of Information Management and Systems, University of California at Berkeley. http://ecai.org/imls2002/time_period_directories.pdf.

Fontaine, T. 2002. Waitukubuli, Dominique, Dominica. *TheDominican.net, 1* (30). http://www.thedominican.net/articles/dominica-independence.htm.

Freundschuh, S. M. 1998. The relationship between geographic scale, distance, and time as expressed in natural discourse. In M. J. Egenhofer and R. G. Golledge, eds., *Spatial and Temporal Reasoning in Geographic Information Systems,* 131–142. New York: Oxford University Press.

Frontiera, P. 2004. *A Probabilistic Approach to Spatial Ranking for Geographic Information Retrieval*. Doctoral dissertation, Department of Landscape Architecture and Environmental Planning, University of California at Berkeley.

Gey, F., and P. Clough. 2005. *GeoCLEF 2005—Cross-Language Geographical Information Retrieval*. http://ir.shef.ac.uk/geoclef2005/.

Global Biodiversity Information Facility (GBIF). 2005. *Website*. http://www.gbif.org/.

Global Change Master Directory. 2002a. *Landsat Thematic Mapper Imagery*. NASA Goddard Space Flight Center. http://gcmd3.gsfc.nasa.gov/KeywordSearch/Home.do.

Global Change Master Directory. 2002b. *USGS Digital Orthophoto Quadrangles*. NASA Goddard Space Flight Center. http://gcmd3.gsfc.nasa.gov/KeywordSearch/Home.do.

Golledge, R. G. 1991. The conceptual and empirical basis of a general theory of spatial knowledge. In M. M. Fischer, P. Nijkamp, and Y. Y. Papageorgiou, eds., *Spatial Choices and Processes,* 147–168. Amsterdam: North-Holland.

Goodchild, M. F., S. Yang, and G. Dutton. 1991. *Spatial Data Representation and Basic Operations for a Triangular Hierarchical Data Structure*. NCGIA Technical Paper 91–8. Santa Barbara, CA: National Center for Geographic Information and Analysis.

Griffiths, A., and M. Lynch. 1987. *Geographic Information Systems: A Library Perspective*. British Library Research and Development Department Project Ref: SI/G/700. Department of Information Studies, University of Sheffield.

Hastings, J., and L. L. Hill. 2002. Treatment of "duplicates" in the Alexandria Digital Library Gazetteer. In M. J. Egenhofer and D. M. Mark, eds., *GIScience 2002 Abstracts,* 64–65. Boulder, CO: Springer. http://alexandria.sdc.ucsb.edu/~lhill/paper_drafts/Hastings&Hill-GISc02-Abstract-Submitted.pdf.

Hausner, A. 1996. *Convex Hulls*. Computer Science Department, Princeton University. http://www.cs.princeton.edu/~ah/alg_anim/version1/ConvexHull.html.

Hill, L. L. 1990. *Access to Geographic Concepts in Online Bibliographic Files: Effectiveness of Current Practices and the Potential of a Graphic Interface*. Doctoral dissertation, School of Library and Information Science, University of Pittsburgh.

Hill, L. L. 2002. *Feature Type Thesaurus*. Alexandria Digital Library, University of California at Santa Barbara. http://www.alexandria.ucsb.edu/gazetteer/FeatureTypes/FTT_metadata.htm.

Hill, L. L., R. Dolin, J. Frew, G. Janée, and M. Larsgaard. 1999. Collection metadata solutions for digital library applications. *Journal of the American Society for Information Science*

(JASIS). Special issue on metadata, *50* (13), 1169–1181. http://www3.interscience.wiley.com/cgi-bin/issuetoc?ID=66001475.

Hirtle, S. C. 1998. The cognitive atlas: Using GIS as a metaphor for memory. In M. J. Egenhofer and R. G. Golledge, eds., *Spatial and Temporal Reasoning in Geographic Information Systems*, 263–271. New York: Oxford University Press.

Holmes, D. O. 1990. Computers and geographic information access. *Meridian, 4,* 37–49.

International Organization for Standardization (ISO), Technical Committee 211. 2003a. *Geographic Information—Metadata* (ISO 19115:2003). http://www.iso.org/iso/en/prods-services/ISOstore/store.html.

International Organization for Standardization (ISO), Technical Committee 211. 2003b. *Geographic Information—Spatial Referencing by Geographic Identifiers* (ISO 19112:2003). www.iso.org.

International Organization for Standardization (ISO), Technical Committee 211. 2005. *Geographic Information—Metadata—XML Schema Implementation* (ISO/CD TS 19139, under development).

Ishikawa, T., and K. A. Kastens. 2005. Why some students have trouble with maps and other spatial representations. *Journal of Geoscience Education, 53* (2), 184–197.

Jackson, J. A. 1997. *Glossary of Geology.* 4th ed. Alexandria, VA: American Geological Institute.

Janée, G. 2003. *Spatial Similarity Function.* Alexandria Digital Library, University of California at Santa Barbara. http://www.alexandria.ucsb.edu/~gjanee/archive/2003/similarity.html.

Janée, G., and J. Frew. 2002. The ADEPT Digital Library Architecture. In G. Marchionini and W. Hersh, ed., *Proceedings of the Second ACM-IEEE Joint Conference on Digital Libraries (JCDL 2002), Portland, OR,* 342–350. New York: ACM Press. http://www.alexandria.ucsb.edu/~gjanee/archive/2002/jcdl-adept.doc (slides for the presentation: http://www.alexandria.ucsb.edu/~gjanee/archive/2002/jcdl-adept-talk.ppt.)

Janée, G., and J. Frew. 2004. *Spatial Search, Ranking, and Interoperability.* Paper presented at the Workshop on Geographic Information Retrieval, ACM SIGIR 2004, Sheffield, UK.

Janée, G., J. Frew, and L. L. Hill. 2004. Issues in georeferenced digital libraries. *D-Lib Magazine, 10* (5). http://www.dlib.org/dlib/may04/janee/05janee.html.

Janée, G., and L. L. Hill. 2003. *ADL Gazetteer Protocol.* Version 1.2. Alexandria Digital Library, University of California at Santa Barbara. http://www.alexandria.ucsb.edu/gazetteer/protocol/specification.html.

Jarvis, H., N. Cross, and I. Johnson. 1999. *ECAI Metadata Manual.* http://www.ecai.org/documentation/ecai_metadata_standard.html.

Jones, P. J., and S. T. Dumais. 1986. The spatial metaphor for user interfaces: Experimental tests of reference by location versus name. *ACM Transactions on Office Information Systems,* 4 (1), 42–63.

J. Paul Getty Trust, Research Institute. 2005. *Getty Thesaurus of Geographic Names Online.* http://www.getty.edu/research/conducting_research/vocabularies/tgn/.

Kornai, A., and B. Sundheim. 2003. *Workshop on the Analysis of Geographic References, May 31, 2003, Edmonton, Alberta, as Part of the North American Chapter of the*

Association for Computational Linguistics and Human Language Technology Conference (NAACL-HLT 2003). http://people.mokk.bme.hu/~kornai/NAACL/.

Larson, R. 1996. Geographic information retrieval and spatial browsing. In L. C. Smith and M. Gluck, eds., *Geographic Information Systems and Libraries: Patrons, Maps, and Spatial Information*, 81–123. Urbana-Champaign: Graduate School of Library and Information Science, University of Illinois at Urbana-Champaign. http://sherlock.berkeley.edu/geo_ir/PART1.html.

Larson, R., and P. Frontiera. 2004. *Ranking and Representation for Geographic Information Retrieval*. Paper presented at the Workshop on Geographic Information Retrieval, ACM SIGIR 2004, Sheffield, UK.

Leidner, J. L. 2004. *Towards a Reference Corpus for Automatic Toponym Resolution Evaluation*. Paper presented at the Workshop on Geographic Information Retrieval, ACM SIGIR 2004, Sheffield, UK.

Livingston, G. 2004. *Too Soon Old, Too Late Smart: Thirty True Things to Learn Before You Die*. New York: Marlowe.

Lloyd, R., and C. Heivly. 1987. Systematic distortions in urban cognitive maps. *Annals of the Association of American Geographers*, 77 (2), 191–207.

Longley, P., M. F. Goodchild, D. Maguire, and D. Rhind. 2001. *Geographic Information Systems and Science*. Chichester: Wiley.

Mammal Networked Information System (MaNIS). 2003a. *Classic Localities*. http://elib.cs.berkeley.edu/manis/ClassicLocalities.html.

Mammal Networked Information System (MaNIS). 2003b. *Manual for the Georeferencing Calculator*. http://elib.cs.berkeley.edu/manis/CoordCalcManual.html.

Mammal Networked Information System (MaNIS). 2005. *Georeferencing Guidelines*. http://elib.cs.berkeley.edu/manis/GeorefGuide.html.

Mark, D. M. 1993. Human spatial cognition. In D. Medyckyj-Scott and H. M. Hearnshaw, eds., *Human Factors in Geographical Information Systems*, 51–60. London: Belhaven Press.

MetaCarta Inc. 2005a. *MetaCarta. Corporate brochure*. http://www.metacarta.com/docs/Corporate_Brochure_06_05.pdf.

MetaCarta Inc. 2005b. *Website*. http://www.metacarta.com/.

Moen, W. E. 1996. The Government Information Locator Service: Discovering, identifying, and accessing spatial data. In L. C. Smith and M. Gluck, eds., *Geographic Information Systems and Libraries: Patrons, Maps, and Spatial Information*, 41–67. Urbana-Champaign: Graduate School of Library and Information Science, University of Illinois at Urbana-Champaign.

Montello, D. R. 1993. Scale and multiple psychologies of space. In A. U. Frank and I. Campari, eds., *Spatial Information Theory: A Theoretical Basis for GIS (COSIT '93)*, 312–321. Lecture Notes in Computer Science, no. 716. Berlin: Springer-Verlag.

Moritz, T. 1999. *Geo-referencing the Natural and Cultural World, Past and Present: Towards Building a Distributed, Peer-Reviewed Gazetteer System*. Paper presented at the Digital Gazetteer Information Exchange Workshop, Smithsonian Institute, October 12–14, 1999.

Morris, B. 1988. CARTO-NET: Graphic retrieval and management in an automated map library. *Special Libraries Association, Geography and Map Division, Bulletin, 152*, 19–35.

Muller, J.-C. 1985. Mental maps at a global scale. *Cartographica, 22* (4), 51–59.

MySQL AB. 2005. *MySQL Manual—Introduction to Spatial Extensions in MySQL.* http://dev.mysql.com/doc/mysql/en/GIS_introduction.html.

Naaman, M., Y. J. Song, A. Paepcke, and H. Garcia Molina. 2004. Automatic organization for digital photographs with geographic coordinates. In H. Chen, M. Christel and E. P. Lim, eds., *Proceedings of the Fourth ACM/IEEE Joint Conference on Digital Libraries (JCDL 2004), Tucson, AZ,* 53–62. New York: ACM Press.

National Geospatial-Intelligence Agency. 2005. *GEOnet Names Server (GNS).* http://earth-info.nga.mil/gns/html/.

National Research Council Mapping Science Committee. 1999. *Distributed Geolibraries: Spatial Information Resources. Summary of a Workshop held June 15–16, 1998.* Washington, DC: National Academy Press. http://www.nap.edu/html/geolibraries.

National Science Foundation, Computer and Information Science and Engineering (CISE). 2005. *Shared Cyberinfrastructure (SCI).* http://www.nsf.gov/cise/sci/about.jsp.

Natural Resources of Canada. 2004. *The Atlas of Canada: Glossary.* http://atlas.gc.ca/site/english/learningresources/glossary/index.html.

Nebert, D. D. 2000. *Z39.50 Application Profile for Geospatial Metadata or "GEO."* Version 2.2. U.S. Federal Geographic Data Committee. http://www.blueangeltech.com/standards/GeoProfile/geo22.htm.

Nygeres, T. L. 1993. How do people use geographical information systems? In D. Medyckyj-Scott and H. M. Hearnshaw, eds., *Human Factors in Geographical Information Systems,* 37–50. London: Belhaven Press.

Open Geospatial Consortium Inc. 1999. *OpenGIS Simple Features Specification for SQL.* http://www.opengis.org/docs/99-049.pdf.

Open Geospatial Consortium Inc. 2001. *Geoparser Service Specification—Draft Candidate Specification.* Discussion paper OGC 01-035, version 0.7.1. http://www.opengeospatial.org/docs/01-035.pdf.

Open Geospatial Consortium Inc. 2002. *Geography Markup Language (GML) Implementation Specification.* Version 2.1.2. http://www.opengis.org/docs/02-069.pdf.

Open Geospatial Consortium Inc. 2003. *Geography Markup Language (GML) Implementation Specification.* Version 3. https://portal.opengeospatial.org/files/?artifact_id=7174.

Open Geospatial Consortium Inc. 2004. *Resources—Glossary of Terms.* http://www.opengis.org/resources/?page=glossary.

Open Geospatial Consortium Inc. 2005. *OpenGIS Specifications.* http://www.opengeospatial.org/specs/?page=specs.

Open Geospatial Consortium Inc. 2006. *Gazetteer Service Profile of the Web Feature Service Implementation Specification.* Implementation specification OGC 05-035rl, version 0.9.1. https://portal.opengeospatial.org/files/?artifact_id=13593.

Orth, D. J., and R. L. Payne. 2003. *Principles, Policies, and Procedures: Domestic Geographic Names.* U.S. Board on Geographic Names. http://geonames.usgs.gov/pppdgn.html.

Peabody Museum of Natural History. 2005. *BioGeoMancer: What It Does.* http://www.biogeomancer.org/yu/bgm-docs/what-it-does.html.

Petras, V. 2004. *Statistical Analysis of Geographic and Language Clues in the MARC Record.* Technical report for the "Going Places in the Catalog: Improved Geographical Access" project, supported by the IMLS National Leadership Grant for Libraries, Award LG-02-02-0035-02. University of California at Berkeley. http://metadata.sims.berkeley.edu/papers/ Marcplaces.pdf.

Princeton University Library. 2005. *Digital Chart of the World Data.* Princeton University. http://www.princeton.edu/~geolib/gis/dcw.html.

Pruett, N. J. 1986. State of the art of geoscience libraries and information services. In E. P. Shelley, ed., *Proceedings of the Third International Conference on Geoscience Information, Adelaide, South Australia,* 15–30. Adelaide: Australian Mineral Foundation.

Rees, T. 2002. *C-squares Specification.* Version 1 (draft as of 01/2002). CSIRO Marine Research. http://www.marine.csiro.au/csquares/spec1.htm.

Rees, T. 2003a. *About C-squares.* CSIRO Marine Research. www.marine.csiro.au/csquares/ about-csquares.htm.

Rees, T. 2003b. "C-squares", a new spatial indexing system and its applicability to the description of oceanographic datasets. *Oceanography, 16* (1), 11–19.

Reid, J. S., C. Higgins, D. Medyckyj-Scott, and A. Robson. 2004. Spatial data infrastructures and digital libraries: Paths to convergence. *D-Lib Magazine, 10* (5). http://www.dlib.org/ dlib/may04/reid/05reid.html.

RLG enters new sphere with geoinformation project. 1989. *The Research Libraries Group News, 19* (spring), 3–9.

Rosenberg, M. 2004. *Geography: Map Scale.* http://geography.about.com/cs/maps/a/ mapscale.htm.

Smith, B., and D. M. Mark. 2001. Geographical categories: An ontological investigation. *International Journal of Geographical Information Science, 15* (7), 591–612.

Smith, D. A. 2002. Detecting events with date and place information in unstructured text. In G. Marchionini and W. Hersh, eds., *Proceedings of the Second ACM/IEEE Joint Conference on Digital Libraries (JCDL 2002), Portland, OR,* 191–196. New York: ACM Press.

Smith, D. A., and G. Crane. 2001. Disambiguating geographic names in a historical digital library. In P. Constantopoulos and I. T. Solvberg, eds., *Research and Advanced Technology for Digital Libraries. Proceedings of the 5th European Conference, ECDL 2001, Darmstadt, Germany,* 127–136. Lecture Notes in Computer Science, 0302–9743; 2163. Berlin: Springer.

Swanson, D. R. 1986. Fish oil, Raynaud's Syndrome, and undiscovered public knowledge. *Perspectives in Biology and Medicine, 30* (1), 7–18.

Swanson, D. R. 1988. Historical note: Information retrieval and the future of an illusion. *Journal of the American Society for Information Science, 39,* 92–98.

Taxonomic Databases Working Group (TDWG). 2005a. *Darwin Core 2 Documentation.* http://darwincore.calacademy.org/Documentation/.

Taxonomic Databases Working Group (TDWG). 2005b. *TDWG Website.* http://www.tdwg. org/.

Tufte, E. R. 1983. *The Visual Display of Quantitative Information.* Cheshire, CT: Graphics Press.

Tversky, A. 1977. Features of similarity. *Psychological Review, 84,* 327–352.

Tversky, B. 1993. Cognitive maps, cognitive collages, and spatial mental models. In A. U. Frank and I. Campari, eds., *Spatial Information Theory: A Theoretical Basis for GIS (COSIT '93)*. Lecture Notes in Computer Science, no. 716. Berlin: Springer-Verlag.

Tversky, B., and H. A. Taylor. 1998. Acquiring spatial and temporal knowledge from language. In M. J. Egenhofer and R. G. Golledge, eds., *Spatial and Temporal Reasoning in Geographic Information Systems*, 155–166. New York: Oxford University Press.

United Nations Group of Experts on Geographical Names (UNGEGN). 2005. *UNGEGN Website*. http://unstats.un.org/unsd/geoinfo/ungegn.htm.

University of California at Santa Barbara. 1994. *Towards a Distributed Digital Library with Comprehensive Services for Images and Spatially-Referenced Information*. Proposal to the National Science Foundation. http://www.alexandria.ucsb.edu/historical/www.alexandria.ucsb.edu/docs/proposal/index.html.

University of California at Santa Barbara, and Stanford University. 2005. *National Geospatial Digital Archive (NGDA)—A Project of the National Digital Information Infrastructure and Preservation Program (NDIIPP), an Initiative of the Library of Congress*. http://www.ngda.org/.

University Consortium for Geographic Information Science. 1998. *Cognition of Geographic Information*. http://www.ucgis.org/priorities/research/research_white/1998%20Papers/cog.html.

University of Tulsa. 2005. *Petroleum Abstracts Website*. http://www.pa.utulsa.edu/.

U.S. Federal Geographic Data Committee. 1998. *Content Standard for Digital Geospatial Metadata*. Version 2. http://fgdc.er.usgs.gov/metadata/contstan.html.

U.S. Federal Geographic Data Committee. 2003. *Geospatial Metadata Standards*. http://fgdc.er.usgs.gov/metadata/meta_stand.html.

U.S. Federal Geographic Data Committee. 2005a. *FGDC/ISO Metadata Standard Harmonization*. http://www.fgdc.gov/metadata/whatsnew/fgdciso.html.

U.S. Federal Geographic Data Committee. 2005b. *National Geospatial Data Clearinghouse*. http://www.fgdc.gov/clearinghouse/clearinghouse.html.

U.S. Geological Survey, Geographic Names Information System (GNIS). 2004. *U.S. Board on Geographic Names*. http://geonames.usgs.gov/bgn.html.

U.S. Geological Survey, Geographic Names Information System (GNIS). 2005. *GNIS Website*. http://geonames.usgs.gov/.

U.S. Geological Survey EROS Data Center. 2005. *National Aerial Photography Program (NAPP)*. http://edc.usgs.gov/products/aerial/napp.html.

U.S. Library of Congress. 2005. *Digital Preservation: National Digital Information Infrastructure and Preservation Program*. http://www.digitalpreservation.gov/.

U.S. Library of Congress, Network Development and MARC Standards Office. 2003. *MARC Code List for Geographic Areas*. http://www.loc.gov/marc/geoareas/.

U.S. Library of Congress, Network Development and MARC Standards Office. 2005a. *MARC Standards*. http://lcweb.loc.gov/marc/.

U.S. Library of Congress, Network Development and MARC Standards Office. 2005b. *MODS: Metadata Object Description Schema: Official Web Site*. http://www.loc.gov/standards/mods/.

U.S. Library of Congress, Network Development and MARC Standards Office. 2005c. *Z39.50 International Standard Maintenance Agency Website.* http://www.loc.gov/z3950/ agency/.

U.S. National Institute of Standards and Technology—Information Technology Lab. 2005. *Federal Information Processing Standards Publications (FIPS PUBS).* http://www.itl.nist.gov/ fipspubs/.

Wegener, M. 2000. Spatial models and GIS. In A. S. Fotheringham and M. Wegener, eds., *Spatial Models and GIS: New Potential and New Models,* 3–20. London: Taylor & Francis.

Weibel, S., J. Godby, and E. Miller. 1995. *OCLC/NCSA Metadata Workshop Report.* http://dublincore.org/workshops/dc1/report.shtml.

Weimer, N. 1998. *The Mercator Conformal Projection.* University of Alberta. http://www. ualberta.ca/~norris/navigation/Mercator.html.

Weisstein, E. W. 1999. *Cartesian Coordinates Entry in MathWorld.* A Wolfram Web Resource. Accessed through GuruNet: http://www.gurunet.com/.

Wieczorek, J., Q. Guo, and R. J. Hijmans. 2004. The point-radius method for georeferencing locality descriptions and calculating associated uncertainty. *International Journal of Geographical Information Science,* 18, 745–767.

Wikimedia Foundation Inc. 2005. *Wikipedia, the Free Encyclopedia.* http://en.wikipedia.org/ wiki/Main_Page.

Wong, C. 2003. *GIS Cookbook: Recipe—How to Geocode Addresses.* Center for Spatially Integrated Social Science. http://csiss.org/cookbook/recipe/7.

Woodruff, A., and C. Plaunt. 1994. GIPSY: Automated geographic indexing of text documents. *Journal of the American Society for Information Science,* 45 (9), 645–655.

Worboys, M., and M. Duckman. 2004. *GIS: A Computing Perspective.* 2nd ed. Boca Raton, FL: CRC Press.

Worldwide Web Consortium (W3C). 2005. *SKOS Core Vocabulary Specification.* Working Draft 2, November 2005. http://www.w3.org/2004/02/skos/core/spec/.

Introduction to Index to Geographic Examples

This index is similar to the index for an atlas; it lists placenames and the pages on which those placenames are used as examples. Unlike an index to an atlas, it contains georeferencing for such named places as "Cambridge and Broad Streets (corner of), London" and "southern California," which will only be found in textual documents, and a named place-based event: Hurricane Katrina. It also contains more forms of the placenames than you will find in an atlas (e.g., "Big Apple" for New York City). Unlike a regular back-of-the book index, these placenames have been linked to geographic footprints (the actual coordinates are not shown in the printed copy). Using this geospatial information, the geographic distribution of the places is displayed in the accompanying coverage distribution map. Potentially an electronic version of this index could be used to represent this book in a georeferenced information system to provide access to the information referring to geographic locations; for example, finding books (or text passages) with information about places within 100 miles of San Francisco. Applied to other textual resources, this approach would provide a wealth of georeferenced information that is ordinarily available only through text searching. Please note that this index is merely a demonstration of the potential uses of georeferenced information. For this book, the placenames are used only as examples. For other books, articles, papers, and reports where georeferencing is linked to substantive information about geographic locations, such indexes would open up access to relevant information using geospatial queries and provide an overview of the geographic coverage of an information object.

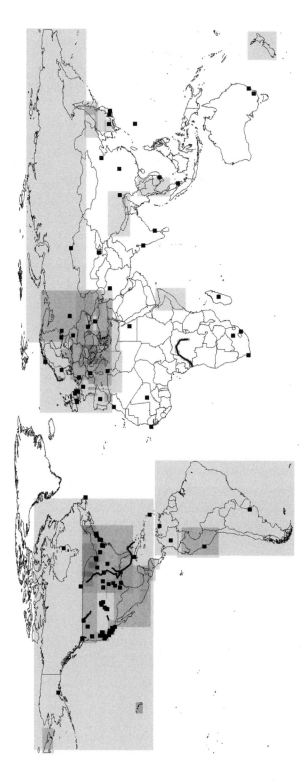

This map shows the geographic distribution of named geographic places listed in the accompanying *Index to Geographic Names Used as Examples*. It consists of a platte carrée map of the world with shading for area locations (e.g., countries), lines for linear features (e.g., rivers and the path of Hurricane Katrina), and points for features such as cities and small lakes. In some cases, a set of boxes was used to represent the location of an area (e.g., the Mediterranean Sea and Florida) in order to better represent its shape. For this book, the distribution map satisfies a curiosity about what geographic examples were used and how they are spread around the world. It is a demonstration of how such distribution maps and the underlying linking between formal and informal georeferencing could be useful for other textual documents. The map was created by Jordan Hastings using ESRI's ArcMap and Microsoft Excel software.

Index to Geographic Examples

Index